W9-AVN-370

THE
EVANGELISM
MANDATE

Also by David L. Larsen

The Anatomy of Preaching
Biblical Spirituality
The Company of the Creative
The Company of the Preachers
Telling the Old, Old Story

THE

EVANGELISM MANDATE

Recovering the Centrality of Gospel Preaching

DAVID L. LARSEN

kregel
PUBLICATIONS

Grand Rapids, MI 49501

The Evangelism Mandate: Recovering the Centrality of Gospel Preaching

© 1992 by David L. Larsen

Published by Kregel Publications, a division of Kregel, Inc., P.O. Box 2607, Grand Rapids, MI 49501. For more information about Kregel Publications, visit our Web site: www.kregel.com.

Cover design: John M. Lucas

ISBN 0-8254-3089-5

Printed in the United States of America

1 2 3 4 5 / 06 05 04 03 02

For
Lorrie and Mark
Tom and Tammy
Dan and Rose
"the children the Lord has given me"

(Isaiah 8:18a)

CONTENTS

APPENDIX: FIVE CLASSIC EVANGELISTIC SERMONS

INTRODUCTION

*Then said Evangelist, If this be thy condition, Why stand-
est thou still? He answered, Because I know not whither
to go. Then he gave him a Parchment Roll, and there was
written within, FLY FROM THE WRATH TO COME.*

*The Man therefore read it, and looking upon
Evangelist very carefully, said, Whither must I fly? Then
said Evangelist, pointing with his finger over a very wide
field, Do you see yonder Wicket Gate? The man said, No:
Then said the other, Do you see yonder Shining Light? He
said, I think I do. Then said Evangelist, Keep that light in
your eye, and go up directly thereto, so shalt thou see the
Gate. . . .*

(John Bunyan, *Pilgrim's Progress*)

People everywhere who have lost their way are asking the big questions about the meaning of life and human destiny. Would God that
a loving Evangelist could intersect their paths and give them needed
direction. Every Christian should be an evangelist in this sense, and
indeed there is mounting evidence of evangelistic resurgence around the
world.

While this book is particularly designed for pastors and Christian
leaders and for students in seminaries and training schools who are exercised about the evangelistic sermon as a unique genre, the case is made
here for an overall evangelistic strategy in every local church which will
embrace all aspects of endeavor—from the primary department to the
pulpit.

The material presented here has been forged in the vigorous give-

and-take of my class on evangelistic preaching taught at Trinity Evangelical Divinity School over a period of years. The positive response of students along with the unswerving encouragement of the administration and my faculty colleagues has put me most gratefully in their debt. The generosity of the Board of Trustees in granting me a sabbatical leave to finish the project and the unflagging support of my wife and help-meet, Jean, occasion praise to God.

The redoubtable Philipp Spener expressed the burden of his heart in six pious desires (*Pia Desideria*, 1675), the last of which is: "That theological education might give better instruction in preaching, particularly stressing that preaching is for saving souls rather than demonstrating one's wit and scholarship." That is the burden of this book and the passion of my own soul. "How beautiful on the mountains are the feet of those who bring good news, who proclaim peace, who bring good tidings, who proclaim salvation, who say to Zion, 'Your God reigns!'" (Isaiah 52:7).

Ad Gloriam Dei.

PART I

Salvation from Sin

1

The Priority of Evangelism

The prime need of the Church in these times is a new sense of its proper task.

(Carl F. H. Henry,
Aspects of Christian Social Ethics)

Witnessing is the whole work of the whole church in the whole world throughout the whole age.

(T. R. Glover)

You have nothing to do but to save souls. Therefore spend and be spent in this work.

(First Methodist Discipline)[1]

Every list of Christian priorities must include evangelism. But how should evangelism be ranked in importance with other crucial responsibilities? Clearly all Christian priorities must be subsumed under the controlling affirmation: "The chief end of man is to know God and glorify Him forever." Christian mission is doxological (cf. Matthew 5:16; Romans 15:6, 9; 1 Corinthians 1:26-31; etc.). The overarching rubric in all Christian experience is the worship of the true and living God. And the first task of the worshiping community is evangelism.

Recent discussions of "holistic mission" in ecumenical circles and among some evangelicals have tended to place certain derivative priorities (such as social justice and the alleviation of human suffering) on par with evangelism; they have thus diluted and denatured evangelism.[2] If everything the church does is evangelism or an equivalent to evangelism, we have obviously lost evangelism in any significant sense. (Analogously, if everything is sacred, then nothing is sacred.) Thus the meaning of evangelism is skewed and distorted beyond recognition.

Our aim in this volume is to describe and understand the nature and place of evangelistic preaching in the church today. Our basic premise is that evangelism is to be pervasive in the church at all times and in all places. Evangelism is to be foundational and fundamental, from the primary department to the pulpit. Because of what evangelism is meant to be for the Christian enterprise, evangelistic preaching has validity and continuing relevancy. The whole case argued here hinges on being able to demonstrate that evangelism is paramount.

The *definition* of evangelism is thus critical. One of the most widely used definitions came, at the end of the First World War, from the Archbishop's Committee in the Church of England: "To evangelize is so to present Christ Jesus in the power of the Holy Spirit, that men shall come to put their trust in God, through Him, to accept Him as their Saviour, and serve Him as their King in the fellowship of His Church."[3] J. I. Packer and others criticize that definition because it closely associates purpose and results.[4] But in point of fact, so does the Scripture (cf. Luke 19:10; John 3:16; 1 Timothy 1:15). The crucial point is, it is God who purposes and accomplishes, and He sometimes does this through us.

Another superb definition comes out of the Lausanne Covenant: "To evangelize is to spread the good news that Jesus Christ died for our sins and was raised from the dead according to the Scriptures, and that as the reigning Lord he now offers the forgiveness of sins and the liberating gift of the Spirit to all who repent and believe."[5] That statement is accompanied by further discussion of the obedient life and responsible service which should accompany conversion, but the primary focus is on the saving acts of God's grace through the Lord Jesus Christ, which is where the emphasis must be.

Even D. T. Niles's memorable definition captures something of the charm and magnificence of evangelism: "Evangelism is one beggar telling another beggar where to find bread."[6] Evangelism necessarily involves the sharing and the proclaiming of the good news. The Christian presence must find articulation in Christian proclamation; that is evangelism.

Our essential argument here is that evangelism so defined must be construed as the chief and uppermost priority in the church and in the lives of all Christians who comprise the church. Evangelism is not simply one of many important things we we are to do, but is in fact the first priority in all we do. All else flows from and follows it. This view rests on four pillars.

THE BIBLICAL PRIORITY

The Bible with all of its pluriformity has an extraordinary unity. Its consistent accent on the gracious, saving initiative of the sovereign God is seen on the earliest pages of Scripture when immediately after the sin of our first parents God comes seeking them. He brings a promise (the *protevangelium* of Genesis 3:15).[7] He clothes them with animal skins made from the sacrifice of innocent life (Genesis 3:21). The whole body of Messianic prophecy in the Old Testament (with its over three hundred predictions concerning the Savior's character and career) is the very warp and woof of the special revelation in the New Testament.[8]

The theme of the two modes of human response to the divine initiative is often in clear focus. For example, in the contrast between Cain's offering and Abel's bloody sacrifice, Abel's faith is commended. And it is God who orders the construction of the ark for the saving of Noah's family and the animals. The builders of the Tower of Babel with their Pelagian ambition to scale the heights of Heaven and make a name for themselves are set against God's election of Abram from Ur of the Chaldees. God's promises to Abram to make a great nation of him and a great name for him have as their objective a blessing for "all peoples on earth . . . through you" (Genesis 12:2, 3). This pivotal passage is the Great Commission of the Old Testament.

Here is the divine plan of redemption for fallen man, through the seed of the woman, through the seed of Abram, for all mankind. The angel's announcement at the birth of Jesus picks up the same strands of God's great missionary heart: "I bring you good news of great joy that will be for all the people. Today in the town of David a Savior has been born to you; he is Christ the Lord" (Luke 2:10, 11). The crucial elements are here; they are joyful, universal, and powerful.

The heartbeat of divine love and grace thus pulsate through the whole Bible. What is its essential theme other than God's "great salvation" (Hebrews 2:3) through the Lord Jesus Christ? But the all too familiar picture of God's own people losing sight of their mission is all too painful and familiar for us. The Lord said to His ancient covenant people, "You are my witnesses" (Isaiah 43:10a). Yet the book of Jonah shows how national self-interest and superpatriotism can eclipse compassion and a burden for those who are doomed to be destroyed.

Except for the remnant the vision was lost in Israel, and only in the person of the Savior Himself do we see the retrieval of what the divine purpose really is. John 3:16 is truly the heart of the Bible: "For God so loved the world that he gave his one and only Son, that whoever believes in him shall not perish but have eternal life." God's "indescribable gift" (2 Corinthians 9:15) in Jesus Christ is earmarked for all who thirst for spiritual life (John 7:37, 38). Jesus has embodied "the tender mercy of our God" (Luke 1:78), and He reached out to the lost, the disenfranchised, the hurting, the sick (and reaches out to them today). But even here the issue of sin and its divine remedy were and are central (cf. Luke 5:24). The parables of Jesus are parables of grace, and His anticipation of the cross was in terms of His being a ransom for sinners (Mark 10:45).[9]

The overmastering and all-consuming priority of our Lord is also apparent in His marching orders to His followers. The Great Commission in its five forms establishes and reinforces the priority of evangelism.

Matthew 28:19ff.—"[G]o and make disciples of all nations."

Mark 16:15—"Go into all the world and preach the good news to all creation."

Luke 24:47—"[A]nd repentance and forgiveness of sins will be preached in his name to all nations."

John 20:21—"As the Father has sent me, I am sending you."

Acts 1:8—"[A]nd you will be my witnesses in Jerusalem, and in all Judea and Samaria, and to the ends of the earth."

The Great Commission is unavoidably the primary responsibility for the Christian church in this age. The book of Acts narrates the blessing of the outpoured Spirit upon the followers of Christ as they obediently carried out His instructions. The epistles provide theological analysis of the ecclesiological implications of evangelism. And Revelation discloses the final triumph of the gospel.

THE THEOLOGICAL PRIORITY

Theological system is the construct in which what Scripture teaches thematically is systematized topologically (the *analogia fidei*). Luther was less of a systematic thinker than was Calvin, but each spoke and wrote from within a system. Every Christian communicator shares from within a system. To have no theology is bad theology. Further, those who disparage theological structure and counsel others to "preach

Christ, not doctrine" fail to realize that *every* statement about Christ is doctrinal. The relevant question about a given statement is, does this statement square with what Scripture says—is it a consistent and coherent part of what Scripture teaches as a whole?

Interestingly enough, the priority of evangelism follows from either a more Calvinistic or a more Arminian theological system or from innumerable variations in between. To put this in different words, the importance of evangelism follows from either a more covenantal or a more dispensational system. While there may be differences in nuance at various points within the respective systems, the primal character of evangelism must be recognized as a given.

Certainly in more liturgical or "high church" settings evangelism sometimes seems to be swallowed up by a strong emphasis on the sacraments. At the same time some teaching on baptism in very "low church" settings can virtually obliterate a repentance/faith response. Nevertheless, Anglicans such as Bryan Green or John Stott could not be sounder on the nature of spiritual conversion, and Episcopalians such as the American preacher John Guest have been mightily used in crusade evangelism. European Lutherans such as O. Hallesby of Norway wrestle deeply with the relationship of baptism and conversion, but Hallesby is unequivocal on the centrality of evangelism.[10] A contemporary Lutheran has trenchantly observed:

> The world into which Luther came was a world in which virtually all were baptized, yet he preached in such a way that people should move from unbelief to faith. He worked to evangelize the baptized. Is anything less needed today? Who violates grace and baptism today—if not those who preach and teach as though baptism were a guarantee of eternal security? In the Larger Catechism Luther clearly taught that baptism was an ark out of which people can and do fall and to which they must return for salvation. The language Luther used was response oriented. That is the other side of Luther, the faith side that is response and which holds people responsible while still seeing faith as a gift and not as a saving work.[11]

Five important points must now be discussed.

1) The evangelistic priority follows from *a right doctrine of revelation and inspiration*. On this point, R. B. Kuiper insists that our theology of evangelism follows from our view of the infallible Word.[12] The initiative in our relationship with God is "from [God] and through him and to him" (Romans 11:36). God has addressed us through His spokesmen, the prophets, but now climactically in the person of His Son

(Hebrews 1:1-3). All who hold to the uniqueness of Scripture and the authority of the divine revelation have no option but to submit to it all. We cannot pick and choose what we like in the Biblical materials. Even in the very last chapter of the inspired canon, the invitation is given: "The Spirit and the bride say, 'Come!' And let him who hears say 'Come!' Whoever is thirsty, let him come; and whoever wishes, let him take the free gift of the water of life" (Revelation 22:17). These words of grace are followed by a warning to not add to or take away from the Word of God (vv. 18, 19). God demands full obedience to His revealed will.

2) The evangelistic priority follows from *a right doctrine of God.* As Kuiper argues, the Triune God is the author of evangelism. The Father, the Son, and the Holy Spirit in that remarkable division of labor within the eternal personal distinctions of Deity accomplish redemption, just as they did in creation and as they will effect the consummation. The Father plans, the Son produces, and the Spirit applies and perfects.

3) The evangelistic priority follows from *a right doctrine of sin.* It has been rightly maintained that 90 percent of doctrinal error results from a defective understanding of sin. The fact is that mankind is more than sick—we are spiritually dead (Ephesians 2:1-3). The Bible clearly teaches that sin is what is wrong with our world, and that is what has brought all the disruption and misery and suffering and death which are the human lot. "I'm O.K., You're O.K." will not bring us through.

4) The evangelistic priority follows from *a right doctrine of salvation.* God in His matchless grace has provided a remedy for our predicament through His Son, Jesus Christ. Christianity is Christ—the supernaturally born, sinless, sin-bearing, triumphant Savior. His death and resurrection brought us atonement (Romans 5:8; Titus 2:11ff.). This is the good news of the entire New Testament. "Believe on the Lord Jesus, and you will be saved" (Acts 16:31). This is not peripheral but quintessential. The gospel feast has been prepared for all who come to Christ. The God-ordained rites of the church—i.e., baptism and the Lord's Supper—set forth the saving acts of God in Christ. Thanks to God's grace, we are at the very center of "his eternal purpose which he accomplished in Christ Jesus our Lord" (Ephesians 3:11). Paul longed to see his own people on the receiving end of all this, even wishing himself cut off for their sake (Romans 9:1-3; 10:1).

5) The evangelistic priority follows from *a right doctrine of the hereafter.* Humankind will either spend eternity in the presence of God, enjoying the felicities of Heaven, or will be eternally separated from God in Hell. This is no figurative sword of Damocles hanging over human-

ity. Jesus spoke more about eternal punishment than anyone else recorded in Scripture. We are dealing here with the eternal destinies of undying souls. God wants people to be saved (2 Peter 3:9). "Do I take any pleasure in the death of the wicked? declares the Sovereign Lord. Rather, am I not pleased when they turn from their ways and live?" (Ezekiel 18:23).

Although we shall give greater attention to theological considerations in the next chapter, it is clear here that evangelism (the proclamation and sharing of the good news about Jesus Christ) must be the compelling priority above all others because of the tenets and convictions of sound Christian theology.

THE CHRONOLOGICAL PRIORITY

The logical priority of evangelism is readily apparent to anyone who considers the *ordo salutis* (the order of salvation). Regeneration, justification, and reconciliation must all precede sanctification. One must be "born from above" (literal translation, John 3:3, 7) and become part of the family of God before one can "grow in the grace and knowledge of our Lord and Savior Jesus Christ" (2 Peter 3:18). Conversion must come first. Since God is the God of righteous judgment *and* of loving mercy, our spiritual life must begin in a relationship with Him (Mark 12:29-31).

The recent emphasis on making disciples has been salutary for the church. Seeing people converted to Christ is just the beginning; they must be taught how to grow and mature in the Lord. The problem of immature believers—stunted and stalemated Christians who are passive and apathetic—is a large part of the inertia in many local bodies of believers. Some of these have not genuinely come to know God through His Son, Jesus Christ. The fact is, people must come to new life in Christ before they can follow Him and become like Him. How can we expect people who are yet dead in their sins to behave and respond like Christians from the heart? One of the most fruitful fields in which to work evangelistically is that of unsaved church members.

As different as B. B. Warfield and Lewis Sperry Chafer are in many respects, each inveighs strongly against any soteriological approach which would compromise the principle made clear in Scripture that salvation is the work of God and not the work of man.[13] Autosoterism, also called Pelagianism, is a persistent heresy that appeals greatly to our pride. It precludes the necessity of casting ourselves totally upon God for His mercy and grace. It allows us to claim the right to put at least a few stitches in the garment of righteousness. It allows for human boasting. It permits us to avoid admitting, "Vile and full of sin am I."

This miracle of regeneration and justification must take place before any further response to God is possible. "Therefore, if anyone is in Christ, he is a new creation; the old has gone, the new has come!" (2 Corinthians 5:17). Apart from this supernatural work wrought in us, prayer and fellowship with God are impossible and admittance to Heaven inconceivable. Spurgeon used to say that if God allowed the unregenerate into Heaven, they would try to pick the pockets of the angels. Heaven would thus become Hell.

Hence we can confidently state the obvious: we must start at the beginning. Square one is evangelism. Nothing beyond it is meaningful without it.

THE PRACTICAL PRIORITY

The focus of evangelism is the proclamation of the gospel—the good news of eternal life through Jesus Christ on the basis of His death and resurrection on our behalf. In the New Testament the Greek word *euangelion* means "good news" or "gospel." The verb form (*euangelizomai*) means "to announce good news" or "to proclaim the gospel." The Old Testament background is the Hebrew word *basar*, which means "to bear good tidings," as in Isaiah 61:1, 2 (which, significantly, was quoted at the outset of Christ's ministry—see Luke 4:16ff.). This Hebrew word is also found in Isaiah 40:9 and 52:7. This word has the connotation of a military conquest or victory. It involves loudly proclaiming good tidings! This is undeniably to assume priority in the practical experience of the people of God.

We must now stress that a person needs to hear the bad news before he or she can appreciate the good news. We live in an age of much bleak and dark news. I recall vividly how during the most desperate days of the Second World War we would love to hear the newscaster Gabriel Heater, who would invariably begin his program with the sentence, "Ah, there's good news tonight." We needed to hear some good news then, and people need to hear good news now—God's good news.

The word "evangelist" occurs three times in the New Testament. Acts 21:8 refers to a specific man who was an evangelist; 2 Timothy 4:5 is a charge to "do the work of an evangelist"; and Ephesians 4:11 indicates that some persons are uniquely gifted by God to do evangelizing.[14] Paul was proud of the gospel (Romans 1:16) and was eager to preach it (1 Corinthians 9:16). We who know Jesus Christ have made a fantastic discovery, thanks to God's revealing Himself to us in His grace. This discovery exceeds even what the ancient Greek Archimedes discovered when he discerned the principle of the displacement of water and rushed out of his bathtub into the streets crying, "Eureka, eureka"—"I have found it, I have found it." We have found the Lord, or rather He has found us, and we can now proclaim a message of joy.

Confusion prevails in many ecclesiastical quarters as to what the gospel really is, even though Paul clearly gave the content of the gospel in 1 Corinthians 15:3, 4. The gospel proclaims that Jesus Christ died for our sins, was buried, and rose again. To withhold a medical remedy from the sick, to withhold warning of a fire from those in a burning building, to withhold critical evidence in a court of law—these are criminal offenses. To withhold the good news from those who so desperately need it is a terrible sin. Sharing the good news of Christ must be our priority.

A young couple outside of Christ who are contemplating marriage need the gospel. A dying man or woman outside the Savior needs the gospel. The guilt-ridden counselee needs the gospel. What is conceivably more important in extremity and duress than the hope of the gospel? Simply in terms of the practical situations of ministry and everyday life, evangelism must be given top importance. From every standpoint we must insist that evangelism is the number-one priority.

Conceding that the North American church desperately needs revival and renewal and that evangelism is one of the outgrowths of revival, we need to remember that revival means "to make alive again." Life is presupposed if there is to be a revivifying. The premise and presupposition of everything Christian is evangelism, and thus it cannot be minimized or ignored.

2

The Theology of Conversion

I wanted to know about doctrine, about what to believe.

(The young Thomas Merton)[1]

God's justification of the sinner is the meaning of the New Testament.

(Frederick Dale Bruner)[2]

Theology in the New Testament is virtually a theology of mission.

(William A. Dyrness)[3]

True history has to do with the saving and losing of souls.

(Frederick Buechner)[4]

I want you to know, brothers, that the gospel I preached is not something that man made up.

(Galatians 1:11)

Can human nature be changed? Undeniably a dreadful and debilitating malady has poisoned all of mankind. We see "man's inhumanity to man" and "nature red with tooth and claw." The violence, misery, greed, and exploitation all around us and inside us attest to the devastation the Bible ascribes to our revolt against God and its consequences. What is true individually and personally is magnified corporately.

Reinhold Niebuhr well argues in his *Moral Man in Immoral Society* that selfishness is exaggerated in nations.

Is there a remedy? "Can the Ethiopian change his skin or the leopard its spots? Neither can you do good who are accustomed to doing evil" (Jeremiah 13:23). "But how can a mortal be righteous before God?" (Job 9:2b). Must we succumb to the pessimism of the ancient preacher—"What is twisted cannot be straightened; what is lacking cannot be counted" (Ecclesiastes 1:15)?

The naive optimism at the end of the last century with its anticipation of a humanly inaugurated golden age was fueled by the evolutionary vision. But it foundered quickly on the reefs of this century's world wars and depressions. Modern depth psychology and the horrors of the Holocaust disclosed the unspeakable darkness of the depravity of humankind. Liberalism's lullabies now seem laughable, as when Newell Dwight Hillis warbled: "Laws are becoming more just, rulers humane; music is becoming sweeter, and books wiser; homes are happier, and the individual heart becoming at once more just and more gentle."[5] The inevitability of progress and the inherent goodness of man were the linchpins of liberal thought. In such a system, no doctrine is more scorned than the doctrine of original sin.[6]

But empirical reality contravened this doomed system. The sensitive and prominent British philosopher C. E. M. Joad totally disdained Christianity and found the Prayer Book's claims that man is born in sin and that the human heart is desperately wicked totally unacceptable. But experience led him to confess most movingly: "My eyes were gradually opened to the extent of my own sinfulness in thought, word and deed; so that, finding that it was only with great difficulty and effort that I could constrain myself to even the most modest degree of virtue."[7] This is the human experience in microcosm in this century.

The brilliant expectation of synthesis in Hegelian pantheism never materialized. Secularists such as Oswald Spengler and Arnold Toynbee wrote apocalyptically of a gloomy future. Karl Barth's *Romerbrief* introduced the neo-orthodox revolution in which sin was taken with much greater seriousness; but even in Barth evil has no objective reality, and there is no Satan in his theology.[8] Though he turned liberalism upside-down, he remained within the framework of Schleiermacher's thinking. Barth's theology did not lead to evangelism.

Historic Christianity has maintained that Jesus Christ can make a radical change in human life. This is the essence of the gospel. Evangelism aims at conversion which results in salvation. As the messenger in Sophocles' writing came crying, "Good news, good news!"

so believers proclaim a solution to the insoluble, an answer for the unanswerable, a prescription for the hopeless predicament of humankind. The total collapse in our time of the Marxist dream of a classless society and state socialism underscores the vacuum for which God's power to save is the only adequate proposal left on the table. "When the disciples heard this, they were greatly astonished and asked, 'Who then can be saved?' Jesus looked at them and said, 'With man this is impossible, but with God all things are possible'" (Matthew 19:25, 26).

DEFINITIONS: WHAT CONVERSION IS

Christ has the power to make bad people good. The process begins with proclamation and appeal; the response is conversion by the grace of God to the glory of God; the result is a changed life and discipleship. The phenomenon we call conversion is set forth by the Hebrew verb *shubh* and the Greek verb *epistrepho*, both of which mean "to turn or return."[9] God is the primary mover (Jeremiah 31:18), although man appears to have a subordinate part (Jeremiah 24:7). Individuals (2 Kings 23:25) and nations (Jonah 3:5-10) are subjects of conversion. God uses His prophets as secondary agents in effecting conversion (Nehemiah 9:26; Zechariah 1:4).[10] How movingly the prophet Isaiah conveys the divine invitation to sinners: "Come, all you who are thirsty, come to the waters; and you who have no money, come, buy and eat! Come, buy wine and milk without money and without cost" (Isaiah 55:1). And what is the desired end of this gracious appeal? "Let the wicked forsake his way and the evil man his thoughts. Let him turn to the Lord, and he will have mercy on him, and to our God, for he will freely pardon" (v. 7). That is conversion!

The simple verb *strepho*, meaning "to turn," is used by our Lord in Matthew 18:3 where He says, "[U]nless you change and become like little children, you will never enter the kingdom of heaven." The verb *epistrepho*, meaning "to turn about" or "to turn toward," is used in James 5:19, 20 and other places (cf. Matthew 13:15; Mark 4:12; Luke 22:32), and the noun (in the original Greek), implying a turning from and a turning to (corresponding to repentance and faith), is found in Acts 15:3.[11]

A pivotal study of conversion in the book of Acts and today is William Barclay's A. S. Peake Lectureship, entitled *Turning to God*. In contrast to pagan pessimism and hopelessness, Barclay carefully examines the Christian hope and power which make possible the supernaturalization of human life. Conversion is a miracle of divine grace! He quotes John Wesley:

> I have seen (as far as a thing of this kind can be seen) very many persons changed in a moment from the spirit of fear, horror, despair, to the spirit of love, joy and peace, and from sinful desire, till then reigning over him, to a pure desire of doing the will of God; him that was a drunkard and is now exemplarily sober; the whoremonger that was, who now abhors the very "garment spotted by the flesh."[12]

We will come back to Professor Barclay, but we want simply at this point to call attention to his finding that "The main means of conversion in the early Church was preaching."[13]

In his epochal treatment of conversion in the ancient world, A. D. Nock of Harvard defines conversion as "the re-orientation of the soul" and points out that there was no missionary zeal in Greek religion and no summons to self-surrender. Not until the rise of the Roman cults (A.D. 70-134) and the desire to penetrate the mysteries of the universe and the hereafter do we really have mention of conversion. Plato does speak of the object of education as "the turning (*epistrepho*) of the soul," but Nock argues that pagan conversions did not involve reorientation, any recoil from the past, or any idea of starting a new life. While Christian conversion as depicted in the New Testament may have different forms (a theme we shall develop in the next chapter), it is uniquely a drastic reorientation of human life to a holy God through Jesus Christ by the Holy Spirit.[14]

The contemporary debate over conversion revolves essentially around the question as to whether salvation is to be seen primarily as corporate or individual, whether the accent is to be placed on humanization or justification. Arguing for the latter in a most timely volume is David Wells, who expounds the historic Biblical position: "Conversion is the doorway that is inextricably linked to the house of Christian faith."[15] Conversion was not unknown in Judaism, but in becoming a proselyte one in effect became a Jew, whereas in Christian conversion all such ethnic, racial, and other barriers are done away with in Christ (Galatians 3:26-29).

The conversion of the Apostle Paul becomes an important case study of what Wells terms the conversion of "insiders." The *theology* of Paul's conversion is normative, not the experience per se.[16] The fact that the conversion story is given three times (Acts 9:1-9; 22:3-21; 26:4-20) reinforces the notion of the prototypical nature of the event (cf. 1

Timothy 1:16). Here is an instance of what William James calls "internal combustion," the turning around of a man from darkness to light—from defiance to obedience, new life, and the forgiveness of sins. We are analyzing here more than the shifting of deck chairs on the *Titanic*. We are witnessing the formation of a new man in Christ! This is what God offers to all.

No one has set forth conversion more powerfully or more popularly than E. Stanley Jones in his magnificent *Conversion*. Jones asserts that Jesus divides humanity into two groups: the converted and the unconverted, the twice-born and the once-born.[17] He quotes Alexander Pope, the author and poet who muttered, "O Lord, make me a better man," to which his page replied, "It would be easier to make you a new man."[18] That is the specialization and expertise of the Lord Jesus Christ.

The Lord Jesus likened the change He proposes to make in human beings to *birth*—the beginning of life and experience in a new realm of reality. This is "birth from above" (literal translation, John 3:1ff.). Asked why he always preached "you must be born again," George Whitefield's reply was: "Quite simply, because 'You must be born again.'" A probing and thorough study of regeneration in relation to conversion is found in Peter Toon's superb volume, *Born Again: A Biblical and Theological Study of Regeneration*.[19] Charles Colson's testimony *Born Again* is *prima facie* evidence of Christ's power to save a most reprehensible rascal. What encouragement for all of us, for we were rascals as well!

Conversion, then, is participation in a new reality. It means embodying in our own experience the model of the re-created world (cf. Genesis 1; 2 Corinthians 5:17). Though derided, the evangelical pietistic idea of the sudden change of the individual's heart is the paradigm of Biblical conversion. The close relationship of the sign of baptism to conversion emphasizes the corporate ecclesial context of the conversion experience and safeguards it from undue individualism.

Richard Baxter, the Puritan preacher, and T. J. Bach, a modern missionary statesman, were both converted through the reading of a tract. Frederick Buechner was converted while listening to a sermon. Augustine heard a voice while working in a garden. Spurgeon responded in a church service on a snowy day. C. S. Lewis was "surprised by joy" while riding in the side-car of his brother's bike on a thirty-mile stretch to Whipsnade Zoo. Sadly, Barth's shrinking back from speaking of "conversion experience" has widely influenced many to a suspicion of evangelism.[20] However, we stand on solid rock when we declare, "Unless you repent, you too will all perish" (Luke 13:3).[21]

BIBLICAL DOCTRINES—
HOW CONVERSION TAKES PLACE

The theological matrix out of which we build our understanding of evangelism and conversion must be the sound doctrine of Holy Scripture. The climate in contemporary theology is not especially congenial or compatible to what we are here undertaking to do. It is in vogue among the avant-garde today to eschew propositional revelation and to take flights of fancy in "story theology" or in "aesthetic theology," thus compromising coherence and fidelity to the faith in the vagaries of subjectivity. We must take this mood seriously in our addresses to the modern mind, but we cannot "give away the store." Dietrich Ritschl has well argued that there is no special gospel for modern man. Concessions in the realm of the supernatural will not ultimately make the gospel more palatable to modern man, but will rather rob sinners of the gospel altogether if we are not careful. Our understanding of conversion rests upon three doctrinal building blocks.

The Character of God

From start to finish, from beginning to ending, conversion is the work of God. The initiative and the capacity for changing human nature is solely His. However, *sola gratia* does not rule out authentic human response, for this is part of the divine proviso. We are dealing here with who God is. We are grappling with the attributes of God. God Himself is a tension-filled synthesis, as Gustaf Aulen maintained, in which we see both the "goodness and the severity of God" ("the kindness and sternness of God") (Romans 11:22, KJV and NIV respectively). How can we resolve this antinomy any more than we can rationally resolve the human and divine natures of our Lord in the hypostatic union or the oneness and the threeness in the triune nature of our God? How can the finite grasp the infinite?

Hence Charles Simeon's position with respect to divine sovereignty and human freedom seems satisfying. The truth is not at either side, nor is the truth in the middle, but the truth is at both ends. The Bible asserts both divine sovereignty and human freedom. I would argue on the basis of Scripture for the validity of the universal call on the one hand *and* the validity of the sovereign initiative of the grace of God as solely and wholly underlying conversion and salvation on the other. The collapse of either of these two coordinates will have disastrous consequences. Perhaps the simultaneity of freedom and sovereignty will be seen in the eleven dimensions of reality known to modern physics and astronomy (as suggested by Dr. Hugh Ross).

At the cross of Christ and in his functioning as the Mediator between God and man, we see that "mercy and truth are met together; righteousness and peace have kissed each other" (Psalm 85:10, KJV). How can a holy and righteous God receive sinful human beings to Himself without compromising His integrity and character? The whole sacrificial system of the Old Testament pointed forward to the vicarious, substitutionary atonement that would be accomplished by Christ, for "it is the blood that makes atonement for one's life" (Leviticus 17:11).[22] That is how God remained just and yet justifies sinners (cf. Romans 3:21-26).

The virulent antipathy of the modern mind to penal satisfaction in the atonement of Christ jeopardizes evangelism. The hostile responses of self-sufficient sinners have long discouraged believers from proclaiming the good news. The cross of Christ is the moral and ethical epicenter of redemption history (Romans 3:24, 25; 1 Corinthians 1, 2; Galatians 6:14; etc.). God imputes the sin of our first parents to the whole race (Romans 5:12-21). And God imputed the sin of the race to Christ as He suffered and died on Calvary. And now God imputes the perfect righteousness of Christ to all who believe. There can be no forensic justification (God declaring the sinner righteous) without the imputation of our sins to Christ as He died for us.

C. H. Dodd is a case in point. This gifted scholar denies the wrath of God in the classical sense in his work on Romans 1. Without the bracing reality of God's anger directed at sinners, he softens propitiation to mere expiation (as seen in his strong influence on the RSV). His realized eschatology defuses human accountability in a future judgment, and thus the gospel has been effectively eviscerated by a well-meaning but blundering academic. An earlier notable on the American scene, Horace Bushnell, evinces a sub-orthodox view of the atonement. He termed penal satisfaction "anathema," and although in a later work he tried to retrieve some ground for objectivity in the atonement, he in effect held a rather weak, exemplarist view of Christ's sacrifice.[23] We are not surprised, therefore, that in his *magnus opus*, *Christian Nurture*, he downplays conversion and advances the idea that children in a Christian home should never know they are anything other than Christians. Here and in the thought of others the idea of crossing a line has evaporated.

Scandinavian evangelicals in North America have long struggled with the vestiges of P. P. Waldenstrom's denial of objective transaction in the atonement. His espousal of Ritschlian ideas (derived from Schleiermacher) was based on a shallow view of the holiness of God and the idea that God's wrath is not personal. "The theory keeps its happy, optimistic tone to the end . . . this generous and happy gospel appealed to the masses . . . those times were spring days . . . happy is the springtime."[24] A sound and Biblical view of the character of God and His attributes builds the foundation for our understanding of what sin is and therefore what the saving acts of God must be to deliver and rescue fallen mankind.

The Nature of Man

Pascal wrote in the seventeenth century: "Christianity is strange. It bids man recognize that he is vile, even abominable; and bids him desire to be like God." The grandeur of man is on account of the *imago dei*; the misery of man is on account of the historical fall of our first parents in the Garden of Eden. To construe the virtual obliteration of the *imago* through sin is unfortunate because it rules out general revelation (as in Barth) or any univocal contact or common ground (as in Van Til and Jay Adams) or any significant exercise of free moral agency (as in Luther's *Bondage of the Will*).

Yet on the other hand, to minimize or equivocate concerning the historicity and reality of the human fall is to undercut the necessity of a historical redemption in Christ (as in Tillich and many others) and to leave us vulnerable to a doctrine of evolutionary origins which makes *homo sapiens* descendants of primates and human life equal to biological function. God becomes virtually extraneous in the whole *schema*. The Bible teaches that man and woman were created perfect in the beginning, "in the image of God," and that their willful disobedience and rebellion seriously defaced that image but did not efface it (cf. Genesis 9:6). A biblical anthropology and hamartiology are crucial for evangelism and conversion.

Charles G. Finney was a trophy of God's saving grace and a powerfully used evangelist. Careful study of his theology indicates, however, that in his "Oberlin perfectionism" he denied the omniscience of God. The diminution of the mighty God always has lamentable consequences. Finney's view of sin and the Fall allowed for human retention of moral ability. This is very close to the inalienable ability advanced by Pelagius, the view that man unaided by grace is able to fully observe the Decalogue. We are not surprised that Finney held a governmental view of the atonement and denied substitution.[25] While he was used to bring many to Christ, his view undermined understanding of the gospel, and those groups most influenced by Finney have been most susceptible to the inroads of liberalism. The following dictum remains: sound, Biblically based theology is the *sine non qua* of evangelism and conversion.

The Meaning of Faith

The doctrinal formulation which aptly captures the prescribed response to the gospel message is expressed in Paul's words, "they must turn to God in repentance and have faith in our Lord Jesus" (Acts 20:21). We have already seen that conversion entails a turning from and a turning to, both of which are implied in a correct understanding of what saving faith is (Ephesians 2:6-9). Neither repentance nor faith is meritorious work, but rather gifts of God through Jesus Christ by the Holy Spirit. We must give further consideration to the interrelationship between these in our later discussion on "Lordship Salvation" and the most regrettable controversy raging among evangelicals over this matter.

No one has more deftly treated the three basic ingredients which constitute faith as such than B. B. Warfield.[26] The elements are: 1) *notitia* (insight); 2) *assensus* (consent and agreement to the truth but not yet saving faith); 3) *fiducia* (commitment, which is demonstrably what the Greek verb *pisteuo* means in its ninety-eight occurrences in John's Gospel). Faith in Christ is receiving what God in mercy offers.

Sola fides in this Reformation sense is hard for modern men to accept. We Americans with our work ethic and our self-reliance find our symbols in Jonathan Livingston Seagull and "the little engine that could." Like Smith-Barney, "We earn it." Effort and energy expended constitute our means of goal accomplishment from the cradle to the grave. But the Word of God says, "[W]e maintain that a man is justified by faith apart from observing the law" (Romans 3:28). "Justifying faith is not a bare intellectualism; that is, it is not merely an assent to the historic facts of the gospel story, a mere belief in its historicity."[27] Failure to maintain a full-orbed, Biblical understanding of what faith truly is leaves us vulnerable to easy-believism and other grievous doctrinal errors.

DEFECTIONS—WHAT HINDERS CONVERSION?

Certain ideologies on the contemporary scene are working at cross-purposes with Biblical teaching on evangelism and conversion. The most nefarious and serious of these challenges are the following:

1) *Universalism.* The ancient heresy of Origen has lifted its head powerfully in our time and has become pervasive in the mainline denominations. Karl Barth's implicit universalism has snared many.[28] J. I. Packer has trenchantly pointed out that universalism ignores all that the Bible says about the importance of decisions in this life and their eternal significance. He quotes Nels Ferre as urging us to "preach hell as having a school and a door in it," but then asks pointedly, "But why did not Jesus preach hell that way?"[29] The "two-covenant" teaching about

the Jews not needing to come through Christ allows for an exception the Scripture does not allow (cf. John 14:6; Acts 4:12).[30] Dear believers such as Hannah Whitehall Smith in her *The Restitution of All Things* got caught in this trap of universalism. Isn't Luke 13:23, 24 final? Did Jesus not mean what He said?

2) *Annihilationism.* Strangely, a growing group of evangelicals are denying the eternal nature of God's retributive punishment. This is built on an emotional and sentimental aversion to what the Bible teaches. It introduces a salad-bar theology which is ominously dangerous. If punishment is not eternal for those separated from God, is felicity for the blessed eternal either? (Cf. Matthew 25:46.)

3) *Social activism.* *The Call to Conversion* by Jim Wallis dilutes the kerygmatic proclamation of the gospel of the grace of God, at great peril. Wallis blurs and obscures true conversion and in fact confuses conversion with discipleship. He rejects instantaneous conversion and dumps in the whole kitchen sink, arguing, "Conversion means to relinquish our wealth . . . our atomic stockpile, etc. etc."[31] Racism, capitalism, and militarism are focal points in that mistaken book. In response, subsidiary involvement must never cloud the main ministry of the church. As Beyerhaus quotes Freytag: "Nothing can be called mission in the Biblical sense which is not . . . directed toward conversion and baptism."[32]

4) *Hypercalvinism.* There is a scholastic hypercalvinism which not only veers into supralapsarian extremes with respect to the divine decree but is suspicious of crusade evangelism and challenges the propriety of assurance in salvation. Certainly this is extreme. For example, Andrew Bonar has been criticized as guilty of "Rowism," the belief that an individual can know with full assurance whether or not he or she is converted. Such a view is arid and sterile evangelistically.

5) *Psychologism.* The human potential movement wed with American pragmatism is peddling another gospel in our times. Pulpit pabulum nowadays is more often good advice than it is good news. "Pop" psychology and health-and-wealth messages are common among us. "Become what you are" is urged rather than Augustine and Calvin's "become what you are not." We know the church is at cliff's edge when a popular proponent of these ideas relegates Paul's teachings in Romans and the commentary of Luther and Calvin on the same to the slag heap in favor of his "new reformation."[33] In truth, the gospel is not the way to self-esteem. The gospel points the way to Christ, forgiveness, and eternal life. What Sidney Ahlstrom calls "harmonial religion" is not the gospel of reconciliation outlined by Paul in 2 Corinthians 5.

6) *Liberationism.* One of the more devious threats to the everlast-

ing gospel is liberation theology, tinctured in various degrees with Marxist presuppositions. It reduces essentially to salvation through sociology. Yet the dialectic process without a transcendent deity will do little against injustice, inequity, and inequality; it merely replaces one oppressive system with another.[34]

7) *Ecumenism.* The emerging theology of the broad ecumenical movement may include snippets of several or all of the above, but the predominate motif may be denominated "Kingdom Theology."[35] This is to be differentiated from what Edmund P. Clowney calls "kingdom evangelism." An effective spokesman for "Kingdom Theology" is William J. Abraham in his influential *The Logic of Evangelism.*[36] Though critical of those secularisms which leave no room for evangelism, he begins by taking a swat at Robert Coleman's *The Master Plan of Evangelism* as "pragmatism . . . not ancient gospels" and at Michael Green's *Evangelism in the Early Church* as "'a tendentious reading of evangelism in the early church."[37]

Abraham advocates a "broader work of evangelism." He accepts the place of proclamation but resists equating evangelism and proclamation. He properly puts evangelism into an eschatological frame of reference (*eschatology* meaning that the meaning of history is not totally within history). Arthur P. Johnston adroitly analyzes the movement as primarily emphasizing "the gospel as practical changing of society by the church."[38] While the Kingdom of God and the church are related to each other, they are not identical, and hence the confusion of equating them is liable to alter the agenda of each of them. The World Council approach to evangelism fixates on "justice as an essential and integral part of the Good News." Failure to see the now and the not-yet tension of the Kingdom of God may well distract the church from her primary task.

In the face of all of this, when like the messenger in Sophocles' play we would shout "'Good news! Good news!'" we need to be reminded that the first serious encounter for Christian in *Pilgrim's Progress* was the Hill Difficulty. But being fully confident he commenced his ascent, as must today's Christians facing their task, saying:

> *Come, pluck up, heart, let's neither faint nor fear.*
> *Better, though difficult, the right way to go,*
> *Than wrong, though easy, where the end is woe.*

Seeking to maintain Biblical standards for evangelism and conversion embroils us in difficult combat, but we have no alternative than to do battle.

3

The Psychology of Conversion

*Surely the arm of the Lord is not too short to save, nor his
ear too dull to hear. But your iniquities have separated you
from your God; your sins have hidden his face from you.*

(Isaiah 59:1, 2)

*To say that I was born again, to use that traditional
phrase, is to say too much because I remained in most
ways as self-centered and squeamish after the fact as I was
before, and God knows remain so still. And in another
way to say that I was born again is to say too little
because there have been more than a few such moments
since, times when from beyond time something too precious to tell has glinted in the dusk, always just out of
reach, like fireflies.*

(Frederick Buechner)[1]

*Structurally, Eliot built the poem on a phrase from Bishop
Andrewes about "the two turnings" which Andrewes had
declared were necessary for a "conversion." The one turning looked ahead to God; the other, appropriate for a pen-
itential season, looked back to one's sinful past.*[2]

*I possess assurance only so long as I see these two
things simultaneously: all of my sinfulness and all of
God's grace.*

(Professor O. Hallesby)

For we also have had the gospel preached to us, just as
they did; but the message they heard was of no value to
them, because those who heard did not combine it with
faith.

(Hebrews 4:2)

Having examined the Biblical and theological underpinnings of our understanding of conversion, we now need to consider the *experience* of conversion itself, to which William James devoted two chapters in his classic Gifford Lectures. There he has defined being converted as "to be regenerated, to receive grace, to experience religion, to gain an assurance ... the process, gradual or sudden, by which a self hitherto divided, and consciously wrong, inferior and unhappy, becomes unified and consciously right, superior and happy, in consequence of its firmer hold upon religious realities."[3] While there are some serious deficiencies in James's understanding of conversion, he does describe actual evangelical conversions such as Sam Hadley's and does quote Joseph Alleine's splendid word to the effect that "Conversion is not putting in a patch of holiness; but with the true convert holiness is woven into all his powers, principles and practice. The sincere Christian is quite a new fabric, from the foundation to the topstone. He is a new man, a new creature."[4]

The English word *conversion* derives from the Latin root *conversio* and generically means "a turning from something to something else." There are purely secular conversions, ideological conversions, and psychological conversions. There are conversions to false religions and cults. Maloney quotes sociologist James Richardson's contention that "ours is 'an age of conversions' in which many, if not most people could be best described as suffering from a hunger for meaning. Thus, people are continually seeking."[5]

Clearly Christian conversion must be understood in a vertical as well as a horizontal sense, for it involves meeting the one true and living God through His Son Jesus Christ by the Holy Spirit. Such an experience is a *miracle*. This is hard for modern depth psychology to process, and so it is quickly reduced to psychologism. Svere Norborg has firmly critiqued William James by insisting that Christian conversion is unique because it takes place in a context of Christian ideas and facts which can be found absolutely nowhere else.[6]

No one has better delineated the irreducible bedrock reality here than Bishop Stephen Neil when he insists:

> Conversion is the beginning of real Christian life. Christian nurture, education and worship may be valuable preparations. But no one is or should be called a Christian until he has personally encountered God in Jesus Christ, until he has personally repented, until he has personally accepted God's gift of salvation through faith in Christ, until by his faith he has individually been born again. The reality of the Church in the world depends on there being enough people who have passed through this experience and through whom it can be passed on to others.[7]

This is spiritual reality.

THE PREPARATIONS FOR CONVERSION

While authentic conversion is instantaneous in the sense that we cross a line from death to life, it does involve predisposing factors of a long-range and also of a more immediate nature. God's foreknowledge (Romans 8:29) and His prevenient grace work together in His searching for and winning sinners to Himself. What Edward John Carnell called "pre-soteric synergism" refers to what may be years of gracious quest and heavenly influence interacting with our wills and dispositions. Quickening—being made alive—comes after constant pursuit. As Francis Thompson so movingly describes it in "The Hound of Heaven":

> *I fled Him, down the nights and down the days;*
> *I fled Him, down the arches of the years;*
> *I fled Him, down the labyrinthine ways*
> *Of my own mind; and in the midst of tears*
> *I hid from Him . . . but with unhurrying chase,*
> > *and unperturbed pace, deliberate speed*
> > *majestic instancy, They beat . . . and a Voice beat*
> > *more instant than the feet.*

The double foci of the Spirit's witness to the unconverted seem to be conviction for sin (John 16:8-11) and God's remedy for our sin and guilt in the finished work of Jesus Christ on the cross (John 12:32, 33; Romans 3:21-26). In our day of no-fault accidents and no-fault divorce and instant solutions and "I'm O.K., you're O.K." philosophy, there is considerable resistance to preaching against sin and preaching on the cross of Christ where God's wrath against sin was climactically disclosed and where His saving solution for sin was provided.

But we cannot be true to what the Bible teaches without emphasizing repentance. How can we challenge the easy-believism of our times if we are unwilling to face the spiritual malady which is destroying us? So what if we are dismissed as guilt-inducing neurotics. The fact remains that "The Christian doctrine of sin is the most comprehensive and satisfying explanation of personal and social ills."[8] Too much "evangelical" preaching is beginning to resemble what H. Richard Niebuhr called "evolutionary optimism" and comes out as "a God without wrath bringing men without sin into a kingdom without judgment through the ministrations of a Christ without a cross."

Though critical of Robert Schuller's recasting our understanding of the basic human problem as a loss of self-esteem, William Dyrness argues, "Awareness of sin is not a precondition of an encounter with God's love in Jesus Christ." He adds that we cannot insist that "A proper understanding of sin is prerequisite to hearing the gospel."[9] Where then is repentance? What about Paul's argument in Romans? Are people ready to hear the good news before they have heard the bad news? Certainly the believer's awareness of sin and its consequences is greater after conversion than before, but facing the sin question at conversion is not optional. (See John Bunyan's *Grace Abounding to the Chief of Sinners* for further treatment of this essential subject.)

Indeed "the popularity of some of the modern psychological hypotheses is due in large measure to the way in which they relieve a man of any need to face the moral problems in his own life."[10] But on the other hand, in his classic work *Whatever Became of Sin?* the late Dr. Karl Menninger, prominent psychiatrist, pled with clergy to "Preach! Tell it like it is. Say it from the pulpit. Cry it from the housetops. Cry comfort, cry repentance, cry hope. Because recognition of our part in the world transgression is the only remaining hope."[11] Similarly Dr. M. Scott Peck calls for dedication to reality in the forthright facing of evil and sin as they are.[12]

Accommodating our message to North American cultural optimism will lead to a downplaying of moral accountability and a depreciation of the atoning sacrifice of Christ.[13] The cross of Christ was foolishness and a stumbling-block in the first century, but that did not persuade Paul to abandon its proclamation (cf. 1 Corinthians 2:2; Galatians 3:1). All of our essential theological categories, including the love of God and the holiness of God, focus upon the necessary and invaluable transaction on the cross of Christ.

When seventeenth-century Jesuit missionaries to China were anxious not to offend the refined taste of the Chinese *literati*, they redrafted the Gospel story, omitting anything to which exception might be taken, especially of course the crucifixion of Christ. What was left? Professor Hugh Trevor-Roper, Regius Professor of Modern History at Oxford, said it was "an unobjectionable residue, with no divine power to win converts." What a contrast to the true gospel, of which the Apostle Paul said, "it is the power of God for the salvation of everyone who believes" (Romans 1:16).

The fact is, gospel witness does not create sin. Rather, it recognizes the reality of guilt, seeing every human being as permeated with sin. Sin and its concomitants of regret and remorse occasion unspeakable suffering in human life and experience. "He who conceals his sins does not prosper, but whoever confesses and renounces them finds mercy" (Proverbs 28:13). Granted, there is excessive and neurotic guilt which is pathological, but genuine release for real sin comes only at the foot of the cross of Christ (1 John 1:7, 9). The answer ultimately is not the psychiatrist's couch but Christ's cross.

The Holy Spirit awakens guilt in order to save. Paul Tournier is right when he affirms that "We can only discover grace when we know the shudder of guilt."[14]

Where are we culturally and psychologically on this? Garrison Keillor, a fantastic communicator, says, "I've heard a lot of sermons in the past ten years that make me want to get up and walk out. They're secular, psychological, self-help sermons. Friendly, but of no use. They didn't make you straighten up. They didn't give you anything hard. . . . At some point and in some way, a sermon has to direct people toward the death of Christ and the campaign God has waged over the centuries to get our attention." These are irreplaceable themes.

THE PROCESS OF CONVERSION

What may be years of preparation in which God brings innumerable influences to bear upon a human life culminate in a decision to receive Christ, a commitment involving repentance toward God and faith in Jesus Christ. This point-in-time experience is *conversion*. Some shrink back from what is sometimes called "decisionism," and certainly there are excessively emotional environments in which there is manipulation and exploitation. This is unacceptable. J. I. Packer insists that

. . . high-speed evangelism is not a valid option. Evangelism must rather be conceived as a long-term enterprise of patient teaching and instruction, in which God's servants seek simply to be faithful in delivering the gospel message and applying it to human lives, and leave it to God's Spirit to draw men to faith through this message in his own way and at his own speed.[15]

If these strictures rule out special times of gospel harvest and the gift of evangelist in the church (Ephesians 4:11), or if the legitimacy of persuasion is questioned, or if the propriety of strong and vigorous invitation to receive Christ publicly is at issue (all of which will be seen in the next chapter to be part of apostolic practice), we have gone too far.

Conversion does involve process, as we have argued; but it is also an *event*. That event may take place on the highway while listening to a gospel broadcast on the car radio. Response to a gospel invitation may occur in a person's home or family circle, in a Sunday school class or youth retreat, in a public service of a local church, or in a great evangelistic rally. Packer admits that in the days of Moody, Torrey, and other notable gospel preachers, there were successful evangelistic campaigns. As I understand what he has written, he speaks with approbation of such, but raises questions about whether organized campaigns in our time are possible or acceptable.[16]

Dr. Martyn Lloyd-Jones some years ago brilliantly engaged Dr. William Sargent's significant book entitled *Battle for the Mind.* Sargent had argued that evangelical conversion was essentially a conditioned reflex, analogous to brainwashing or the reaction of Pavlov's dogs. This is to make conversion "the rape of the mind." In his masterful treatment, Dr. Lloyd-Jones convincingly shows that what Sargent pejoratively terms "softening-up" is really a kind of education or instruction such as is employed not only in religion but in politics and all kinds of training.[17] Lloyd-Jones vigorously critiques Sargent's psychologizing of Paul's and Wesley's conversions with an understanding which comes from within the framework of Biblical thought on the reality of the resurrection of Jesus Christ. As Christians we do not dismiss conversion phenomena as hysteria, but rather see with the eye of faith the power of the living Christ transforming human lives.

Then Dr. Lloyd-Jones, reflecting his own serious reservation about modern mass evangelism, as did Packer later, indicted "much of the modern approach to evangelism, with its techniques and methods."[18] Abuses have indeed existed historically. George Whitefield himself used a trumpeter at the end of a sermon on the Second Coming and judgment day, throwing a vast throng into virtual panic.[19] But both Christ and the apostles spoke to large audiences. To step back from seeking revival because there have been abuses in revivals would be a serious mistake. Unfortunately, Dr. Lloyd-Jones was never able to participate in, for example, a Billy Graham crusade. We shall deal later with his forceful criticism that "so many fall away."

We are indebted to these brothers for their caution, for they voice concerns we dare not ignore. We concur with the Puritans that hearts must be prepared; we must not pick fruit that is not yet ripe. We must seek God's time—and there are "seasons of refreshing" from the Lord. The Day of Pentecost, when three thousand were baptized, was such a day, as was the following day when five thousand came to the Lord. Process became event.

A striking parallel exists with the phenomenon of revival itself. In the face of much criticism for excess and abuse, Jonathan Edwards described and evaluated the moving of God in his *A Faithful Narrative of the Surprising Work of God in the Conversion of Many Hundred Souls in Northampton, Mass. A.D. 1775*. We must not throw out the baby with the bathwater!

THE PATTERNS OF CONVERSION

Unquestionably the format in the conversion experience varies. Conversions recorded in the Bible demonstrate no uniform type of experience to be expected or sought. Christian biography and autobiography further attest to the fascinating divergence of outward circumstance and configuration within the dynamic of spiritual rebirth.

Dr. Gordon Allport of Harvard reported some years ago concerning a group of college students who had experienced conversion. Seventy-one percent indicated their conversion was a gradual awakening; 15 percent experienced conversion after an emotional stimulus in relation to a specific event; and 14 percent described a crisis kind of conversion.[20] Allport further observed an ever-lowering age for conversion. This would contrast with older studies—such as that of Starbuck in 1899, at which time conversion very definitely usually occurred in later adolescence.[21]

Psychological and sociological factors accompany the spiritual dynamics of conversion just as surely as they did in the great spiritual movements of history (for example, the Protestant Reformation or the great revivals which swept across Scandinavia in the last century). Factors which influence the shape and format of the conversion experience include: 1) parental relationship, and the nature and kind of adolescent rebellion experienced; 2) identification figures; 3) personality structure (to be addressed subsequently); 4) the spirit of the times and the cultural milieu; 5) group expectation (how the group defines the format of the conversion experience will greatly influence how individuals in that group develop their own experience).

George Albert Coe, a devotee of Bushnell, felt strongly at the turn of the last century that conversions in their more traditional form were dying out. He stated that 82 percent of those who had experienced a crisis-type of conversion experience had a sensitive, emotional, and high-strung, manic-depressive kind of personality.[22] He would be shocked indeed to see in our day the resurgence of crusade evangelism around the world. But at the same time, temperament does have a pivotal role in determining the format of individual conversions.

For some persons, conversion has a substantial intellectual and cerebral component. The mind and its grasp of certain basic facts must be engaged for all, to be sure. But for some, conversion is largely the resolution of doubts and intellectual struggles. Clearly the conversion of C. S. Lewis was of this order, and T. S Eliot as well. T. S. Eliot, this century's most significant poet in the English language, was early drawn to Bishop Lancelot Andrewes. "Andrewes' emotions were controlled by his intellect. Eliot found he felt more sympathy for the cool, cultivated temper of Andrewes than for John Donne's flashing brilliance."[23] In both these cases, God opened the eyes of the understanding. Apologetics looms large in the process the Spirit uses to reach such persons.

Others evince a heavier emotional component. Emotion is a rich part of human life and experience. After all, love itself involves emotion. Some persons weep easily and express their feelings with little inhibition, so we are not surprised that for them conversion entails much more feeling and fervor. It would be a serious mistake to view this format as normal for all, but it is legitimate for some. Dr. Gordon H. Clark, a highly respected evangelical philosopher and theologian, had little esteem for emotion and felt it had no place in evangelism. For him, evangelism is the exposition of Scripture. He speaks of Stott's "non-theological views" in pressing for more than intellectual assent. Clark also finds Charles Hodge deficient because he insisted "Faith is more than simple assent." Indeed, Calvin himself made a slip in wanting to include the heart as well as the head. All of which is to say that D. L. Moody, in Clark's view, had very little gospel and Billy Sunday even less (although Clark himself came to Christ under the ministry of Billy Sunday).[24] Does not this limit the sovereign Holy Spirit of God?

For still others, the conversion experience is more a volitional shift in which the will seems under particular address, as in the case of St. Augustine's coming to Christ. Augustine had been under effective preaching in Milan and was intellectually challenged. His mother's prayers haunted him. Then one day, sitting in the garden, he heard a voice tell him to take and read the Scripture. The passage to which he gave attention was a direct summons to action—Romans 13:11-14. He went to his Heavenly Father and found new life in Christ.

Carl G. Jung, the eminent analyst, testified that every solution to human problems was, from his point of view, essentially religious. He said rightly that if some antagonist challenges your testimony of spiritual experience, you have only to say, "I have had this experience." The discussion and debate are ended there. What can be disputed?[25] Conversion is not a violation of human personality; it is the *integration* of human personality. Said Henry Martyn, pioneer missionary to India and Persia, "Since I have known God in a saving manner, painting, poetry and music, have had charms unknown to me before. I have received what I suppose is a taste for them: for religion has refined my mind and made it susceptible of impressions from the sublime and beautiful."[26]

SOME PROBLEMS IN CONVERSION

While a variety of implications rising out of the conversion experience will be explored at various points in this book, several major areas of special concern will be pinpointed here.

1) *Generational problems.* The writings of Piaget, the French educational psychologist, and Lawrence Kohlberg, the Princeton psychologist, have raised many issues with respect to what children can and do understand morally. All who are concerned about the conversion of children realize how susceptible to suggestion little children are. Great care and much prayer must be exercised by and on behalf of those who work with children.[27] The importance of relationships within the child's home also cannot be overemphasized.[28] James Y. Fowler has been especially helpful in tracing the stages of faith in relation to conversional change.[29] And Robert Coles of Harvard continues to do very important research and writing on the spiritual life of children.[30] I believe we are all agreed that we want children to come to Christ, but we must seek this cautiously and wisely.

2) *Cross-cultural problems.* The tremendous movements of God in the Two-thirds World, with people coming to Christ in unprecedented numbers, raise important issues about the format of conversion experience. When we realize the scope of the Protestant explosion in Latin America, with Brazil and Guatemala now being perhaps 20 to 30 percent Protestant and three-quarters of the converts Pentecostal, we perceive a situation from which we can learn about what "takes"

cross-culturally.[31] What about evangelism and conversion in African-American churches in the U.S.?[32] The quality of preaching and music preferences and styles are indeed central. What distinctive patterns must be built and used in ethnic groups both within and beyond our borders?

3) *Communicational problems.* The Biblical gospel message with its transforming salvation through the supernatural Christ has been deemed of no value by our culture intellectually, psychologically, and methodologically again and again. Yes, we have made horrendous blunders and have failed abysmally in one way or another. Yet, God's truth marches on, and people are being saved. How tragic it would be if we were to now emasculate the gospel in order to communicate to modern listeners. Yes, we need to creatively shape our presentation for our particular audience, but never at the expense of the good news Christ has commissioned us to proclaim. So much of what the church publishes and preaches today is the pabulum of narcissism and veiled hedonism. Charles Hodge worried about preaching in his day, and so might we. His concern—"Conviction of sin is made of little account, Christ and His Atonement are kept out of view, so that the matter of salvation is not distinctly presented to the minds of the people"[33]—ought to be our concern in these days in which we live as well.

PART II

Sent to Preach

4

The Ancestry of
Evangelistic Preaching

Like cold water to a weary soul is good news from a distant land.

(Proverbs 25:25)

And he sent them out to preach the kingdom of God. . . .

(Luke 9:2)

So they set out and went from village to village, preaching the gospel. . . .

(Luke 9:6)

He welcomed them and spoke to them about the kingdom of God. . . .

(Luke 9:11)

Jesus said to him, "Let the dead bury their own dead, but you go and proclaim the kingdom of God."

(Luke 9:60)

Since the first priority of the worshiping community is evangelism, and since the goal of evangelism is conversion—that is, the radical rewriting of each person's spiritual autobiography—we must now explore the documents which provide our basic norms and paradigms. While Holy

Scripture does not give us detailed instructions for evangelism, just as it does not give us a precise model for church government or the exact format for the worship of God, we do find essential principles clearly expounded and helpfully exemplified in both the Old and New Testaments, and especially in the latter.

While it is true that the word *evangelism* was not generally used in relation to the ministry of the church until the nineteenth century, nevertheless the Bible is an evangelistic book in which evangelism is seen taking place. Certainly verbal proclamation is the very essence of evangelism, but we all agree that alone it is not enough.[1] Strategization for world evangelization involves both Christian presence and Christian proclamation. We shall be giving careful attention to the broader thrust of evangelism in our time and a total strategy of evangelism for the local church, but at this point we want to examine with some care the genealogy of evangelistic preaching.

While excluding no sound or wise methodology in evangelism, I would maintain with Dr. Vernon L. Stanfield that "the pulpit is our supreme evangelistic opportunity,"[2] whether that pulpit be in the local church, the rescue mission, the prison, an evangelistic crusade in a community, or whatever. As the Apostle Paul stated it: "God was pleased through the foolishness of what was preached to save those who believe" (1 Corinthians 1:21b). The current evangelistic dormancy in many local churches and among many Christians can be traced in large part to deficiency in the pulpit—and specifically a diminution of both evangelistic fervor and theological substance.[3]

OLD TESTAMENT ANTECEDENTS

> Out of the crooked timber of humanity no straight thing was ever made. (Immanuel Kant)

The overwhelming testimony of that two-thirds of our Bible we call the Old Testament indicts the tragic lostness and sinfulness of humanity. This tragedy was the consequence of the disobedience of our first parents and our involvement in their revolt against God. Human history would be essentially inexplicable were the third chapter of Genesis to be excised. Apart from a historic fall by a historic Adam and Eve in a historic Garden of Eden, the human predicament would have to be explained as the result of our being created as finite beings, and thus God would be ultimately responsible for our plight. (This is precisely what Reinhold Niebuhr argues in his Gifford Lectures, *Human Nature and Destiny*.)

In arguing that human sin is man "*incurvatus in se*" ("turning in upon himself"), Luther articulated what is clear on every page of the Old Testament: "The heart is deceitful above all things and beyond cure" (Jeremiah 17:9).The violence, the cruelty, the rapacious greed and great wickedness we read about in Holy Writ—it all mirrors the depravity in our own hearts. These are but specimen pages in the long dirge of human despair, a relentless litany of human woe and wickedness.

But—praise God!—immediately upon the debacle of our first parents' deviation, the sunlight of divine grace and love burst through, for we see the forgiving God in pursuit of guilty sinners and His provision of clothing through the death of innocent animals. "The Lord made garments of skin for Adam and his wife and clothed them" (Genesis 3:21). Even more, He promised them a Savior who was to be born of woman (Genesis 3:15, the *protevangelium*).

While we do not find find a great deal of formal discourse (i.e., formal preaching) in the Old Testament, there is proclamation aplenty—by seers, sages, and prophets.[4] Indeed, the good news of forgiveness for sin and restoration of fellowship with God is on virtually every page of the Old Testament. Paul assures us: "The Scripture foresaw that God would justify the Gentiles by faith and announced the gospel in advance to Abraham: 'All nations will be blessed through you.' So those who have faith are blessed along with Abraham, the man of faith" (Galatians 3:8, 9). The way of salvation is indeed revealed in the Old Testament. For example, we read concerning Abraham, "Abram believed the Lord, and he credited it to him as righteousness" (Genesis 15:6). The soteriological nexus is stated by Habakkuk: "But the righteous will live by his faith" (Habakkuk 2:4b; cf. Romans 1:17; Galatians 3:11; Hebrews 10:38).

Embedded in the sacrificial system with its axiom, "It is the blood that makes atonement for one's life" (Leviticus 17:11b)—enshrined in the psalmnody of God's ancient covenant people (as in Psalms 32; 51; etc.)—extolled by the prophets (Isaiah 1:18; 55; Jeremiah 31; Ezekiel 36; etc.)—the gospel is found in the Old Testament, because Christ is there! (Cf. Luke 24:27; John 5:39.) God's promise to save all who repent and believe is enunciated and elucidated again and again. Who can say how much any specific Israelite understood as he placed his hand on the head of the sacrificial victim, thus transferring guilt? However, the idea of vicarious atonement is powerfully stated in the Old Testament (cf. Isaiah 53:4-6) and developed further in the intertestamental period.

Those who were saved in Old Testament times believed the promise of God and looked forward to the Messiah who was to come. Paul teaches that God was forbearing with regard to "the sins committed beforehand" (Romans 3:25) in order "to demonstrate his justice at the present time, so as to be just and the one who justifies the man who has faith in Jesus" (Romans 3:26). While the sermon as such did not find formal shape until the synagogue service in the time between the Testaments, the good news was proclaimed in the rituals of the Tabernacle and the Temple, in the revelatory interpretation of God's mighty acts in the history of Israel (for example, the Exodus and Passover), and in the oral repetition of the unique story of God's saving engagement with the human race.

Even though the preaching office as such was not to be established until New Testament times, the words of Abraham to the rich man in torment are significant: "They [the rich man's brothers, still alive on earth] have Moses and the Prophets; let them listen to them" (Luke 16:29). Alford well observes: "This verse furnishes a weighty testimony from our Lord Himself of the sufficiency then of the Old Testament Scriptures for the salvation of the Jews."[5] R. K. Harrison, the distinguished Old Testament scholar, advocating gospel preaching from the Old Testament, puts it well when he says, "I have no difficulty in seeing His presence, both in prefigurement and prophecy, in the Old Testament Scriptures."[6]

God's very election of Israel was missionary in purpose. Chosen in her weakness (cf. Deuteronomy 7:7ff.; 9:5ff.), Israel was chosen to serve. Rowley makes the point well that those who are chosen are not always so choice.[7] Nevertheless, God elected Israel to be His witnesses to the nations (Isaiah 43:8-14). But again the book of Jonah shows how easily God's servants allow narrow, selfish interests to supplant the mission of witness and testimony. Scot McKnight has demonstrated how Jewish missionary activity was virtually nil during the Second Temple Period. There were a few "evangelists" but *no* aggressive missionary instinct.[8]

GOSPEL PRECEDENTS

To escape the wrath and curse of God due to us for sin, God requires of us faith in Jesus Christ, repentance unto life, with the diligent use of all the outward means whereby Christ communicates to us the benefits of redemption. (*Westminster Shorter Catechism*, question 85)

The Lord Jesus Christ came to preach the gospel; but even more, He came so there would be a gospel to preach. His forerunner, John the Baptist, came "preaching in the Desert of Judea and saying, 'Repent, for the kingdom of heaven is near'" (Matthew 3:1). The Lord Jesus continued that ministry, as we read in the next chapter: "From that time on Jesus began to preach, 'Repent, for the kingdom of heaven is near'" (Matthew 4:17). When we agree with Ozora S. Davis, one-time president of Chicago Theological Seminary, that "Christian preaching is still the compelling engagement of the Church,"[9] we are arguing on the basis of what Jesus Himself did. Thirty-three different terms are used in the New Testament to speak of communicating the gospel. There is a vital oral dimension to what Christ and the apostles did.

Certainly Jesus engaged in personal encounters in one-on-one settings—for example, He conversed with the Samaritan woman at the well. Jesus always had time for individuals. The Gospel of John especially pinpoints some of the interviews Jesus had with a most intriguing variety of sinners, with eternal consequences. Certainly Jesus invested much time with the Twelve and other immediate followers. He gave them what amounted to a three-year course in pastoral ministry and evangelism. But He also spoke to the multitudes which continually crowded in upon Him.

Jesus was a *preacher*. The message which He brought did not fit His times or His world, His *sitz im leben* or the traditions which developed around Him. But He preached with authority. He analyzed his audiences (as in the Parable of the Sower) and skillfully and vividly addressed His hearers. Ninety-eight percent of His gospel preaching is identified as to specific audience, and Baird has analyzed the four basic audiences Jesus addressed.[10] He spoke simply and directly to the common people, who heard Him gladly. His powerful metaphors and similes and His humorous sense of the incongruous arrested His listeners and led them into spiritual truth. Raymond Bailey in a recent study has admirably shown how our Lord captured the power of language and harnessed it to communicate the good news.[11]

The centrality of the preaching/teaching ministry of Jesus (words which are used virtually synonymously in the Gospels) is seen in a careful inductive study of the Synoptics. Matthew makes twelve specific references to preaching. Mark also makes twelve references (including two to the worldwide preaching of the gospel—13:10; 14:9). And Luke makes twenty-four references to preaching (including two references to the universal appeal of the gospel—2:10, 31). Dr. Luke underscores the importance of gospel preaching in the ministry of Jesus in the memorable words: "But he said, 'I must preach the good news of the kingdom of God to the other towns also, because that is why I was sent.' And he kept on preaching in the synagogues of Judea" (Luke 4:43, 44). The watershed passage in Luke shows the Savior just about to reach Jerusalem on His final journey—the triumphal entry is next—and then comes Jesus' meeting with Zacchaeus and the tax-collector's conversion and the pungent summary, "For the Son of Man came to seek and to save what was lost" (Luke 19:10).

Jesus preached about the lostness and sinfulness of all people (see, for example, Matthew 7:17-23; Luke 11:13; 15). He preached the love of the Heavenly Father and prophesied repeatedly concerning His substitutionary death for sinners (Mark 10:45). He taught about Heaven and Hell. He taught that people ought to repent and believe on Him (John 3:16, 36; 5:24). He taught about regeneration (John 3:3, 5) and justification (Luke 18:9-14). He taught about conversion and becoming like a little child in order to enter the Kingdom (Matthew 18:1ff.). He invited sinners to come to Him for rest and forgiveness (Matthew 11:28-30). It is no wonder that godly pastors and evangelists have through the centuries preached on conspicuous conversions in the Gospels—Nicodemus, the Samaritan woman, blind Bartimaeus, Zacchaeus, the dying thief, etc.[12] On page after page of the Gospels we see the beauty and miracle of God's saving grace.

A sample discourse of our Lord, recorded in the Gospel of John, shows Jesus taking His hearers beyond a focus on the natural and the visible to the spiritual and the invisible (John 6:32ff.), speaking of Himself as the life-giving Bread of God. On that occasion Jesus enunciated an essential principle: "No one can come to me unless the Father who sent me draws him" (v. 44a). Clearly, the initiative is solely God's. Jesus quoted the prophet Isaiah: "'They will all be taught by God'" (v. 45). The Father has decreed that "everyone who looks to the Son and believes in him shall have eternal life" (v. 40). As a consequence, "Everyone who listens to the Father and learns from him comes to me [Christ]" (v. 45). Being drawn by the Father does not overrule human free will. As Augustine says in this regard: "If a man is drawn, says an objector, he comes against his will. [We answer] if he comes unwillingly, he does not believe: if he does not believe, he does not come. For we do not run to Christ on our feet but by faith; not with the movement of the body, but with the free will of the heart. Think not that thou art drawn against thy will: the mind can be drawn by love."

Sadly, some claim that the gospel cannot be defined. But as a well-known bishop honestly asks, "If there is no unchanging truth, what do we evangelize about?" Some ecumenical pluralists fault "the evangelical pietistic idea of the sudden change of the individual's heart" and assert, mistakenly, that recent Biblical and historical studies indicate this is a rather modern concept. A Roman Catholic writer more accurately indicates that conversion in the New Testament was indeed a one-time event. But sadly he then separates himself from the Biblical norm by asserting that now conversion is process, not event.[13]

Another critical issue relating to Jesus' pattern for evangelism is raised by John Wimber and the "signs and wonders" movement of our time. In his book *Power Evangelism* he essentially argues for a Gospel hermeneutic (similar to classic Pentecostals who would argue from a book of Acts hermeneutic that we need to experience and re-create the book of Acts).[14] No serious student of Scripture would deny that in both the Gospels and in Acts basic principles are laid down, but the pressing question is: What in the Gospels and in Acts is principial, and what is accidental or time-bound? The sense in which Scripture is our model is an exceedingly important issue. The baby leaping in its mother's womb (Luke 1:41) is not a permanent phenomenon we are to try to duplicate. The sound of a mighty rushing wind on the Day of Pentecost is not a permanent requirement for the church. However, principles of spiritual leadership and Spirit-led witness are meant for the entire church of all ages.

Leaning heavily on Mark 16:9-20, John 14:12, and the concept of the overlapping of this age and the age to come, Wimber argues that effective evangelism must be accompanied with corroborating signs and wonders. However, we need to balance this expectation with the words of Jesus in Matthew 16:1-4. Why do we not see resurrections from the dead in the Wimber movement? (Then again, even a resurrection—Christ's or another's—would not convince some; see Luke 16:31.) Also, John 10:41, 42 describes a mighty ministry without miraculous attestation: "And many people came to him. They said, 'Though John never performed a miraculous sign, all that John said about this man was true.' And in that place many believed in Jesus."

Signs and wonders are given or withheld according to the sovereignty of God. In special times there have indeed been breakthroughs of supernatural happenings to accredit Christian testimony (especially where gospel rains are falling for the first time), but nothing in Scripture or church history would lead us to believe that such are normative in evangelism. The power in evangelism is the power of the cross of our Lord Jesus Christ and the transforming power of the gospel (Romans 1:16). The inherent power in the gospel of Christ seems displaced in this "third wave" movement, as Peter Wagner calls it. The Great Commission of our Lord (Matthew 28:19, 20) gives us our necessary marching orders.[15] Obeying His command in the power of the Holy Spirit—that is all we need.

VIGNETTES FROM THE BOOK OF ACTS

The Spirit of God maketh the reading, but especially the preaching of the Word, an effectual means of convincing and converting sinners, and of building them up in holiness and comfort, through faith unto salvation. (*Westminster Shorter Catechism*, question 89)

The book of Acts describes for us what one writer has called "an explosion of divine dynamite continuing page after page, life after life." Acts pictures an unhindered gospel unleashed through the Holy Spirit. The context for this spiritual conflagration is preaching. As James said, "For Moses has been preached in every city from the earliest times and is read in the synagogues on every Sabbath" (Acts 15:21). The apostolic preachers preached the Word, preached the gospel, preached Jesus Christ, and preached the Kingdom of God—and all who follow in their train do likewise.

The daunting task of evangelism in an idol-filled world is movingly portrayed by Michael Green in his epochal work *Evangelism in the Early Church*.[16] Evil supernaturalism was (and is) frenetically opposed to the advance of the gospel. A complex Gentile society confronted the Pauline mission.[17] The message being preached was Jesus Christ, the Sin-bearer, crucified and raised from the dead. The early Christian proclaimers quoted much from the Old Testament, even when they were preaching to largely Gentile audiences. The challenge of contextualization was met without sanitizing the gospel of its less attractive components. As Dietrich Ritschl well put it for us today: "There is no special gospel for modern man."

Not only did the apostles preach, but we read, "Those who had been scattered preached the word wherever they went. Philip went down to a city in Samaria and proclaimed [preached] the Christ there" (Acts 8:4, 5). Several words are used to set forth such promulgation (cf. Acts 11:19, 20). In addition to preaching, evangelism is visitation evangelism and personal evangelism and educational evangelism.[18]

C. H. Dodd drew a sharp distinction between preaching (*kerygma*) and teaching (*didache*) in the early church. The specific Christocentric content of the former (the age of fulfillment has come—Christ came, died, rose again, is now exalted, and will return—therefore you must repent and believe) is contrasted with the basically ethical message in Christian teaching. Robert Worley, Robert Mounce, and Jesse

Weatherspoon have all critiqued Dodd as oversimplifying the data.[19] In my view all good preaching has a substantive teaching element and all good teaching becomes preaching at some point. The *kerygma* includes teaching, and, as Stendahl correctly argues, preaching has ethical content.

Michael Green points out that for a hundred and fifty years the early church had no buildings as such, and "there was the greatest variety in the type and content of Christian evangelistic preaching."[20] Portions of eleven sermons are to be found in Acts, all but one of which were essentially addressed to the unconverted. These sermons were saturated with Old Testament Scripture (with the one exception being Paul's sermon in Athens, which shows the skill of adapting—but not compromising—the message for a unique setting),[21] were heavily doctrinal, were Christ-centered, were plain and direct calling for a commitment, were both thinking and feeling, and were kindled by prayer and empowered by the Spirit. Careful study of the actual samples of preaching in the book of Acts is not only spiritually invigorating but imperative for charting a course for evangelistic preaching in our time.[22]

The Apostle Peter's mighty sermon on the Day of Pentecost, like the other sermons, was carefully built on a single theme: *Jesus Christ is Lord!* (cf. Acts 2:14-40). After making his point of contact with his hearers by referring to the immediate situation, Peter proceeded: An ancient prophecy was quoted, vv. 16-21 (here was the authority for that which was being proclaimed). A supernatural person was proclaimed, vv. 22-24 ("God raised him"). Conclusive proof was cited, vv. 25-31 (Scripture was quoted again). The fulfilled promise was announced, vv. 32-36 ("God has made this Jesus . . . both Lord and Christ!"). And then to those who were cut to the heart under the conviction of the Holy Spirit, Peter pressed for a response. He warned, and he pleaded, and many accepted his message.

At the heart of what we might call the Antioch analogy (Acts 13:1-4) is the remarkable vision and aggressiveness of the Apostle Paul. Green quotes Professor Chadwick as saying, "Paul's genius as an apologist is his astonishing ability to reduce to an apparent vanishing point the gulf between himself and his converts, and yet to 'gain' them for the Christian gospel."[23] In the remarkable study *Paul the Convert*, written by the Jewish scholar Alan F. Segal, the author recognizes the authenticity of Paul's conversion.[24] Paul's sense of the dissonance between the Pharisaic Jewish community of his upbringing which he left behind and the Christian community of Jesus was resolved in submission to Christ and a resultant passion for evangelism.[25]

Paul's conversion became a model for all conversion (i.e., the theology of his conversion, not its format). In this connection note 1 Timothy 1:12-17. Argues Segal: "Conversion provided the dynamic for a true religious revolution in the late Roman Empire and a startling innovation in religious patterns."[26] And, "For Paul, the Jew as well as the Gentile must be converted, and the new community that Jesus founded must be a community of converts."[27] That is the book of Acts in a nutshell, and it is still the truth today. Thus, evangelistic preaching is yet part of the picture, and the revivalistic pattern is not irrelevant.

The preaching of Paul in the synagogue in Pisidian Antioch laid bare a strategy for reaching out both to Jews and Gentiles who feared God (Acts 13:16), but warms up to the latter (13:26). And virtually all distinctions have vanished by verse 38. This message is not dissimilar to Stephen's in Acts 7:

I. An Old Testament retrospect, 13:17-22.
II. The glorious Redeemer, 13:23-39 (Christ is the heart and center).
III. A most pressing and urgent reminder, 13:40, 41.

Another of Paul's sermons, that given in Athens (Acts 17:22-31), again launches appropriately from the immediate situation and is not an example of his infidelity to the gospel, as some have argued, but is rather evidence of his consummate skill as an evangelist. The sermon strategy is most impressive:

I. God is the Creator, 17:22-26.
II. God is the Sustainer, 17:27-29.
III. God is the Judge, 17:30, 31. And Christ is the climax!

EPISTOLARY ACCENTS

Whose glory it was to proclaim the gospel of our Lord Jesus Christ. (Plaque of the preachers in First Presbyterian, Pittsburgh)

Even as the risen Christ addressed letters to the seven churches of Asia Minor (Revelation 2, 3), so the inspired Apostle Paul addressed seven churches before coming to certain more personal correspondence. The order is not accidental.[28] The letter to the Romans almost hyperventilates with Paul's passion—"I am so eager to preach the gospel also to you who are at Rome" (Romans 1:15). Paul longs for a spiritual harvest, and in this most theological of all of his statements of the divine plan of salvation he leads us step by step from universal condemnation to the sinner's justification, sanctification, and glorification. The Romans road is the road all Christians have taken, and the preacher needs to know it well.

Apostolic Strategization

We're looking at what Adolf Harnack called "missionary preaching" as he traced the mission and expansion of Christianity in the early centuries. Paul basically developed an urban strategy. He traveled over ten thousand miles, from city to city. He exercised geographic and social mobility as he touched a remarkable cross section of society. The church emerged as a rich mixture of varied social strata.[29] The contours and configurations of the underlying strategy are profitably analyzed for our own strategizing. Paul was flexible in format (1 Corinthians 9:19-23) but was unyielding as to the purity of the gospel in a syncretistic world (Galatians 1:6-10).[30] The working paradigm is set forth clearly in Romans 10:14-21:

1) Our objective is to send.
2) Those who are sent are to preach.
3) Those who hear are to believe.
4) Those who believe will be saved.

Apostolic Evangelization

Paul wanted to do pioneer evangelism and church planting (Romans 15:17-20). The "work of the evangelist" (2 Timothy 4:5) is never depicted as separate from the corporate life of a local assembly. Paul spoke of ninety-nine different persons in his epistles, showing his deep concern for individuals. He prayed continually for the churches, even for the congregation at Colosse which he had not visited at the time he wrote to them. All of his labors were with reference to the will of God (Romans 1:9, 10), an ever-deepening sense of his total dependence on God's Spirit (1 Corinthians 2:1-5; 1 Thessalonians 1:4, 5), and a mounting sense of the urgency of the evangelistic task in light of the imminent return of Jesus Christ (1 Thessalonians 4:13-18). Paul was a firebrand for God.

Apostolic Instruction

Paul rejoiced to see individuals converted to the Savior, but he did not then abandon them. The epistles were an important part of his follow-up. New babes in Christ must be nurtured and cared for "as a father deals with his own children" and "like a mother caring for her little children" (1 Thessalonians 2:7-12). Paul's kinship language in reference to the Thessalonians is moving and exemplary. But it is all predicated on a *bona fide* conversion experience. The balance of the New Testament epistles round out the kind of pastoral care necessary in the Christian community.[31]

From the *protevangelium* in Genesis 3:15 to the final chapter and climactic invitation in the Revelation, we see God's invitation to guilty rebels: "The Spirit and the bride say, 'Come!' And let him who hears say, 'Come!' Whoever is thirsty, let him come; and whoever wishes, let him take the free gift of the water of life" (Revelation 22:17). This constitutes the heritage bequeathed to the church and all Christians today. May we not hesitate or equivocate in our fidelity to "the faith that was once for all entrusted to the saints" (Jude 3).

5

The Continuity of Evangelistic Preaching

Day after day, in the temple courts and from house to house, they never stopped teaching and proclaiming the good news that Jesus is the Christ.

(Acts 5:42)

I preached what I felt, what I smartingly did feel.

(John Bunyan)

I gave them Christ.

(John Wesley)

Through the infinite goodness of God, I felt what I spoke.

(David Brainerd)

To preach Jesus is to preach peace, joy, life. The evangelist, that is, the bearer of the glad tidings, "opens his mouth, and beginning at (whatever) Scripture, preaches Jesus" (Acts 8:35, 10:36).

(Adolph Saphir)[1]

The pylons of the evangelistic enterprise (and of evangelistic preaching, its critical component) are sunk deeply into Holy Scripture and its supernatural revelation of Jesus Christ as Savior and Lord. All who subsequently preach the gospel stand in the succession of Acts 8, where we see *preaching* evangelism as Philip goes to Samaria and proclaims "the good news of the kingdom of God" (Acts 8:12) and also *personal* evangelism as Philip leads the Ethiopian eunuch to the Lord and into the waters of baptism (Acts 8:27ff.). We see the further enlargement and extension of the circle as Peter preaches to Gentiles in the house of Cornelius (Acts 10, 11).

The basic New Testament idea is seen in Romans 15 where Paul describes his passionate preaching over a period of time: "I have fully proclaimed the gospel of Christ" (v. 19b). This is a strategic element of the building of the church in a wide geographic area. By the end of the first century, church historians estimate, there were one million believers in the ancient Roman world. It is valuable for us to trace the essential continuity in the evangelistic message and motive from that time to the present.

THE SURGE

> Be thorough in your study of church history and of the great things which God has done in various eras and periods. (D. Martyn Lloyd-Jones)[2]

The powerful spiritual thrust mounted by the early Christian church was based on the absolute certainty of the bodily resurrection of Jesus Christ. The Easter event was the launching pad for what ensued in the thought and life of the church.[3] The Holy Spirit moved powerfully on the apostles and their successors to propel them into powerful witness, in fulfillment of Jesus' words recorded in Acts 1:8. Particularly striking is the clear continuity in gospel proclamation from the apostles to the early fifth century. This witness was in the family circle and in society as a whole and not infrequently led to martyrdom.[4]

In his classic treatment *The Decline and Fall of the Roman Empire*, Edward Gibbon attributes the rise of Christianity to a number of factors, one of which was the extraordinary zeal of the early believers for their faith.[5] There was much lay preaching.[6] Indeed, Origen was invited to "expound the sacred Scriptures publicly" before he was ordained an elder. In commenting on Psalm 36, likening Christian preachers to arrows, Origen said: "All in whom Christ speaks, that is to say every upright man and preacher who speaks the word of God to bring men to salvation—and not merely the apostles and prophets—can be called an arrow of God. But what is rather sad, I see very few arrows of God. There are few who so speak that they inflame the heart of the hearer, drag him away from his sin, and convert him to repentance."[7] (Origen lived A.D. 185-254.)

Bible reading and preaching were the chief elements in early Christian public gatherings.[8] Irenaeus (c. A.D. 135-185) argued, "The preaching of the truth shines everywhere and enlightens all men that are willing to come to a knowledge of the truth."[9] There was no effort to keep this proclamation from being doctrinally explicit. As Michael Green aptly characterized this preaching: "Primitive evangelism was by no means mere proclamation and exhortation; it included able intellectual argument, skillful study of the Scriptures, careful, closely reasoned teaching and patient argument."[10] Christianity presented ideas which required a choice. Yale historian Ramsay MacMullen helpfully analyzes "evangelical campaigns and publicity" which by A.D. 313 (the time of the conversion of Constantine) brought the church to five million adherents.[11]

While there were variations in approach and style, there was a fundamental ongoing identity in the message of Jesus and His resurrection which thundered forth into the spiritual battle.[12] Eusebius, the early church historian (A.D. 260-340), described evangelism in this period:

> They augmented the means of promulgating the gospel more and more, and spread the seeds of salvation and of the heavenly kingdom throughout the world, far and wide ... afterwards leaving their country, they performed the office of evangelists to those who had not yet heard the faith, whilst with a noble ambition to proclaim Christ, they also delivered to them the books of the holy gospels ... so that as soon as the gospel was heard, men voluntarily gathered in crowds, and eagerly embraced the true faith with their whole minds.

He later spoke of "many evangelists of the word, who were ardently striving to employ their inspired zeal after the apostolic example to increase and build up the divine word."[13]

It is not our purpose to analyze the sermon or specific preachers as such during this period, nor how the Biblical message increasingly took on Greek rhetorical form. But we can discern the struggle for the purity of the gospel which was taking place then, as throughout the history of the church.[14] So quickly did the message of *sola gratia* recede. T. F. Torrance has shown how rapidly sacramental and philosophic ideas threatened to smother the doctrine of grace even in the apostolic age. "Failure to apprehend the meaning of the Cross and to make it a saving article of faith is surely the clearest indication that a genuine doctrine of grace is absent."[15]

Nonetheless, the expansion of the church in the first five centuries is a most thrilling demonstration of the Spirit's power.[16] What started with the twelve apostles, a group lacking in background, education, and skill (what management consulting firm would have chosen them?), caught fire, and a mighty spiritual conflagration raged for centuries afterwards. Hallelujah!

THE SLUMBER

How did Christianity rise and spread? Was it by institutions and establishments and well-arranged systems of mechanism? No! It arose in the mystic depths of man's soul; and was spread by the "preaching of the Word," by simple, altogether natural and individual efforts; and flew, like hallowed fire, from heart to heart. . . . (Thomas Carlyle)[17]

After the collapse of the Roman Empire, the wreckage wrought by the barbarians, and the doctrinal divisions in the church came a thousand years known as the Dark Ages or the Middle Ages. The Constantinian age was one of accommodation and compromise, of worldliness and the secularization of the church. The rise of the bishop of Rome and the imperial papacy threatened to snuff out the light of the gospel in such excesses as the Crusades. Ignorance, superstition, and corruption, along with the rise of Islam and pernicious errors such as Pelagianism, seemed about to extinguish spiritual vitality. "The light that failed" could be written over many geographic areas as the church seemed to be in retreat.[18]

Gregory the Great (A.D. 540-604) embodied the contradictions and calamities of his age. This powerful spiritual leader was the architect of the medieval papacy, veered toward a ransom theory of the atonement, was the first to define purgatory, and yet held strongly to a high view of Scripture (as did all for a thousand years except Theodore of Mopsuestia). He was the first preacher "to make systematic use of illustration and anecdote,"[19] and he inaugurated the movement which led to the evangelization of the Germans, Great Britain, and northern Europe. So even in this most disheartening epoch, God faithfully blessed His Word, and many came to Christ. Such preachers as Gregory the Illuminator in Armenia, Ulfilas among the Germanic tribes, St. Patrick in Ireland, and Ansgar (the French missionary to Scandinavia) were on the honor role of those who proclaimed "the unsearchable riches of Christ" (Ephesians 3:7).[20]

A sovereign God using His strategy of divine providence was graciously at work even in this benighted time of violence, plagues, and oppression. Through more enlightened kings (for example, Charlemagne who fostered literacy) and clarion voices (such as Peter Waldo and the Florentine Savonarola), God was working His good plan. Bernard of Clairvaux (A.D. 1091-1153) was a preacher of great power who inveighed against the infallibility of the Pope, the intemperance of monastics, and atrocities against the Jews. He claimed, "To know Jesus and Him crucified is the sum of my philosophy."[21]

Though not as well known as his eighty-six sermons on the Song of Songs, his course of preaching on conversion is most striking. "He was the ambassador of Jesus crucified, the Savior of the world. It is not astonishing then that, himself entirely aflame with the love of God, his greatest desire was to save souls, to urge them to conversion, and to win them over to Christ in the monastic life."[22] These messages on conversion abound with Scripture, and we are told that Bernard would often ask for a show of hands in response to his preaching.

Anthony of Padua (A.D. 1195?-1231) drew huge crowds both indoors and outdoors. He traveled widely in his native Portugal and in Africa. He used extensive illustration and allegory and carefully divided his sermons into key headings. It was not uncommon for him to draw crowds of twenty thousand to thirty thousand. He built huge bonfires in which to burn up playing cards after his preaching. He was known as "the friend of the poor."[23]

Another free-lance evangelist who felt the call of God "to repair His house" was Francis of Assisi (A.D. 1182-1226). Francis himself had a dramatic conversion. His life and ministry were very Christ-centered and focused on the suffering and agony of the crucified Savior. He would visit four or five places a day proclaiming the gospel. Walker observes, "His sermons were described as 'penetrating the heart like fire.'"[24]

Many others punched holes into the darkness of this period in history, among whom should be cited John Wycliffe, Berthold of Regensburg (whose principal theme was repentance), John Tauler of Strasburg, John Geiler of Kaisersberg, and Gerhard Groot of the Netherlands.[25] God never leaves Himself without a witness, and even in the centuries of greatest darkness God sends emissaries of light. The signs and evidences of a fresh visit of God to the world were multiplying even in the agony and death throes of an age.

THE STIRRING

The Reformers re-introduced preaching and put preaching at the center instead of ceremonies and sacraments. (D. Martyn Lloyd-Jones)[26]

The Evangelical Revival several centuries later was, Philip Watson argues, "fundamentally a renewal and extension of the work of Luther's Reformation." [27] Luther's study of Scripture, and especially of Paul's epistle to the Romans, brought him to freedom and what Watson calls a Copernican revolution in theology, in which the center was now God rather than self, toward which medieval moralism had tended. He found in the cross of Christ the resolution to the tension between God's wrath and God's mercy.[28] Bainton traces the way Luther traveled to his Damascus Road experience.[29] *Sola Scriptura* (only the Bible) was his principle of authority. This led to three glorious related truths: *sola gratia* (only grace), *solo Christo* (only Christ), and *sola fide* (only faith). This spiritual revolution brought a revival of Biblical preaching such as had not been seen for a long time.

This soteriological clarification was nothing less than the recovery of the gospel. Little wonder that Luther preached with such power and results. "Hence true faith in Christ is a treasure beyond comparison, which brings with it all salvation and saves from every evil."[30] The preaching of the Reformer was Christ-centered. His statements "Nothing except Christ is to be preached" and "Where the devil does not find Christ he has already won the game" typify the kind of influence Luther would exert on subsequent generations.[31]

While some Lutheran scholastics would bog down, and some medieval philosophy would lead to the hardening of certain categories, Pietists with roots in Bengel's exegesis would through Spener and Franke sustain the essential elements of Luther's epochal insights. What was said of the situation prior to the Reformation could now be said after the Reformation: "While Meister Eckhart continued to focus on the experience of the Christian life, the dominant Scholastic mode of theology effectively lost the experience of conversion in metaphysical analysis."[32]

John Calvin likewise did not find morality enough to feed his undying soul and at age twenty-three experienced genuine conversion and, except for a brief exile, worked from 1536 until 1564 as a minister of the gospel in Geneva. The Bible was his authority and Christ's saving work the only answer to man's depravity.

A direct descendant of Calvin was John Knox in Scotland, of whom Lloyd-Jones pungently observed: "He preached with fire and power, alarming sermons, convicting sermons, humbling sermons, converting sermons, and the face of Scotland was changed."[33]

This is the positive legacy of the Protestant Reformation after a thousand years, when evangelistic preaching had almost been abandoned. Though there was a healthy re-emphasis on the resurrection of Christ, Perry and Strubhar well quote A. T. Pierson: "The main weakness of the Reformation was its failure to revive evangelistic activity, although there was a renewal of evangelical faith."[34] It remains for others to evaluate this in light of the New Testament paradigm, in which gospel facts are stated and response is solicited.

THE SLOWDOWN

> Our method in proclaiming salvation is this [written of the Moravian revival of 1727]: To point out to every heart the loving Lamb, who died for our sins, by the preaching of His blood, and of His love unto death, even the death of the cross; never, either in the discourse or in the argument, to digress even for a quarter of an hour from the loving Lamb. (Count Zinzendorf)

Even with the doctrinal retrieval, the heirs of the Reformation found themselves embroiled against one another in disputation (Lutherans against Anabaptists, etc.). Feeling the impact of the Enlightenment and its skepticism, western culture was facing moral and spiritual collapse and the kind of nihilistic destruction seen in the French Revolution.

Though Cranmer and company sought the subjection of the church to the Bible in England and enshrined "justification by faith alone" in the *Book of Common Prayer* and the Thirty-nine Articles, England was sinking low spiritually. In response, God sent the Puritans in the seventeenth century and the first Evangelical Awakening in the eighteenth century.

The Puritans were immensely dissatisfied with the Reformation as it had become embodied in the Elizabethan church. They insisted on a conversion experience for every person, and this set Puritanism against the Church of England as it was then constituted for the most part.[35] They preached for such conversion, sought it, and testified of it. "The pangs of new birth" frequently involved a long struggle and intense turmoil. They had clear reservations about "high-speed" evangelism.

Richard Baxter's Puritan formula was, *every pastor is to be an evangelist.* As J. I. Packer helpfully summarizes, the three R's of Puritan preaching were: ruin, redemption, and regeneration.[36] Echoing the Reformation, Robert Bolton insists: "Jesus Christ is offered most freely, and without exception of any person, every Sabbath, every sermon, either in plain and direct terms or implied at the least."[37] Those Puritans transplanted to North America embodied the same concerns as properly preoccupied their British counterparts.

The Evangelical Awakening of the eighteenth century came out of the Reformation, the Pietistic recovery of the Reformation, and the Puritan Revolution.[38] The combustion took place in Northampton, Massachusetts, where Jonathan Edwards was the pastor and where three hundred came to Christ in six months.[39] Vitiated by the disastrous Half-way Covenant, New England was ripe for something special from God.[40] Also at the epicenter in America and Britain was George Whitefield, the "trumpet-voice." The conversion of John and Charles Wesley supplied the Awakening with its genius. The Awakening then moved to Scotland, significantly impacted the Church of England, and gave birth to the modern missions movement and the Sunday school and led to major societal changes (including the abolition of slavery).

Although differing substantively in theological nuancing, Whitefield and Wesley worked together and agreed on the essentiality of the new birth.[41] Progeny of these deep movings of the Spirit of God multiplied through the Tennents in the Middle Colonies[42] and Christmas Evans in Wales.[43] While further analysis of central issues in these divine visitations will come later, we sense God's faithfulness to bless His Word in fulfillment of His marching orders to the church. May the prayer of all our hearts be, "Lord, do it again!"

THE STARTS AND STOPS

> There are too many persons who have imbibed and propagated this notion, that it is almost the only business of a preacher to teach the necessary doctrines and duties of our holy religion by a mere explication of the Word of God without enforcing these things on the conscience by a pathetic address to the heart. (Isaac Watts)

The nineteenth century saw waves of spiritual renewal both in North America and abroad. The early spiritual giant Charles G. Finney (1792-1875) is often called the father of modern evangelism.[44] Finney's revivalism is well-flavored with Jacksonian democracy. An attorney by training, Finney traveled widely and was responsible for the so-called "new measures" in evangelism—evangelistic music, the anxious seat or mourner's bench, the participation of women, and the protracted meeting. The great Rochester, New York, revival was conducted from September 10, 1830 to March 6, 1831. Over ten thousand people made professions of faith in Christ, and the community was deeply impacted and the churches were demonstrably increased.

We have already made brief critique of some aspects of Finney's theology. Both his message and his methods were controversial. Gardiner Spring and Lyman Beecher, both American Presbyterians, led the frontal assault. Criticism of evangelists is nothing new. The apostles were criticized; the Erskines faulted Whitefield; William G. McLoughlin has moved in on Billy Graham from the left, as many have from the right.[45] We shall have occasion to examine these issues in subsequent sections. Finney traveled widely (itinerant evangelism was now accepted by both Presbyterians and Congregationalists), ministered as pastor of the Broadway Tabernacle in New York City, and served as president of Oberlin College in Ohio.

The Layman's Prayer Revival of 1857-58 brought a great harvest of souls. J. Edwin Orr has traced the widespread awakening variously focused in the nineteenth century.[46] Sometimes the evangelist was a local pastor—for example, Charles Haddon Spurgeon who in his thirty-seven years as pastor of the Metropolitan Tabernacle took in fourteen thousand new members and saw three hundred million copies of his books and sermons distributed.[47] He was called "the last of the Puritans" by the British prime minister William E. Gladstone.

In the United States Lyman Beecher was much used as a pastor and later as a seminary president.[48] He had been converted as a student at Yale University, where Timothy Dwight was the president and saw much transformation in the lives of students. (Dwight was the son of one of Jonathan Edwards's daughters.) Now revivalism was being increasingly adopted as a method of evangelism.

Certainly Dwight Lyman Moody epitomizes the evangelist as we now understand such a role. The great Chicago revival of 1876 saw many confess Christ. At this time half of the population of Chicago was unchurched. The crusade began in October 1876 and lasted for three and a half months. The city was ripe for proclamation; the great Chicago fire of 1871, the Great Panic of 1873, and the Henry Ward Beecher scandal in Brooklyn had all tilled the soil. Nine hundred thousand people attended the tabernacle built for the occasion (seating eight thousand). Four hundred thousand responded to the invitation, of which six thousand joined Chicago churches.

Following Moody's ministry on two continents came J. Wilbur Chapman, R. A. Torrey, William E. Biederwolf, Billy Sunday, Mordecai Ham, B. Faye Mills, John R. Rice, Bob Jones, Sr., and many others. Billy Sunday came to Christ at the Pacific Garden Mission in Chicago; Charles E. Fuller came to Christ through Paul Rader; Jerry Falwell came to Christ through Charles E. Fuller.[49] Local Baptist pastors such as John Roach Stratton of New York City, J. C. Massee of Boston, W. B. Riley of Minneapolis (whose magnificent *The Bible of the Expositor and the*

Evangelist extends through the whole Bible), and George W. Truett of Dallas epitomize what a local pastor can do through pulpit evangelism.

Dean Willard Sperry of Harvard complained in 1946, "We are tired of revivals." One critic observed, "It is unlikely that any professional revivalist will play a major role in future spiritual awakenings." Then in 1949 came the Los Angeles Crusade of Billy Graham. Faithful to the Word of God and true to the message of the cross, Billy Graham has been used around the world in crusades in which millions have made decisions for Christ. His books, television and radio ministry, films, and other outreach approaches have modeled evangelism for thousands of pastors and laypersons. The sovereign God continues to do His work however He chooses.

Furthermore, on every continent itinerant evangelists, pastors, and laypeople are evangelizing in obedience to Christ's command (cf. Matthew 28:19, 20; Acts 1:8). And so it will be until Christ returns for His own. With all of the cultural, ethnic, geographical, and methodological differences, the message of Christ is the same, and the power of God to change human lives and bring them into conformity to the will of God remains the same. So let us lift our hearts and voices in agreement with the Apostle Paul: "I am not ashamed of the gospel, because it is the power of God for the salvation of everyone who believes" (Romans 1:16).

6

The Sociology of Evangelistic Preaching

*Of whom, what thou speakest, and to whom, take fre-
quent heed.*

(The Latin poet Horace)

*The glorious Gospel of the blessed God our Saviour is the
great object of our attention as minister and people; this only
am I allowed to preach, this only are you allowed to hear.*

(William Jay, 1769-1853)

*The preacher, when he preaches his sermon, does not
whisper, even to his wife, his belief that thousands may
perhaps be turned to repentance by his words; but he
thinks that the thousand converts are possible.*

(Anthony Trollope, in *Can He Forgive Her?*)

*A passionate tumultuous age will overthrow everything,
pull everything down; but a revolutionary age that is at
the same time reflective and passionless leaves everything
standing but cunningly empties it of significance.*

(Soren Kierkegaard)

God wants people to be saved. This has been His purpose from all
eternity. For this reason the eternally begotten Son of God took

on humanity "when the time had fully come . . . to redeem those under law" (Galatians 4:4, 5), to effect salvation for sinners (cf. John 3:17; 1 Timothy 1:15). The loving and gracious God desires that sinners be saved. "God our Savior . . . wants all men to be saved and to come to a knowledge of the truth. For there is one God and one mediator between God and men, the man Christ Jesus, who gave himself as a ransom for all men—the testimony given in its proper time" (1 Timothy 2:4-6). Furthermore, there is Scriptural evidence that the Second Advent of our Lord is being delayed so more people will be added to the church of Jesus Christ. "The Lord is not slow in keeping his promise, as some understand slowness. He is patient with you, not wanting anyone to perish, but everyone to come to repentance" (2 Peter 3:9).

The Christian communicator must thus have a passion to see men and women come to Christ. But if we are going to find and rescue lost sheep, we must know something about sheep and their wandering ways. We must make contact with them. If we are going to be fishers of men (and not just keepers of the aquarium), we need to be shrewd judges of the habits of fish and will need to present our bait at the most opportune time and place. The local library's scientific volumes on fishing are analogous to the church growth movement's extensive studies on responsive and unresponsive people groups. Analyzing those we are attempting to reach can be very helpful. To quote from a fishing classic: "Of course, the nature of the sport, the very delicacy of it, requires the fly-fisherman to be utterly attuned to nature's rhythms: to water temperature, hatching cycles, sunlight, barometric pressure, and so on."[1] Analysis of sinners in modern culture is even more valuable.

Some have denied the relevance of cultural exegesis, and certainly we must recognize the dangers attending such *prolegomena*. Karl Barth (consistent with his repudiation of general revelation) believed that the preacher of the Word is essentially speaking to stones. Following his lead, Dietrich Ritschl felt nothing could be learned from secular data which would help the communicator intersect with the contemporary hearer.[2] Jesus, however, analyzed the different kinds of soil into which the sower committed the seed. Also, we have already noticed how earlier and later preachers addressed specific situations (consider Paul in the synagogue and Paul in Athens). As we have been warned, preaching to our age must not reflect or include the mistaken ideas of our age. It is to these issues that we now address ourselves.

CULTURAL ANALYSIS

Massive social and political changes are impacting opportunities for gospel proclamation throughout the world. The collapse of state socialism and communism in Eastern Europe and in the Soviet Union have completely altered the geostrategic nature of the situation we face. The world missionary task is not pursued in a vacuum; each continent and each nation presents its own unique set of circumstances which must be weighed in strategizing for gospel advance.[3]

Certain identifiable trends in western Europe have more direct relevance to the North American church since we seem to be on a track which could be called "the Europeanization of the church." Hence a *Sunday Express* poll of 1,101 adults in fifty-five representative parliamentary constituencies through the United Kingdom indicated that 34 percent did not know what happened on the first Easter Sunday; 39 percent did not know what happened on Good Friday; 50 percent were unable to state outside which city Jesus was crucified. Clearly this shows the shape of things at hand for our own culture, if not already present.[4] The implications of this gross cultural ignorance of anything Biblical or Christian are immense as we seek to shape our communication of the everlasting gospel.

Though the United States has emerged as an uncontested superpower and enjoys relative prosperity among the nations (although having some very painful pockets of poverty), our nation is undeniably on fire within. With one murder every twenty seconds and a rape every four minutes, with millions living in dread of molestation, violence, or harassment, our great cities have become fortresses of fear and our placid small towns and countryside have only an appearance of gentility. As we seek to contextualize the ageless gospel, to translate it into the idiom of our generation, as every previous generation has had to do, to decode it and encode it accurately and effectively, we sense a general feeling of foreboding. Jonathan Weiner in *The Next One Hundred Years* gives an in-depth study of "one of the most dangerous periods since the origin of life." Sixty-nine percent of those polled in a *Time*/CNN study wanted to "slow down and live a more relaxed life." Sixty-one percent noted that "earning a living today requires so much effort that it's difficult to find time to enjoy life."[5] These findings are germane to the communicator who is looking for points of contemporary contact with the modern mind.

We easily observe that the basic paradigms in our society are changing. Alvin Toffler in *Powershift* observes: "We live at a moment when the entire structure of power that held the world together is now disintegrating. A radically different structure of power is taking form. And this is happening at every level of human society." We are seeing a shift from violence to wealth and now to knowledge, Toffler posits, with mass customization replacing mass production. Christians see opportunity in the current crisis because we have *knowledge* that is *life* (John 17:3). The very depersonalization of modern life, even as it alienates and agonizes, opens a door for Christian testimony. As we can infer from John Naisbitt's *Megatrends* axiom, high-tech times give opportunity for high-touch. Thus what we must honestly admit to be a time of serious cultural decomposition and decay affords the Christian proclaimer a multitude of opportunities to minister the message of the changeless Christ. Paganization is depressing, but we must not cower in the face of it all. Factor analysis of the present mind-set is called for as we face the spiritual malaise of our times. Key components and pieces include the following:

1) *Pluralism.* We live in a society which, in theory at least, accepts an incredible variety of ideas and beliefs. Ours is also quite a religious society. The sociologist Peter Berger has noted that the U.S. and India are among the most religious societies in the world (Sweden being the least religious).[6] But the ever-increasing pluralism in our society has brought a noticeable unraveling of any sense of our historic moral moorings, which lay chiefly within the Judeo-Christian ethic. As C. E. M. Joad has suggested, the principal characteristics of a society without moral standards are "luxury, skepticism, weariness and superstition [read New Age spiritualism]."

Multiculturalism easily becomes a code word for the denigration of historical heritage. Relativism then reigns resulting in a theology "in which," as one writer has put it, "the Supreme Being resembles nothing so much as a goo-goo politician with a 100 percent approval rating from the liberal lobbying organizations." In this regard Samuel Johnson, when told of a gentleman who maintained that virtue and vice were indistinguishable, contented himself with observing, "Why, sir, when he leaves our houses let us count our spoons."

Thus in the interest of inter-religious dialogue we are urged to abandon "exclusive claims" and adopt a "revised Christianity."[7] Hence gays and lesbians are being ordained, mainline denominations lean toward approval of homosexual, premarital, and extramarital relations, and Christopher Columbus is castigated by the National Council of Churches for his "invasion" of the western hemisphere. Ironically, along with increasing pluralism and its permissiveness we see the development of growing intolerance by leftists with their insistence on "politically correct" points of view. In this complex climate there is a desperate need for Christian communication.

2) *Secularism.* The word *secular* comes from the Latin *saeculum* ("this age") and refers to the tendency to expunge all elements of the transcendental from conscious awareness and custom. Incongruously, while our society bans manger scenes and crosses from the public square, we turn a blind eye to abortion, pornography, and crime. But sadly, rationalism and the scientific method have not yielded satisfaction in the human quest for meaning.

As powerful as aggressive humanistic secularism is, we must also recognize the emergence of the post-secular mind. A primary consideration here is that one of ten Americans is caught up in the "New Age" movement. Typical of this phenomenon is Marianne Williamson, a liberal, Jewish, ex-lounge singer from Texas who preaches about Jesus, Jung, and the S & L crisis and who is taking Hollywood and New York City by storm, serving up a mishmash of religious chop suey.[8] The appeal of this guru of the "New Age" epitomizes the bankruptcy of secularism. Her *Course of Miracles* is altruistic and fosters social activism (she reaches out to AIDS victims very caringly), but Christ is for her merely a metaphor—"all that Christ is is the unconditionally loving essence of every person."[9] Will we allow "New Agers" to preempt our address to the sterilities and futilities of vacuous secularism, or will we proclaim the truth effectively and courageously?

As we contemplate preaching the good news of the Lord Jesus Christ we must recognize that the misbeliefs of our age have given rise to a tremendous religious confusion. George Gallup, Jr., finds that 33 percent of the American people say they have been born again. Seventy-four percent of adults over eighteen say they have made a commitment to Christ; this is up from 66 percent in 1988. Scrutiny of this data has led Gallup to assert that less than 10 percent of Americans are, however, deeply committed Christians. He states: "Most Americans who profess Christianity don't know the basic teaching of the faith, and they don't act significantly different from non-Christians in their daily lives."[10] This is the spiritual condition of those whom we address; they (and we) have been corrupted by exposure to massive doses of the secularism of our time.[11]

3) *Privatism.* Robert Bellah and company in *Habits of the Heart* have classically defined the exaggerated individualism which is the bane of significant spiritual commitment. Nowhere do we see this as poignantly as among the "baby-boomers," the seventy-six million Americans who were born in 1946 to 1964. There is evidence of some

religious reactivation in this, the largest generation in American history. Books are pouring from the presses which dissect their moods and moves, and we are foolish if we do not take advantage of the analysis.[12] This is a multiple-choice generation for whom the bottom line is not loyalty or principle so much as it is self-fulfillment.

Privatism is just another word for narcissism, obsessive preoccupation with self. What Christopher Lasch wrote about in 1979 in *The Culture of Narcissism*, and what Robert Nisbet lamented in an earlier classical article on the trend toward subjectivism and egoistic states in this "twilight of authority,"[13] were picked up and developed further by Etzioni's *An Immodest Agenda: Rebuilding America Before the 21st Century* (in which the villain is "ego-centered mentality") and Yankelovich in his *Searching for Self-fulfillment in a World Turned Upside-down* (in which he argues that for 80 percent of the American people the old self-denial ethic has given way to the pursuit of self-fulfillment).

The degree to which religious conservatives have succumbed to this cultural drift (totally in contravention of Romans 12:2) is seen in James Davison Hunter's *American Evangelicalism: Conservative Religion and the Quandary of Modernity*.[14] Clearly we have opted for selfism—self-help and a therapeutic culture rather than the lifestyle enjoined by Christ in Matthew 16:24 and John 12:24. Denying self and dying to self are not popular. While we do not today worship a golden calf, we do worship the golden self. Even secular observers— for example, David Riesman of Harvard—maintain that our society is suffering from a decline in national morality as a direct result of our narcissistic preoccupation.[15]

This era of soft living and the failure of discipline have led to the present descent into chaos. The rising rule of appetite and our surrender to irrationality have brought us into the morass in which we languish. It was Perry Miller's opinion that the Puritans excelled because of their "deadness to the world."

4) *Cynicism*. The most unobservant persons detect the increasingly pervasive cynicism in American culture. Many people feel the political system is unresponsive—too much influence peddling, too many golden parachutes. And this cynicism transfers over to religious enterprises as well. The gross materialism and raucous hedonism of the psychedelic sixties have brought a harvest of emptiness and bitterness. Reflective of this nihilism is the widely read *The Day America Told the Truth*. This study's basic finding is that yesterday's moral and spiritual verities have vanished and we are in moral and spiritual chaos; we feel alone; we lie

to those who are closest to us; we have no heroes or models anymore; we are a law to ourselves. Sadly, the authors have no remedy to propose.[16] We, however, have an answer—the gospel of Christ.

Books today abound with such titles as *Images of the Future: The Twenty-first Century and Beyond: Religion 2101 A.D.* and *Understanding Tomorrow.* We can read pollster George Barna's findings in *Vital Signs* and *The Frog in the Kettle* and the thoughts of dozens like him and obtain significant forecasts of the future. Alan Bloom in *The Closing of the American Mind* tells us that the solution is a return to the classics of western civilization, especially the Greek philosophers. Gene Roddenberry, creator of "Star Trek," found comfort in our ability to double human knowledge every six or seven years. This is the new gnosticism. But gnosticism wasn't the answer in the days of the Apostle Paul, and it is not now either.

Laying aside the broad strokes of cultural analysis for a moment, we must observe that individuals are caught in the cultural coils in various ways and with various effects. Each person is an unrepeatable personal event—a unique individual made by the Creator according to His sovereign design. Samuel R. Schutz of Gordon-Conwell Seminary helpfully speaks of four groups to which we can minister the truth of God: 1) skeptics (the unreceptive), 2) prodigals (converted but backslidden), 3) seekers (receptive but unconverted as yet), and 4) pilgrims (believers on the move for God).[17] The larger picture should not obscure the individual and personal picture. Each man or woman, boy or girl, is our audience.

CHRISTIAN RELEVANCE

The foregoing analysis of the formidable communications task of our time might seem overwhelming. But is it any more so than the early church faced in the first century, or than Whitefield and Wesley faced, or than our missionaries face today as they contextualize God's truth into totally alien cultures? My essential premise is that *we do not need to make the gospel relevant to modern man.* The gospel is relevant. J. A. Davidson insightfully identifies "relevance anxiety" as one of the foremost occupational hazards of the clergy. He writes:

> Relevance anxiety develops when a clergyman strives frantically to keep up with the latest religious fashions and cultural vogues. Its victims would as soon put saw-dust on their yogurt as be caught being irrelevant. They tend to be very high on communication, celebration, rapport, sensitivity, and the like—and sometimes they go blue in the face striving for them. A rather conspicuous symptom is the

unholier-than-thou pose of some of its victims when in the presence
of their stodgier brethren.[18]

The larger issue is that of the Christian's relationship to culture, an
issue deeper than the relationship of the Christian to popular cultural
forms, although that becomes an ancillary concern.[19] The classic treatment remains that of H. Richard Niebuhr in *Christ and Culture*, in
which he outlines five diverse approaches to this thorny question:
1) Christ against culture (1 John, Tertullian, Tolstoy, Karl Barth); 2) the
Christ of culture (the gnostics, Abelard, Schleiermacher, Ritschl);
3) Christ above culture (the synthesists: Clement of Alexandria, St.
Thomas, Joseph Butler, Roger Williams); 4) Christ and the culture in
paradox (Marcion, Luther, Kierkegaard); 5)Christ, the transformer of
culture (Augustine, Calvin, Wesley).[20] However we may feel about the
classification of this or that person, we need to have a clear understanding of the pressing issues.

It seems to me that the crisis of the North American church right
now is not the church in the world so much as it is the world in the
church. We are in danger if our sociology becomes our theology, if we
marginalize the gospel in a frantic effort to get a hearing for the gospel.
Some reply that the message stays the same, but methods change. That
is true. Evangelicals who have been willing to attempt innovation, particularly with respect to communication of the message, have done
well.[21] But preaching is not a method which is up for grabs. McLuhan
has helped us see that the medium is the message; i.e., how it is done
bears heavily on the message itself.

Christ stands against culture in the interest of transforming culture—this is the inescapable foundation of our message. There are two
basic traditions in preaching—preaching in the tradition of the
Enlightenment (which is man-centered), or preaching in the tradition of
the Reformation (which is God-centered). There is no possible fusion or
compromise at this point. Our message is not an improvisation; it came
by divine revelation (1 Corinthians 15:3-8; Galatians 1:11, 12). Biblical
and church history teach us about the reefs and shoals on which many
have foundered. We will now discuss some of these.

1) *Religious liberalism—the danger of accommodation.* The whole
higher critical approach to Scripture was engendered by a vain and futile
attempt to accommodate the Bible to German rationalism; but in the
process men lost the Bible and they lost Christ. J. Gresham Machen
clearly demonstrated that liberalism shorn of the supernatural is not
Christianity at all.[22] Henry Ward Beecher is a case study in accommodation. As one author put it: "He packaged ideas and style in response

to the market."[23] His object was to "mass produce personal religion," and he sought to do so with his "gospel of love" and freedom, but left out any article on Scripture in his statement of faith.[24] Sadly, Phillips Brooks must be put in the same category (as George Marsden has recently recognized).

2) *Other religions and the cults—the tragedy of distortion.* The dangerous mysticism of eastern religions—a viewpoint which erases the Creator-creature distinction and which presents a caricature of the true and living God (for example, in Islam)—shows that the accommodation in the minds of some is the mistaken idea that various religions are merely different roads to the same destination. Many of the cults began because of a reluctance to accept the triune nature of the Godhead or because of an aversion to Biblical teaching on judgment and eternal punishment.

3) *Dead orthodoxy—the peril of omission.* Churches which have stagnated in ritual or fixated in creedal nit-picking easily obscure the authentic gospel. The gospel is more than a theological slogan. The gospel may be preached simply, but it is not simple. As Henry Alford said of "the word of faith we are proclaiming" (Romans 10:8): "The anxious follower after righteousness is not disappointed by an impracticable code, nor mocked by an unintelligible revelation: the word is near him, therefore accessible, plain, simple, and therefore apprehensible."[25] We must be careful to not bury the gospel beneath mountains of empty religious profession and activity.

Proponents of modern-day "church therapy" are in grave danger: don't talk about sin or judgment—avoid words like "ought" or "should"—we need new wineskins and should not try to talk people into belief. To agree to such drivel is to accept the end of preaching, passion, and persuasion. Why did Jesus and the apostles so recklessly open their mouths, without consideration of consequences? We may well need some new wineskins, but remember: "the packaging can affect the product. Improperly bottled wine will spoil."[26]

Frankly, I like what the Cardinal Archbishop of Paris, Jean-Marie Lustiger, a convert from Judaism, said during a visit to our country a while back:

> As things stand now, to say you believe Jesus is the Son of God is going to become an enormous act of courage. How do we resist being beaten down by cultural and ideological campaigns? How, as a Christian, do you consent not to be like everybody else without going someplace far away to raise goats? How do you stand that no one says anything good about you? And how do you live a dissident's life in the name of a conviction that you receive from God?[27]

He sees his mission as "spiritual conversion, not reform." "[T]he wisdom of this age [is] coming to nothing" (1 Corinthians 2:6), but our Lord Jesus Christ is "the power of God and the wisdom of God," even though His cross is a stumbling-block and "foolishness to those who are perishing" (1 Corinthians 1:24, 18).

CONTEXTUALIZED SUBSTANCE

The Christian communicator needs to know his or her audience and must recognize and develop significant points of contemporary contact. Every effective pastor knows the truth of this within ministry to his own congregation. But we must be wary of psychologizing the gospel—for example, substituting Abraham Maslow's levels of human need for the Biblical view of sin. We must beware of placebo preaching which does little more than reflect the drivel of the human potential movement.

What we are up against was reflected in a survey taken a while back on the question, "What are your chances of going to Heaven?" In the poll, 96 percent professed to believe in God, 72 percent indicated they expect to go to Heaven, and 70 percent felt God would be satisfied if they lived a good life.[28] Here we face a deeply entrenched works-righteousness bias—blatant Pelagianism. How do we catapult across this chasm?

What we have going for us (apart from the supernatural agency of the Holy Spirit, which we shall explore in Chapter 10) is a very critical point of contemporary contact. Pascal put it this way: "There is a God-shaped vacuum in the heart of every man which only God can fill through His Son, Jesus Christ." The fact is, Christ and Christianity are magnificently obsessed with people. And thoughtful people cannot avoid or evade Jesus Christ even in the acute paganization of our times.

The basic human problem is *alienation from God*.[29] Substantiating this thesis is the cover story in *Time* magazine, June 10, 1991. It is simply entitled "Evil" and is basically a vigorous grappling with the problem of evil—essentially in the terms of classical theology. Earlier (March 25, 1991) *U.S. News and World Report* carried a cover article, "The Rekindling of Hell," which argued that record numbers of Americans now believe in a netherworld and in a wide variety of after-death punishments. The preacher on these themes has an open door, thanks to the media in our country.

We have unexpected allies in seeking to remain faithful to the Biblical message. In a recently issued volume of essays (the book is significantly entitled *The Crooked Timber of Humanity*), the distinguished Oxford thinker Sir Isaiah Berlin says:

The constant theme of utopian thought, Christian and pagan alike, is that once upon a time there was a perfect state, then some enormous disaster took place. The rest of human history is a continuous attempt to piece together the fragments in order to restore serenity, so that the perfect state may be realized once again.[30]

I say, *Hallelujah!*

Think how the theme of human sin and guilt runs through Hawthorne's *The Scarlet Letter* and Melville's *Moby Dick*, in which we see Captain Ahab obsessed with sin and the white whale representing universal evil. It comes crashing through too in Dostoyevski's *Crime and Punishment*—oh, the anguish of Roskolnikov. We see a wider (group) dimension of sin in William Golding's *Lord of the Flies*, and a few hopeful symbols in Albert Camus's *The Fall*. In Graham Greene's *A Burntout Case* we have a study of spiritual deformity, and in Harper Lee's *To Kill a Mocking Bird* we confront personal and societal evil. These are realities in every human life. It is no use for a psychiatrist to tell us we aren't sinners and we aren't guilty. We *know* we are sinners; we know the scalding tears of remorse and the pain of guilt. And it is still true:

> *What can wash away my sin?*
> *Nothing but the blood of Jesus.*
> *What can make me pure within?*
> *Nothing but the blood of Jesus.*

Now, that message has to be explained, interpreted from the Scripture, illustrated, applied. But it *preaches*, and it preaches well. It preaches powerfully. It preaches to the eternal salvation of human souls.

7

The Technology of the Evangelistic Sermon

Veritas plateat, veritas placeat, veritas moveat. (Make truth plain, make truth interesting, make truth moving.)

(An old Latin text)[1]

So ought the preacher to fulfill his task that he teaches, attracts and turns.

(St. Augustine)[2]

And we also thank God continually because, when you received the word of God, which you heard from us, you accepted it not as the word of men, but as it actually is, the word of God, which is at work in you who believe.

(1 Thessalonians 2:13)

By this gospel you are saved, if you hold firmly to the word I preached to you. Otherwise, you have believed in vain.

(1 Corinthians 15:2)

". . . so that they may be saved" (1 Corinthians 10:33b) was ever the drive shaft and passion of the Apostle Paul. While pulpit evangelism is by no means the only way evangelism is to be done, it has been a central and very significant method in the program of God down through the history of the church and continues in the present time. We have attempted to delineate something of the modern mind-set with which the gospel communicator must intersect, but we also recognize that gospel categories are no more congenial to the unconverted today than they were in the first century. As someone has observed, "The good news did not fit Jesus' times or His world, his *sitz-im-leben* or His traditions." Chesterton had it right when he said, "If the church marries the spirit of the age, she will soon become a widow."

We must turn now to analysis of the evangelistic sermon itself and the praxis of evangelistic preaching today. Studies continue to show that preaching is the number one factor in church growth.[3] Yet many pulpit proclaimers would readily identify with the preacher who asserted, "Peter preached one sermon and three thousand were converted. I preach three thousand sermons and one person is converted." If like Charles Haddon Spurgeon we "expect [conversions] and prepare for them," what must sermons be like to win souls? What is conversion preaching?

THE CHARACTERISTICS OF THE EFFECTIVE EVANGELISTIC SERMON

> And at [God's] appointed season, he brought his word to light through the preaching entrusted to me by the command of God our Savior. (Titus 1:3)

The best analogy for the development of a sermon is not that of constructing a building but of giving birth to a baby. All is predicated on the life-giving Spirit's enlightening and energizing the preacher at every step. In fact, the ministry of the Holy Spirit is so critical in *everything* having to do with evangelism that we will devote an entire chapter to a survey of His involvement (Chapter 10). In this chapter we recognize that there are three levels of communication: 1) the level of *meaning*—what does the Biblical text really say?; 2) the level of *feeling*—where truth stated grips and moves the hearers; and 3) the level of *action and obedience*—where felt truth compels change. We are concerned with accomplishing more than merely charming our hearers—we desire profound *change*. What kind of preaching brings such a result?

1) *The effective evangelistic sermon must be Biblical.* God has promised to bless His Word (cf. Isaiah 55:10, 11). Billy Graham's recurring cry—"The Bible says"—reverberates in our minds and hearts and provides us with a good model to follow. Preaching is not improvisation of religious philosophy but is rather careful presentation of the truth

of God from the Word of God. The sermon may be expository (in which a whole natural thought unit—several paragraphs in some cases—is carefully dealt with, all main points and subpoints being drawn from the text in its context). Or the sermon may be textual (a single verse or two, with the main points being supplied by the text). Or the sermon may be textual-topical (in which the basic seed thought is supplied by the text, but there is not enough text to shape the trajectory of the sermon). Or the sermon may be fully topical (in which the basic theme is supported by various passages as an effort is made to represent what Scripture as a whole teaches on a given subject).

Clearly, any of these types of sermons can be Biblical and any of them can be un-Biblical. Most evangelistic preaching has tended to be textual or textual-topical. Careful exposition of a good kerygmatic text is ideal for evangelistic preaching. The generally shorter timeframe for the evangelistic sermon in many settings has disinclined many evangelists to preach expositorily. In a previously cited study of preaching, the highest point total was given to "the Biblical content of the messages."[4] The gospel, after all, is not good advice—it is good news! The authority of the message derives from the Biblical revelation.

2) *The effective evangelistic sermon must be doctrinal.* One denominational director of evangelism urged preachers to "preach Christ and not doctrine." But to preach Christ is to preach doctrine. It is not a question of whether we will present doctrine or not, but of what kind of doctrine we will present.

J. H. Jowett contended that "We must preach on those tremendous passages whose vastness almost terrifies us as we approach them." The grand themes of redemption, sin, salvation, and much more are necessary themes. People are tired of trifles; they hunger for life-changing truth. T. S. Eliot's J. Alfred Prufrock lamented, "I have measured out my life in coffee spoons." We have the privilege of preaching texts with Grand Canyonesque dynamics of infinity and eternity.

3) *The effective evangelistic sermon must be Christological.* All gospel preaching from all parts of the Scripture should be Christ-centered.[5] Christ is the theme of both Testaments—prospectively in the Old and descriptively in the New. Martin Marty questions why Christian contributors seem to make so little reference to Jesus:

> It is strange that in public discourse, there is gulping when the name comes up. Some megachurches, even of evangelical sort, I am told, avoid reference to Jesus Christ in their huge public services when they are out to lure the unchurched. Bring up the scandal later, we are advised. I think that's unfair.[6]

At this point I agree with J. F. Powers, who maintains that Christ crucified is like DNA. Without DNA, there would not be any human life. "The cross is like that. It is the very essence of human existence."[7] In a recent Lutheran debate on theological integrity, Robert Jenson warned about a new "gnosticism" which "balks at the specificity of Biblical particularity and yearns for categories more amenable to the contemporary mind." At the same conference, Carl Braaten called attention to the trend of temporal concerns, good and proper in their own right, which sometimes threaten to displace the gospel. This is a grievous error, he argued, for "*soteria* [salvation] is more than *shalom*, not less. Its corollaries include the salvation of the sinner; it includes reconciliation with God, removing the guilt of sin; it includes the promise of everlasting life, for the wages of sin is death; it means deliverance from the wrath of God, in exchange for the acceptance of his love."[8] The content of the gospel is Christ!

4) *The effective evangelistic sermon is apologetical.* It is desperately intent on building bridges of thought to the unconverted mind. Many people do not want to think; they are narcotized through the mass media, numbed by the continual sense of crisis in the world about us. We must arrest them in their torpor. We need to engage and capture attention in the sermon's introduction. We must be inductive in our approach and must be concerned about being imaginative. Illustration is so important, as we shall develop later in this chapter. We also need to use persuasion effectively in evangelistic preaching as we move toward the call for a decision.[9] After all, preaching is application, and application has to begin in the introduction. We need to learn to use questions skillfully, for asking the right questions is crucial.[10] Is it not significant that the longest article in *Great Books of the Western World* is the article on God? Realizing that the average person in our country is at the tenth grade educational level, we must take pains to make the message clear. Overuse of the language of Zion can obscure the great truths we have been commissioned to share.

5) *The effective evangelistic sermon is passionate.* The sermon must not be dull and bland but should have a hook in it. Richard Baxter complained in his day that "Few, if any, preach with all their might." Within the unique individuality of each preacher, we need to preach as dying men calling out to dying men. There needs to be effective intensity—the intensity of the love of Christ for lost men and women. Robert Frost used to say that poetry begins with a lump in the throat. Similarly—in fact, more so—evangelistic preaching calls for the investment of feeling and loving and caring. A survey in Great Britain found that 42 percent

of churchgoers dozed during services; 10 percent looked frequently at their watches; 62 percent wished they had stayed home; only 11 percent attended regularly.

In the evangelistic sermon we need to effect a good launch and reach heavenly altitude. We need to move deliberately but positively. We need to end strongly. The sermon is more than a therapeutic talk. We are not hawking junk. We need the spare rigor of a Thucydides and then some volcanoes and a whirlpool. We need to see clearly the need of sinners and the calling of Christ to preach the good news to all. The "me first" generation of which we are a part is on a pleasure-seeking and pain-avoiding track. The issue for many is, how much sin can I get away with and still get to Heaven? Evangelistic preaching intersects with this mood and should never be nonchalant or casual. "Since, then, we know what it is to fear the Lord, we try to persuade men" (2 Corinthians 5:11a). We do not have unlimited time in which to reach those in great spiritual need. With warmth and passion we must press the claims of Christ whenever we can. "[N]ow is the time of God's favor, now is the day of salvation" (2 Corinthians 6:2b).

THE CRAFTING OF THE EFFECTIVE EVANGELISTIC SERMON

> If anyone speaks, he should do it as one speaking the very words of God. (1 Peter 4:11)

The actual preparation of the sermon itself must begin with a thoroughgoing time of prayer and personal devotion to Christ. Then comes the selection of the text. If the preacher is proceeding *lectio continua* through a Bible book, the decision has already been made. Either way, the text needs to be read and reread in the original language (if the preacher has the tools or training to do so) and in various translations. The preacher should never go to the commentaries too quickly and thus be deprived of exploring the text lexicographically on his or her own. Similarly, the preacher should not read the sermons of others on the text too soon. There is a proper time for commentaries and for sermons but not prematurely so as to skew original thinking and research. We need to take the time to luxuriate in the richness of the passage in its context and for creative brooding over its meaning.

Out of this wrestling and grappling emerges the sense of "the big idea" (Haddon Robinson) or "the intention" (David Buttrick) or the "proposition" (John Broadus). This carefully focused sentence will succinctly summarize the main thrust of the sermon and should be developed and argued in a series of main points drawn from the natural order of the text. This outline is the body of the sermon (or "the plot," as Buttrick terms it, also preferring "moves" to main points, to deemphasize the punctilious sense of discourse). The current overuse of inductive preaching (induction being the move from the specific to the general, deduction being the move from the general to the specific) reflects to a degree the aversion of our times to Biblical authority. Once the text has been read, pure induction is impossible; the conclusion has been announced for the believer in the Scripture read. Fred Craddock's classic set the tone for this discussion (and is appropriately entitled *As One Without Authority*, 1971) and has been answered by Craddock's predecessor at Candler, John Brokhoff (aptly entitled *As One With Authority*, 1989). Yet, in preaching evangelistically we are addressing those who have not yet submitted to divine authority or are in process of doing so. Hence inductive elements need to be utilized, especially in the sermon's introduction as we strike points of contemporary contact with our audience.

Interpretation of the Biblical text has much to do with applying the truth of that text to today's world. To move from the meaning of the text to the significance of the text (ala E. D. Hirsch) the essential steps are:

1) Understand the original situation.
2) Find the general principles.
3) Apply the general principles to today—to identical situations, to comparable situations, to different situations. Great care and skill need to be employed in applying Biblical commands, Biblical examples, and Biblical promises.[11]

From a previous generation comes good advice from Henry Sloan Coffin, long-time president of Union Theological Seminary in New York City, who pressed the thesis that evangelism is the supreme duty of the Christian preacher:

1) Select great and moving themes.
2) Choose haunting and wooing texts.
3) Use language which makes people see.
4) Press them to a decision.

The basic skills learned in all preaching apply to the minister seeking to preach an evangelistic message.[12] As we endeavor to target armchair atheists and barroom agnostics and schoolroom skeptics, Coffin's summons to more visual preaching strikes a responsive chord. The novelist Joseph Conrad spoke of his ambition: "by the power of the written word to make you hear, to make you feel—it is, before all, to make you see. That—and no more, and it is everything."[13] Our visual society makes the powerful narrative sections of Scripture particularly appealing for the gospel communicator.

Storytelling is "in" today throughout our culture and in preaching. This new orality is sweeping the communications field,[14] for images are more appealing than ideas. Our affectively starved and more feeling-oriented culture responds positively to right-brained address (the imagistic, the metaphorical, the pictorial). Children too love stories.[15] Human experience itself has a narrative quality. Barbara Hardy convincingly states that "all of life is lived in the narrative mode." Those who have loved the Word of God have always been intrigued with the powerful stories in the Bible. But we have sometimes been so drawn into a more didactic and syllogistic approach to Scripture that we haven't done quality work in handling the narrative sections. The preacher should not do poorly what the Bible does so well.

The road to the contemporary obsession with narrative may go back to H. Richard Niebuhr's chapter "The Story of Our Life," in his *The Meaning of Revelation* (1941). The result in some circles has been "aesthetic theology," with Paul Ricoeur and Stephen Crites insisting that the sacred story is symbolic without carrying literal truth or historicity. Thus Crites declares that "But God raised Him from the dead is not a factual statement at all."[16] Hans Frei, using Tillich's method of correlation, seeks abiding Christian symbols in the Biblical story—again without the story having to be literally true. The more conservative Gabriel Fackre is writing a systematic theology in terms of narrative theology.[17] A new genre called "narrative ethics" has sprung up as well. Clearly some of the appeal of all this is that it provides an escape from questions of criticism and historicity; the jumble of images pretty much leaves every person on his own. For Thomas Long of Princeton, interpretation itself becomes an act of the imagination.

Bible preachers can profit much from a close and careful study of what narrative is.[18] The expositor's early task is to pick the lock of the story and discover what is the central point of reference. As Frank Kermode argues: "A text will offer, at some point, a hint, an index or emblem of the whole, as a guide to our reading of the whole."[19] This is what should be preached. Almost invariably the narrative loop involves "a bind"—i.e., a complication—and the story addresses the situation and the solution.[20] Basically this means to put the leading characters up a tree, throw stones at them, then bring them down from the tree. Although many variations are possible (for predictability in narrative is as lethal as anywhere else), it is perhaps best to identify a series of narrative blocks and then preach through them with continuing application, coming to a sense of climax in the story-line as you conclude. We need to avoid "narrative wobble" (the intrusion of something unreal) and "narrative thickness" (bogging down in a morass of details). What we want is narrative "zip" in which we allow the power of the story-line to surge and soar. The use of cinematographic techniques such as cross-cutting, closeups, and dramatic flashback lend further stylistic diversity and potency to the skill.

"Story" is a "hot" medium. Many evangelists—for example, D. L. Moody and Gypsy Smith—were great storytellers. Today's preachers could well afford to emulate such contemporary tellers of tales as Garrison Keillor, Walter Wangerin, Calvin Miller, Frank Peretti, and Frederick Buechner. A story relates something that has happened, beginning with a point of tension and then leading to a resolution of that tension. "The old, old story of Jesus and His love" is powerful narrative with eternal potency and life.

In our view of preaching, the preacher is like a concert violinist or pianist. The score is given to us, but the author's intention courses through our thought and life process, and we convey what has been written. Yet the interpreter is responsible for loud or soft, fast or slow within the author's instructions and symbols. No two violinists will play a symphony exactly the same, but the brilliance and genius of the composer will be set forth by the faithful artist. This is the task of the gospel proclaimer—to process and package the truth of the evangel for listeners of our time. No greater challenge or opportunity exists anywhere.

THE COMMUNICATION OF THE EFFECTIVE EVANGELISTIC SERMON

> His word is in my heart like a burning fire, a fire shut up in my bones. I am weary of holding it in; indeed, I cannot. (Jeremiah 20:9b)

In no kind of preaching is it more important to not sound like we are reading our sermon than in evangelistic preaching. Our preparation needs to be committed to what Clyde Fant calls the "orascript." That is, do not read or declaim from memory the message which has been prepared, but seek to be free to flow in undulating hills and valleys with a strong move toward a starburst of conviction and declaration.

Listeners need to feel they are being personally addressed. Spurgeon used to say you have not really preached until you've said, You! We must remember in our preaching how delicious the present tense is. We see this in effective creators of fiction. John Updike has used the present tense, as has Joyce Carey in *Mister Johnson*. Damon Runyon always wrote in the present tense. Content which is high-density or a flood of profound knowledge may cater to the preacher's pride, but there is little flow or movement. An overpowering display of pulpit pyrotechnics puts listeners under a steamroller.

How can we reach the pagans of our day, some of whom are not even aware they need to be reached? Because the love of God floods our hearts through the Holy Spirit (Romans 5:5), "Christ's love compels us" (2 Corinthians 5:14). Christ's compassion for sinners moved Him to seek them, to spend time with them, to tell them the truth about their sins and their souls. Souls were not scalps on his belt or notches on his gun or statistics for his records or announcements for his advance man. Do our hearers sense an authentic and genuine love for their undying souls? May it be so. R. W. Dale used to remark that the thing that drew him to D. L. Moody was that he never spoke about lost souls without tears in his eyes. Wilfred Grenfell, that dear English doctor who labored forty years in Labrador, testified: "Now I know that the real fun lies in seeing how much one can put into life for others."[21]

The popular musical adaptation of Victor Hugo's *Les Miserables* was hailed by the drama critic of the *Chicago Tribune*. He spoke of it as a message of hope and indicated, "We are desperately hungry for words of inspiration in an era where little shred of hope exists. This presentation fervently conveys these sentiments. It is a god-send. The finale whose words hold out hopeful promise of a better tomorrow would have had no impact at all if they had not been written, staged and sung with splendor." Form affects content as much as content affects form. How can we improve and develop those intensely creative instincts which will enable us to communicate the gospel in appropriate splendor?

Quoting Ruskin's famous dictum that in preaching we have thirty minutes in which to raise the dead, Calvin Miller, in *Leadership* magazine's issue on evangelism, sought to come to terms with the zeal/art tension in evangelistic preaching. Urgency can have class, he argued, terming it "enlightened urgency."[22] An artist is sharing his dilemma. Only the Holy Spirit can open a person's heart, but He uses us (frail "jars of clay," 2 Corinthians 4:7ff.) to transmit the message. Miller quotes Somerset Maugham's characterization of certain writers: "Their flashy effects distract the mind. They destroy their persuasiveness; you would not believe a man was very intent on ploughing a furrow if he carried a hoop with him and jumped through it every other step."[23] There is the danger.

Imagination is one aspect of creativity. It consists of impulses, flashes of insight, ideas which creativity blends and fashions for the end product. Northrop Frye has insisted rightly, regarding our effectiveness, that the way we say things is as important as what we say. Imagination is a kind of seeing. David Tracy defines imagination as the productive process of art. Campbell Morgan held that imagination is the supreme work of preparation. Baudelaire called imagination "the Queen of the faculties." H. W. Beecher believed that "Imagination is the first element upon which your preaching will largely depend for power and success."

Creativity is doing it the way other people don't, and we desperately need this in our preaching. How can we obtain and weave the stories, analogies, and images which constitute effective discourse? Many of us are image-poor. Edward Casey argued that "the habit of suppressing mental imagery characterizes those who deal with abstract ideas." Blackwood traced three kinds of imagination: 1) descriptive—what's there, 2) constructive—what's implied, and 3) creative—what could be there.

Recognizing that imagination needs to be under the control of reality and not fancy, imagination can also be stimulated. "And the Lord asked me, 'What do you see, Amos?'" (Amos 7:8). This is how Thomas Troeger begins his fascinating little book *Imagining a Sermon*.[24] Without agreeing with his theological position, we can be encouraged by his perspective that governed imagination is a special gift from above. Bach wrote a cantata every week. How was he able to use his gifts so abundantly? Through the same Spirit who so desires to speak through us as we walk in obedience and faith.

Denise Shekerjian believes that creativity requires risk-taking. The philosopher Herbert Ryle spoke of imagination as some "special sort of seeing in the theater of the mind."[25] Related to this is William James's contention that "The mind is at every stage a theater of simultaneous possibilities." Key here is the fact that this type of seeing has a cousin: curiosity. This too must be cultivated. Imagination relies on the art of connection, the perception of patterns. But overfamiliarization comes too easily and stifles us. How can imagination and creativity be fueled and stoked?

1) Learn to see. Carl Rogers says creative people are open to experience.
2) Read much, and read widely. Literature refines our sensibilities.
3) Ponder and meditate. Incubation must begin early and must be an ongoing process.
4) Work at finding just the right words.
5) Look to the Lord, the Creator, who says, "Listen, I tell you a mystery" (1 Corinthians 15:51).

Evangelistic preaching is no easier than the other kinds of preaching. It may even be more difficult in our day and age. But I can identify with Samuel Chadwick who said:

> I would rather preach than anything else in all the world. I would rather preach than eat my dinner. It has its price of agony and sweat and tears, but I thank God that of His grace He called me into this ministry. Is there any joy like seeing a soul saved from death? Any thrill like opening blind eyes? It is a glorious privilege to share the travail and wine of God. I wish I had been a better minister, but there is nothing in God's world or worlds I would rather be.

Praise God! "Do the work of an evangelist" (2 Timothy 4:5).

8

The Controversy over the Evangelistic Appeal

Christ a propitiation is the inmost soul of the gospel for sinful men. . . . It meets the requirements, at the same time, of the righteousness of God and of the sin of man.

(James Denney)

We are to preach all the riches of Scripture, but unless the center holds all the bits and pieces of our pulpit counseling, of our thundering at social sins, of our positive or negative thinking—all fly off into the Sunday morning air. Paul was resolved to know nothing at Corinth but Jesus Christ and Him crucified. Let others develop the pulpit fads of the passing seasons. Specialize in preaching Jesus!

(Edmund P. Clowney)

But the righteousness that is by faith says: "Do not say in your heart, 'Who will ascend into heaven?'" (that is, to bring Christ down) "or 'Who will descend into the deep?'" (that is, to bring Christ up from the dead). But what does it say? "The word is near you; it is in your mouth and in your heart," that is the word of faith we are proclaiming: That if you confess with your mouth, "Jesus is Lord," and believe in your heart that God raised him from the dead, you will be saved.

(Romans 10:6-9)

The Christian communicator is called to proclaim the gospel of Christ, not with fuzziness but with forcefulness. Essential to this mission is certainty of message and clarity in articulation. The gospel is not "almost undefinable" as some maintain. We must part company with those who seem to revel in uncertainty.[1] It is little wonder that many mainline denominations are hemorrhaging to death.

We dare not stammer or stutter as to the essential content and core of the redemptive gospel. To say in effect, "If you, in a manner of speaking, will put your faith, so to speak, in God or something or other, you will be saved, hopefully" is to look at a cloud through a fog. To assert "Unless you believe in Christ you will perish in hell, I think" is a tragic abrogation of Christian responsibility.

The saving word is near us, and it is not unclear. The sophists and cults of our times deny this gospel and obscure it with their sacred-mushroom occultism and their pantheistic spirituality ala Matthew Fox and now Veda Land in Orlando, Florida, with its focused Super Radiance Effect (global impact from the collective emission of good vibrations). We are not surprised at satanic efforts to obfuscate the simplicity and necessity of the gospel.

But are we also clear as to the way to receive God's salvation—i.e., the nature of the human response to the divine initiative? Before James Whitcomb Riley began to write, he traveled as a patent medicine agent. Once he came upon a rock on which an evangelist had painted the Philippian jailer's question, "What must I do to be saved?" Riley painted underneath it, "Take Barlowe's Stomach Bitters." Passing the same place some time later, Riley saw that the evangelist had returned and had painted beneath Riley's line, "And be prepared to meet thy God." Belief in Jesus Christ brings forgiveness and new life—and nothing else will.

The Apostle Paul was not in the least bit confused when he answered the jailer's anguished cry. He did not say: "Dear fellow, in view of our present knowledge of the Bible, you have asked a meaningless question. This selfish business of personal salvation is a bit primitive. Christianity is not about being saved; rather it involves identifying oneself with the forces of love and justice in the reconstruction of society." Of course what he actually said was: "Believe in the Lord Jesus, and you will be saved!" (Acts 16:31). This was undeniably an accurate and sufficient answer, as the subsequent account indicates (Acts 16:32-34).

Tragically and lamentably, there has arisen among Christians today a controversy as to what it means to believe, resulting in a confusion which is most regrettable. We cannot grapple with evangelistic preaching in our time without coming to grips with the issue of "Lordship salvation" and the divisive situation we are facing.

CONCUSSION: JOHN MACARTHUR'S VIEW

John F. MacArthur's vigorously argued views espousing "Lordship salvation" have had concussive force. His sometimes feistily argued insistence that a person is saved only if Jesus is accepted as both Savior and Lord has garnered the strong endorsement of J. I. Packer, James Montgomery Boice, R. C. Sproul, David Hocking, and many other notable Bible-believing luminaries.[2]

Of course, the issue is not new. In an article in the September 1959 *Eternity* magazine the question "Must Christ Be Lord to Be Savior?" was argued negatively by Everett F. Harrison and positively by John R. W. Stott. The question has had urgency both then and now because of a malaise of "easy-believism" which has devastated the church. That there are true believers and also make-believers is not a new phenomenon (cf. John 2:23-25; 8:31, 44), as Harrison pointed out. We would all agree that mere profession is not possession. Even saying, "Lord, Lord" is no guarantee of admission to Heaven (cf. Matthew 7:21-23). Gary R. Collins has probed this whole question most provocatively,[3] and Paul Kenyon has helpfully spoken of the deficiencies of "superficial believism."[4]

It is in response to this background that MacArthur strongly inveighs against the heresy of salvation through "the barest intellectual assent." We earlier argued (in Chapters 2 and 3) that both Calvin and Hodge were correct in their insistence that saving faith is more than intellectual assent. We are not talking about acceptance of propositions but reliance upon a person, the person of our Lord Jesus Christ. True repentance and trust in Christ's finished and atoning work of redemption will without exception result in a transformed life (2 Corinthians 5:17). Then the regenerated/justified believer begins a growth process which leads to maturity in Christ.

Much in MacArthur is helpful and salutary, though there are areas of concern. He asserts (but does not demonstrate) that "most of modern evangelism—both witnessing and preaching—falls far short of presenting the biblical evangel in a balanced and biblical way."[5] I don't believe that Billy Graham or Luis Palau or John Guest are preaching "a diluted gospel." MacArthur's strong emphasis on the new birth has been the very essence of all true gospel proclamation. Certainly turning to Christ and trusting in Christ constitute a commitment, but what level of conscious awareness is necessary for salvation to be genuine? And can any of us judge that? When MacArthur asserts that "all who are saved are true worshipers. There is no possibility of being saved and then not worshiping God in spirit and truth,"[6] is he not making a descriptive out of what he himself calls an objective? Can our assurance of salvation be tested by the authenticity of our worship?

MacArthur is right in calling for confrontation on the sin issue, although in speaking of "the debacle in contemporary evangelism" (i.e., failing to deal with the sin question), we find him again asserting but not demonstrating. (Evangelism Explosion, Campus Crusade's *Four Spiritual Laws*, etc. all face the sin question.) When I was converted at age nine, I received Christ as my Savior, but only subsequently came to understand the dimension of His Lordship and of the fullness of the Holy Spirit. Was I not genuinely converted?

As over against modern evangelism's preoccupation with decisions, statistics, aisle-walking gimmicks, prefabricated presentations, pitches, emotional manipulation, and even intimidation (and no one could deny all of these exist, though MacArthur's rhetoric here is too sweeping and unqualified),[7] MacArthur advances the idea that becoming a Christian and becoming a disciple are one and the same.[8] But becoming a Christian occurs at a point in time when one crosses the line and passes from death to life; becoming a disciple, however, is a lifelong process of pilgrimage and growth. To equate the two is to confuse regeneration/justification with sanctification. Who has ever yielded all in an absolute sense? While MacArthur denies the category "carnal Christian," Christians do in fact sometimes commit carnal acts and live backslidden lives. This is unfortunate, but it does happen and always has. It was so for John Mark and for Peter (cf. Peter's denials recorded in the Gospels and his double standard recorded in Galatians 2:11-14) and for believers in Corinth (e.g., 1 Corinthians 11:27-32).

Along this line the Formula of Concord affirms:

> We believe, teach and confess also that notwithstanding the fact that many weaknesses and defects cling to the true believers and truly regenerate, even to the grave, still they must not on that account doubt either their righteousness which has been imputed to them by faith, or the salvation of their souls, but must regard it as certain that, for Christ's sake, according to the promise and immovable word of the holy Gospel, they have a gracious God.[9]

If the assurance of my salvation is based on my performance or obedience, I have good cause to tremble; but that is not the basis of my continuing salvation. There are immature Christians, and there are immaturities in all Christians. I appreciate MacArthur's concerns, but I do not agree with his point of view on this matter.

It is significant that MacArthur's argument is based almost wholly on the four Gospels, with epistolary data being relegated to an appendix. Though Peter proclaimed Jesus as both Lord and Christ on the Day of Pentecost, Everett Harrison correctly asserts that "A faithful reading of the entire book of Acts fails to reveal a single passage where people are pressed to acknowledge Jesus Christ as their personal Lord in order to be saved."[10]

Confessing Christ as Lord (Romans 10:9, 10) means acknowledging His authority and submitting to it insofar as one understands and grasps it. If this passage means that the sinner must totally surrender all to Christ in order to be saved, we must ask, who then can be saved? Has anyone ever yielded to Christ's mastery totally? MacArthur has sharpened our awareness of the "demand" texts of the New Testament, but he leaves us puzzled in a number of crucial areas. The challenge for growth and continuance in the Christian life is seen in Bengel's exquisite statement: "It is the foundation of being a Christian to become a disciple of Christ; it is the completion of being a Christian, to be a disciple of Christ" (cf. John 15:8).

CONSTERNATION: CHARLES C. RYRIE'S VIEW

With Chafer and Ryrie taking quite a hit, we are not surprised that Charles Ryrie has issued a positive statement to the controversy in his customary gracious and lucid style.[11] Supporting his view, in addition to his former Dallas Seminary colleagues generally, are such worthies as Warren Wiersbe, Erwin Lutzer, Earl Radmacher, and Bruce Wilkinson. At the root of their position is a supreme concern for the preservation of *sola gratia*—grace alone—"by grace . . . not by works, so that no one can boast" (Ephesians 2:8, 9; cf. Romans 4:5). Should works righteousness intrude at all, should reference to what we do become in any sense a basis of our acceptance before God, we have abandoned our soteriological center—i.e., the finished work of Jesus Christ on the cross and in His resurrection (cf. 1 Corinthians 15:3, 4). Alford has not overstated the critical antithesis:

> These cautions of the Apostle are decisive against all attempts at compromise between the two great antagonist hypotheses, of salvation by God's free grace, and salvation by man's meritorious works. The two cannot be combined without destroying the plain meaning of words.[12]

The depth of the chasm on this issue is increasingly evident as we see not only persons but institutions and movements becoming polarized. Rich Wager, a member of the Awana Board of Directors, writes on "Lordship Salvation: Another Gospel?" in *Signal.* He argues most curiously that neither repentance nor the Lordship decision can be made until after conversion.[13] In a series of three articles Dave Breese, president of Christian Destiny, analyzes evangelistic invitations and concludes that surrendering one's life to Christ is not an appropriate invitation for sinner or saint.[14] Here, as elsewhere, the Lordship issue is seen as relevant only for the Christian, and issues of discipleship when presented to unbelievers or brand-new believers are viewed as endangering the gospel of the grace of God. Saved sinners first, committed followers later. Unquestionably this point of view has arisen out of a genuine concern to preserve the purity of the gospel, but at the same time the sole emphasis on the "invitation" texts tends to unnecessarily constrict the meaning and scope of the conversion experience.

Ryrie is magnificent in his delineation of the nature and necessity of grace. He is correct in maintaining that the gospel is good news because it addresses the basic human problem—namely, sin and our wrong relationship to God because of it. The gospel is the good news of Christ's death, burial, and resurrection for sinners.[15] Ryrie shows that the rich young ruler is not the paradigm MacArthur claims since Jesus did not ask him if he were willing to sell all, but in fact told him to sell all and give to the poor.[16] At many points Ryrie offers a very satisfying and convincing exegesis of central passages which lie at the heart of this controversy.

I do not find that Ryrie is a follower of Robert Sandeman, as Packer is too quick to imply about those who do not hold to "Lordship salvation."[17] Ryrie and Bock would agree with Warfield and Berkhof that *assensus* must be followed by *fiducia,* "the determination of the will to obey the truth."[18] Calvin and Hodge hold to the same position—i.e., intellectual assent is not sufficient. To reduce faith to mere acceptance of doctrinal statements is to overintellectualize faith.

Ryrie understands repentance as changing one's mind about Christ—not sorrow for sin.[19] This seems wide of the mark. "Godly sorrow brings repentance that leads to salvation and leaves no regret, but worldly sorrow brings death" (2 Corinthians 7:10). Kromminga defines repentance as "that inward change of mind, affections, convictions and commitment, rooted in the fear of God and sorrow for offenses committed against him, which when accompanied by faith in Christ, results in an outward turning from sin to God and his service in all of life."[20]

Beyond doubt this school of thought has problems with repentance. A. C. Gaebelein wrote in his commentary on Acts:

> What then about repentance? Are faith and the Spirit's work enough? Or is not repentance no less a necessity if men are to be saved? I meet this question boldly and at once by denouncing it as based, not so much on ignorance as on deep-seated and systematic error. The repentance which thus obtrudes itself and claims notice in every sermon is not the friend of the gospel but an enemy. Faith and repentance are not successive stages on the road to life.

On the contrary, repentance and faith are complementary and necessary for each other. John the Baptist preached repentance, and so did the Lord Jesus (Mark 1:4; 6:7, 12; Luke 13:3). Jesus indicated that "repentance and forgiveness of sins will be preached in [My] name to all nations" (Luke 24:46ff.). This is a dominant theme in the book of Acts as well (see, for example, 2:38; 3:19; 5:31; 8:22; 11:18) and in the preaching of Paul (see, for example, Acts 17:30; 20:21; 26:19, 20) and in the other epistles (see, for example, Hebrews 6:1; 2 Peter 3:9).

Some might ask why Paul did not speak of repentance to the Philippian jailer. We can only reply that this wretched man was shattered and could not in himself make a 180-degree turn in his life. Repentance is granted by the Holy Spirit (see Romans 2:4) and involves turning away from our sin and turning toward God. The Philippian jailer was called to put his whole-souled reliance and trust in the person of the Lord Jesus Christ, of whom he had probably heard earlier that day (cf. Acts 16:17, 18), but did that aboutface only through the power of the God who was bringing him into salvation. Godly sorrow over sin is as impossible for the natural man as is the exercise of saving faith.

Ryrie's weakness on repentance is worrisome in a day when Mickey Cohen thought he could be a Christian gangster and Larry Flynt supposed he could be a Christian pornographer. There are many today who profess to come to Christ who have no intention of turning their backs to the world. Antinomianism carries the idea that one can be a Christian and not follow Christ—"cheap grace," as Bonhoeffer called it. The response expected in the New Testament to the *kerygma* was faith, repentance, and baptism. Allegiance to Christ from that point entailed following Jesus, testimony, prayer, and the proper use of material possessions.[21] In our time we need more, not less, emphasis on true repentance for the sinner *and* for the saint. Ryrie's position is helpful but truncated.

CONVOLUTION: ZANE C. HODGES'S VIEW

Hodges, who taught Greek at Dallas Theological Seminary for twenty-seven years, has made a reply to MacArthur's case, similar in some ways to Ryrie but different at several key junctures.[22] He categorically rejects the idea that "a commitment to obedience must be a part of true spiritual conversion."[23] But does not the sinner, like the prodigal son, in turning to the Father's house signal a desire for a changed life? "He got up and went to his father" (Luke 15:20) describes repentance over which there is joy in Heaven. Are not faith and obedience companions (cf. Romans 1:5; 16:26; Hebrews 11:8)? Stott rightly points to Jesus in Matthew 11:28-30 as not only calling us to "Come to me" but to also "Take my yoke upon you."[24] A disjunction between faith and obedience is too extreme.

Hodges does us great service in warning us of the danger of becoming overly dependent on Puritan theology. Though we are indeed in debt to the Puritans, we cannot view the recovery of their system as the nostrum for our times. We shall see this in the next chapter in respect to evangelistic methodology, but we see it here in regard to faith and assurance.[25] On the one extreme is "Martinism" as seen among the Southern Baptists, in which the sense of assurance is itself salvation; in this view one may be rebaptized to obtain assurance/salvation. Though rigorously opposed by B. H. Carroll, this view is experiencing a contemporary resurgence. On the other extreme is the Puritan notion that assurance is impossible, for "He that endureth to the end shall be saved." Although Luther and Calvin held to assurance on the basis of the promise of the Word, Dabney, following the Puritans, rejects this out of hand.

Understanding faith as appropriation is helpful. Is the "look" described in John 3:14, 15 enough? Clearly so. But I cannot accept the idea that discipleship is optional for the regenerate.[26] If discipleship is required of all believers, then it is a concomitant of conversion; i.e., the fruit-bearing life must of necessity be a consequence of union with Christ. More deeply troubling is Hodges's strong rejection of repentance as no part of the saving transaction and in no sense a condition for it. The fact that John does not specifically mention repentance in his Gospel (what about John the Baptist's ministry and John 3:5ff.?) no more negates what Scripture as a whole teaches about repentance than Mark or John's failure to mention the virgin birth negates its factuality. Notwithstanding the many fine features of Hodges's treatment, it seems out of the mainstream and falls short of the full data of Scripture.

A PROPOSAL

How then should we shape the gospel appeal? What response does the Lord ask of those who are convicted of their sins and whose wills are quickened to reply to the R.S.V.P. of the gospel feast? I believe MacArthur overstresses the "demand" texts and that Ryrie and especially Hodges overstress the "invitation" texts. Is there a *media res*?

As Samuel Shoemaker once stated: "To be a Christian means to give as much of myself as I can to as much of Jesus Christ as I know." There must be a response which recognizes we are not the authors of our own being and cannot pull ourselves up by our own bootstraps. A commitment must be made which acknowledges Christ as Savior and as Lord. Repentance and faith as accomplished by the Holy Spirit do totally turn one's life around. But it is also true that a little child with drastic limitations of understanding spiritual reality, or a mentally retarded person, or a person in a cross-cultural context with very limited understanding because of cultural or linguistic gaps, can within those limitations genuinely respond to the claims of Jesus Christ. I came into salvation at age nine, and I am still exploring and discovering the ramifications of that decision I made over fifty years ago.

The present polarization is not healthy, for it has in many instances become acrimonious and *ad hominem*. Perhaps the two extremes should sensitize us to the rich and fertile middle ground which we need to till and harvest. We can learn from both perspectives. This is similar to the situation of Trinitarian theological controversy. The tritheists on the one hand and the Sabellians or modal monarchians on the other, though both in error, help us construct a difficult but necessary definition. Likewise, with this matter we have been considering may we faithfully cry out, "Repent and believe the good news!" (Mark 1:15).

9

The Methodology of the Evangelistic Invitation

Now, brothers, I want to remind you of the gospel I preached to you, which you received and on which you have taken your stand.

(1 Corinthians 15:1)

Whether, then, it was I or they, this is what we preach, and this is what you believed.

(1 Corinthians 15:11)

[B]y setting forth the truth plainly we commend ourselves to every man's conscience in the sight of God.

(2 Corinthians 4:2b)

It was through a sermon that nine out of ten of the elect caught the first hints of their vocation, and by continued listening to good preaching they made their calling sure.

(Jonathan Edwards)

With John Knox and his successors, he knew that 'the tongue and lively voice' are the chief means to which God has promised His power in the recovery of lost mankind ... every great movement of the Spirit will be found to be bound up with the giving of men who preach 'with the Holy Ghost sent down from heaven.'

(Iain Murray, writing about Dr. Martyn Lloyd-Jones)[1]

The proclamation of the gospel of Christ is more than a creative statement of the facts of redemption history. Evangelistic preaching, like all preaching, necessarily involves elements of passion, persuasion, and pleading. In faulting the modern evangelistic appeal with its "wheedling for 'decisions,'" J. I. Packer quotes the Puritan Gurnall on a point which is basic and with which we must all agree: "God never laid it upon thee to convert those he sends thee to. No; to publish the gospel is thy duty. God judgeth not of his servants' work by the success of their labor, but by their faithfulness to deliver His message."[2] Indeed, God is the one who converts and God alone. On this there can be no equivocation. For one thing this means that the timing is ultimately with God, although the messenger freely urges that "Now is the time of God's favor, now is the day of salvation" (2 Corinthians 6:2).

Even Packer concedes, however, in an earlier work, that "the message begins with information and ends with an invitation."[3] To be faithful to the full message of Holy Scripture, we must affirm both divine sovereignty and human responsibility. The witness of God's people is a link in His plan. Neither presenting information nor issuing an invitation infringes on divine sovereignty. Packer himself urges us to press the invitations of Christ upon the unconverted.[4] We may have differences of opinion as to how and when to do this, but that we should do so is incontrovertible. Stott compellingly argues that there can be no authentic proclamation without appeal and there can be no legitimate appeal without proclamation.[5]

Spurgeon urged: "Mean conversions, expect them, and prepare for them." Luther, in discussing the discharge of the herald's duty, insisted that faith both springs from verbal declaration and leads to verbal declaration. Calvin pointed out, "The gospel does not fall like rain from the clouds"; rather it is brought by the hands of men, generally through preaching (1 Corinthians 1:21). And preaching must by definition urge men and women and children to make a decision of faith. Broadus held that if there is no summons, there is no sermon. Christ's appeal "Here I am! I stand at the door and knock" (Revelation 3:20) is the preacher's passion. Campbell Morgan argued that "the minister of Jesus Christ ought occasionally to hold meetings where he urges immediate decision, and gives the opportunity for the same."[6] "We are out to storm the citadel of the will and seize it for Jesus Christ," he said. Sangster agreed, asserting that "the final task is persuasion to capture the will." James Stewart, affirming that we preach for a verdict, quoted Beecher: "A sermon is not a Chinese fire cracker to be fired off for the noise it makes. It is the hunter's gun, and at every discharge, he should look to see his game fall." Finney expressed it in this way: "The infinite God waits for your consent."

This point is reinforced by Bergsma's well-honed insistence:

> The sermon must also have a contemporary purpose as its objective. It must elicit a response. The response must engage the hearer at the point of the emotions, the intellect and the will . . . we are created as response structures, able to respond to the divine address. In fact, we must respond either in joyful obedience or willful disobedience.[7]

> *One ship drives east, another west,*
> *With the self-same winds that blow.*
> *'Tis the set of the sails, and not the gales*
> *That tells them the way to go.*

PREMISES

Since, then, we know what it is to fear the Lord, we try to persuade men. (2 Corinthians 5:11)

The urgent issuance of an invitation to receive Christ is integral to gospel preaching. Nevertheless, dear friends in Christ berate what they term "decisionism," which they believe to be incipient Pelagianism. Packer properly cautions us against "forcing tactics" but also alleges that "high-speed evangelism is not a valid option. Evangelism must be conceived as a long-term enterprise."[8] Yes, in urging people to respond to the gospel we must beware of picking unripe fruit. But as God's witnesses our aim is to reach those who are now ripe. Some—for example, the thief on the cross—do not have great amplitude of time. The point is, in personal evangelism and in pulpit evangelism we have not only the right but the solemn duty to press carefully and sensitively (through the Holy Spirit) for commitment to Christ.

No one has put it better than the Australian Alan Walker: "Evangelical preaching is preaching for a verdict. Its conscious purpose is to win an immediate commitment to Jesus Christ. Its aim is conversion. It seeks to make new disciples, setting them on the road to maturity and holiness."[9]

In the specifics of how and when invitations were given in the fledgling church, the Scriptural account does not have much to say. In regard to worship in the early church, we do not find evidence of a uniform liturgy, though we know there was worship. Similarly, though we cannot precisely reconstruct the methodology of extending an invitation, we know invitations were given by evangelists and preachers of that day.

While R. Alan Streett has probably strained a bit in amassing his case, his classic (but unfortunately out of print) summation of the evidence reaches back to God's direct address to our fallen parents in the Garden of Eden—to Moses calling for the disobedient Israelites ("Whoever is for the Lord, come to me. And all the Levites rallied to him," Exodus 32:19, 20, 26)—to Joshua's public appeal (Joshua 24:15, 16, 24-27)—to Elijah's public invitation on Mount Carmel (1 Kings 18:21)—to Josiah's call in response to which "all the people pledged themselves to the covenant" (2 Kings 23:3)—and to other Old Testament instances such as Ezra, Nehemiah, Joel, and Jonah. Jesus too invited people to come to Him and to follow Him. Zacchaeus came down from the tree to do just that (Luke 19:5, 6).[10]

In some cases these outward actions occurred in a more private context (as probably the leper who fell down before Jesus in Luke 17:15-19), but in other instances there were numbers of other people present. An outward action is frequently tied to and seen as attesting to the inward exercise of faith.[11] William James affirmed that "The performance of a physical act, which is under direct control of the will, makes a mental decision easier." Such appropriate response patterns are often important and subsequently become "defining moments" for the assurance of salvation and bring opportunities for follow-up and discipling.

There is in the book of Acts and in the epistles a strong emphasis on persuasion (which is to be carefully differentiated from any form of manipulation).[12] The word "exhort" is used 108 times in the New Testament. Thus on the Day of Pentecost exhortation was given by Peter and a recognizable response was registered—"Those who accepted his message were baptized, and about three thousand were added to their number that day" (Acts 2:41). Again on the following day, "[M]any who heard the message believed, and the number of men grew to about five thousand" (Acts 4:4). When these great numbers of persons came into personal relationship with God through Christ, it was possible to identify the converts and their baptism. This phenomenon can take place one on one or in a local assembly of believers or in a large public situation analogous to the mass evangelism we have seen in our time.

Streett aptly quotes L. R. Scarborough, that delightful Southern Baptist: "The term 'drawing the net' is applied to the preacher's invitation at the close of his sermon, to the unchurched, the indifferent, and the unsaved to make a public response to the claims of Christ. It has reference to the destiny-determining action to be taken by those 'fishing for men.'"[13] (In this regard consider additional Biblical references to public response to the gospel—Acts 5:14; 6:1, 7; 8:6, 12; 10:44, 48; 11:21, 24; 12:24.)

In a carefully reasoned presentation, R. T. Kendall describes how he introduced "the public pledge" in Westminster Chapel, London. He prefers the word "pledge," which John Calvin used in relation to the assurance of salvation. "The public pledge" is a solemn promise which, though never replacing baptism, may be a temporary replacement for that ordinance when baptism is not physically possible.[14] Coming forward or some equivalent action is a public confession of faith in Christ. Thus while the New Testament picture is not altogether clear, there is a pattern which suggests the importance of identifying those who are coming to know Jesus Christ.

As previously noted, Anthony of Padua would invite listeners to throw vestiges of the old life into a bonfire. Bernard of Clairvaux would ask for the raising of hands. We are addressing here the question of how to implement the appeal of the sermon. The gospel is an invitation to which sinners are to R.S.V.P. A response is called for. James T. Cleland lamented the collapse of many sermons because the preacher himself does not know what the objective of the sermon is. And as he put it, "If there's a mist in the pulpit, there's a fog in the pew." Clifton J. Allen commented: "The invitation is not a gimmick to catch souls. It is not a fetish to insure results. It is not a ritual to confirm orthodoxy. It is simply the call of Christ to confront persons with the offer of his redemption, the demands of his lordship, and the privileges of his service."[15] Even radical preachers and scholars who have long since abandoned the historic gospel will look longingly at that clear call to decide and act (see, for example, Rudolf Bultmann's commentary on the Gospel of John).

The point here is put clearly by the late Roy L. Laurin:

> We dare not fix our attention on the mechanics and say that people cannot be saved unless they pass through the channel of our particular method. But while we can be and should be liberal in our concept of mechanics, we must be certain about one thing, namely: that no one can ever have life who does not deliberately and personally receive Jesus Christ as his or her Savior. The mechanics and the methods may differ, but the essential to salvation is Jesus Christ. We must have Him no matter what the method or mechanics.[16]

Neither Wesley nor Whitefield used "altar calls" in their vast gatherings, which numbered upwards of thirty thousand people. Of course the logistics made that very difficult. However, both urged seekers to meet them after the services, and Wesley used exhorters to deal with those who were under conviction. These two preachers were very different. Wesley felt Whitefield was too oratorical and dramatic.[17] Dargan, on the other hand, called Whitefield the greatest evangelist since the Apostle Paul. "He had a most peculiar art of speaking personally to you in a congregation of 4000 people."[18]

Various "phenomena" were present in these great services, but we must be wary of making any "phenomena" normative. Curiously, Dr. Lloyd-Jones expressed great disappointment in the lack of emotion at Billy Graham Crusades, and that, along with the theological reservations he had (from the standpoint of his "imperial Calvinism," to use Max Stackhouse's superb phrase), disinclined him to support any of the Graham Crusades in Britain.[19] It is difficult to judge emotional depth in others and dangerous to nostalgically import criteria from several centuries earlier as a basis for comparison. At this point Lloyd-Jones seems to me disappointingly narrow. Philippians 1:15-18 indicates that we should rejoice whenever the gospel is proclaimed, whether or not we agree with the preacher's methods or even motives.

Jonathan Edwards advocated earnest pleading with sinners, saying, "Sinners should be earnestly invited to come and accept of a Savior, and yield their hearts unto him, with all the winning, encouraging arguments for them that the Gospel affords."[20] Spurgeon used the inquiry room and personally interviewed converts on Thursdays prior to approving them for baptism and admission to the church. Spurgeon supported the Moody-Sankey meetings.[21] It is true that he never asked seekers "to come forward" at the Tabernacle as did his successor, Dr. A. C. Dixon. But like the Bonars in Scotland, who similarly identified with Moody, he did not try to reconcile divine sovereignty and human responsibility because, as he put it, "There is no need to reconcile friends." The complaint made against some evangelists that the converts don't last and the results are sparse is sometimes heard; but aren't the results in God's hands? We will later discuss the issue of results in evangelism, but we have only to remember that one of the many converted under D. L. Moody's ministry in England was Dr. Wilfred Grenfell, who became "Grenfell of Labrador" and was used by God in a mighty way. We can only bow gratefully before our gracious and sovereign God and rejoice in "such a great salvation" (Hebrews 2:3).

Thus Charles G. Finney's "new measures" (the mourner's bench, evangelistic visitation, and the inquirer's room) were really not so new. There have been many critics of mass evangelism in and out of the church. George Bernard Shaw mocked revivalism in *Major Barbara*. William G. McLoughlin is very critical and sarcastic as he speaks of "the young tycoons of the revival trade."[22] R. B. Kuiper inveighs against mass evangelism, as do Lloyd-Jones and Iain Murray on theological grounds or Erroll Hulse as a separatist.[23] But Scripture, church history, theology, and psychology, as well as practical issues facing the church today, uphold the legitimacy of a public response to Christ in many settings and situations despite the dangers and pitfalls that surround us. Isn't this the story of Christian ministry at all times and in every place?

PERILS

> We are therefore Christ's ambassadors, as though God were making his appeal through us. We implore you on Christ's behalf: Be reconciled to God. (2 Corinthians 5:20)

That much blessing attended Puritan preaching is abundantly clear, and Iain Murray gives a vivid example of it. He relates how George Wishart preached on one occasion for three hours out on a moor in Scotland (he was martyred in 1546). One of the most wicked men in the country was converted, a Laurence Rankin by name. "The tears ran from his eyes in such abundance that all men wondered. His conversion was without hypocrisy, for his life and conversation witnessed it in all times to come."[24]

Gospel proclamation, thanks to God, does result in changed lives. But even here pride or wrong attitudes can creep into our lives. Given our sinful natures and our penchant for ego aggrandizement, every aspect of ministry is fraught with peril. For example, there has been much misuse and outright abuse of the invitation, so much so that some disdain any consideration of it whatever. But we must beware of overreacting and missing out on part of what God means for us to experience and practice. In a parallel situation, even though there have been pathetic distortions of the prophetic truth of our Lord's return as set forth in the Scripture, we must nevertheless give careful and reverent attention to this vital area of divine revelation. We ever need to be subject to the Holy Spirit's control and guidance (the subject of the next chapter).

Some, of course, are overly fastidious and finicky. Peter Masters, in proper concern for theologically accurate nomenclature in the invitation, faults those who speak of "receiving Christ as their Lord and Savior" (even though this is eminently Biblical language—see John 1:11, 12) and curiously reflects on C. H. Spurgeon's succumbing to the influence of D. L. Moody in picking up the same phrase. This seems extreme.[25]

In a memorable article some years ago, D. Bruce Lockerbie has called on the evangelical world to rethink the altar call. Criticizing the "no-holds-barred" hucksterism found in evangelical circles, he pinpoints the conglomerate invitation, the use of "spotters," and an utter predictability and lack of variety as the chief culprits. Yet Lockerbie stoutly maintains that there "are good reasons for conducting a dignified, orderly and wholly sacred period of invitation to public confession."[26]

Leighton Ford put his finger squarely on one of the chief issues in his fine article "How to Give an Honest Invitation." He wisely puts the discussion in the context of the spiritual battle we are waging and our attempt under the Holy Spirit to challenge unbelief and indifference in a field of resistance. He points out how Billy Graham begins giving the invitation in his opening prayer, which is only to affirm that preaching is application. Nothing is sprung on the audience because the entire message is building toward the climacteric of spiritual decision.[27]

We must be open and honest, avoiding any bait-and-switch. We should seek to avoid embarrassing anyone. One of the most offensive tactics is the endlessly protracted invitation in which the presiding pastor tells one lie after another about this being "the last stanza." I am also uneasy about lowering the lights in the interest of encouraging those to come who will only do so if there is semi-darkness.[28] Is this not capitulating to the philosophy that any means to get people forward is justified by the end in view? As followers of Him who is "the truth" (John 14:6) we cannot subscribe to that approach.

When people are writhing "under the arrows of the Almighty," we disappoint our Lord if we abort the Spirit's convicting work by prematurely offering assurance. Not all who come are ready to make their decision, though some are. To offer nothing after the service except the congestion and commotion of the church foyer quickly agog with chatter about sports and weather and business is most likely a quenching of the Spirit. Dr. Lloyd-Jones, when ministering in Sandfields, would meet after the evening service with folk who would come to sit in the front pews, and at Westminster he would retire to the vestry and receive people one by one in his office, just as a doctor would. All of these matters should be prayerful concerns of the spiritual leadership in a congregation.

The danger for the veteran minister is to become perfunctory in the use of the invitation. The danger for the younger minister is not to use the invitation at all, or very seldom. The embarrassment and disappointment of getting no response is real. But we must try to see ourselves as links in a chain of the Lord's making. On occasion ours is the privilege and joy of harvest. Few things hearten a congregation like seeing conversions. As we share the Word we should *expect* to see sinners coming to Christ. Spurgeon heard a young preacher complain that conversions were not occurring regularly under his ministry. Spurgeon asked him, "You do not expect to see conversions at every service, do you?" The young man answered, "No." Spurgeon then remarked, "Then you never will have them."

PROCEDURES

As God's fellow workers we urge you not to receive God's grace in vain. (2 Corinthians 6:1)

The marks of an effective public invitation are suggested by Vernon L. Stanfield, who says the invitation should be given clearly, honestly, courteously, confidently, earnestly, and pleadingly.[29] I would add, positively. Say, "Will you come?" rather than "Why won't you come?" The invitation should be as carefully prepared and as prayed over and as varied as all the other components of the service. In my tradition we are not bound to a specific form and can vary the procedure considerably. I believe it is important to offer seekers the opportunity to come to the Lord and to obtain counsel and help and prayer. Whether or not people walk the aisle, they can come to the front of the sanctuary or into a prayer or inquiry room. Trained, Spirit-filled men and women should be ready to help them pray to receive Christ or, if they are believers, to pray with them concerning specific problems and issues or to anoint them with oil for the healing of the body (James 5:14, 15).

The platform leader must exercise maximum spiritual discernment The after-meeting is a precious and holy opportunity to do work for the Lord. Generally men should pray with men and women with women. We need to be available for "the mumps and measles of the soul" or for the greatest decision anyone can make—for or against Christ, for Heaven or for Hell. Streett tells of how young John Dillinger came forward after a service, but no one came to pray with him. He was an ill-behaved boy who had a very negative reputation. He waited a few minutes and then went out saying, "I'm never going into a church again." He became a notorious gangster whose life ended when he was shot dead on Lincoln Avenue in Chicago. We need to be spiritually ready to wrestle with souls and to travail as spiritual babies are born into the Kingdom of God.

The transition—the bridge from the sermon to the invitation—is very critical. On one occasion after preaching on the Second Coming, Billy Graham moved from the message into the invitation by asking the question, "Well, Billy, what do I have to do to get ready?" Graham has a special gift of giving the invitation; God just takes over as hundreds come without any raving or ranting.[30] Another important part of effective invitations involves the use of apt Scripture quotations. Variations in the invitation which can be used in the local church today include inviting hearers to:

1) Walk forward during the closing hymn or come up after the service.
2) Come forward and sign a book of discipleship (Alan Walker).
3) Raise hands for prayer. (You will not get the names for follow-up this way unless you know your audience especially well.)
4) Come forward and obtain a booklet to be handed out by the pastor.
5) Come forward to sign a card of commitment. (Some speak of the danger of confusing what is done with the way of salvation, but that is true even of praying with the seeker.)[31]

The preacher can also:

6) Invite praying Christians to stand, then the unconverted.
7) Invite people of various ages to stand.
8) Invite the burdened to come forward for prayer or counsel.
9) Invite Christians to bring their unsaved friends and loved ones forward with them.
10) Invite Christians to come forward to recommend Christ to others (Criswell).

Even more liturgical churches can adopt methods which are suitable for their situations. Evans Hopkins, the Anglican, used the after-meeting. Billy Graham has called Dr. Walter Maier, long-time speaker on "The Lutheran Hour," the most effective evangelist of this century.

Ralph Turnbull quotes a strong statement by Daniel Jenkins concerning the preached Word:

Preaching is to be taken seriously as proclamation of the living Word of the regnant Christ . . . in its essence it is nothing less than an eschatological event, an act in which, for a moment, the kingly rule of Christ stands revealed among men, and He is shown forth before them as indeed *Christus victor*. It is an act whereby we see, as in a mystery, Satan falling like lightning from heaven and the Son of Man crowned with glory and honor . . . something happens in Church proclamation. It is not merely a meditation or a commentary upon the sacred history, but a continuation of the sacred history, a further step in the reduction of the strongholds where "every high thing exalted against the knowledge of God entrenches itself." It is altogether proper to speak of the pulpit as the throne of the Word of God and of the sermon as the "Monstrance of the Evangel." [32]

> *Happy if with my latest breath*
> *I may but speak His Name,*
> *Preach Him to all and gasp in death*
> *Behold, behold the Lamb!*

PART III

Strategy for Evangelism

10

The Energy for the Evangelistic Enterprise

As I listen to sermons, I am impressed by the fact that over and over again preaching fails in effectiveness not because of defects in the preparation of the subject-matter, but because the preacher is not putting his whole self into the delivery of the message. One recognizes that the material is good, well and carefully thought out and put together. But it fails to catch fire and kindle answering sparks in the congregation because its utterance gives the impression of being the performance of a routine duty. It has been a great help to me personally to realize that what I have to pray for to the Holy Spirit, as I kneel before entering the pulpit, is that for the next twenty minutes or so I may be enabled to forget everything except this message and this congregation, and to put my whole self into bringing it home to them. The gift of the Spirit for which we need to pray is the gift of concentration. The fruit of the Spirit is to be found in our power to bring our whole mind to bear upon the matter at hand.

(Leonard Hodgson, in
The Doctrine of the Trinity)

This is what we speak, not in words taught us by human wisdom but in words taught by the Spirit, expressing spiritual truths in spiritual words.

(1 Corinthians 2:13)

> *Ministers must needs have the Spirit upon them [for] the*
> *receiving of the people.*
>
> (Rev. Timothy Edwards, father of
> Jonathan Edwards)

The whole of the evangelistic enterprise is humanly impossible. From its inception to its broadest and fullest implementation, the proposal to radically transform and reorient human nature is on the very face of it patently ridiculous. Given man's moral inability and indeed his total spiritual disability, we are talking about something that is impossible apart from the mighty work of God Himself in the gospel of Christ through the power of the Holy Spirit. We must not fail to view the supernatural and miraculous work of the Spirit as essential to every aspect of evangelism; "we are God's fellow workers" (1 Corinthians 3:9a).

Each conversion is a unique demonstration of the Spirit's genius. Eric August Skogsbergh was known as the "Swedish Moody" and was powerfully used of God in his homeland. As a boy in Sweden he sneaked out on a Lord's Day morning before anyone in the house was up and skated all morning, missing the service. But his conscience smote him as he walked home, and hesitatingly he went to the afternoon cottage meeting. A little white-haired preacher was reading the text as he entered. He had heard hundreds of sermons, but this message spoke to his heart in an unusual way. He slipped out quietly and went home to receive Jesus Christ as his own personal Savior.[1]

Karl Olsson tells of an eighteenth-century minister, Jacob Otto Hoof, in the state church in Vastergotland in Sweden. This preacher spent his Saturday nights in the saloon drinking and was often unable to preach on Sunday as a consequence. His last debauchery was so terrible, he was unable to make it home, so he was placed in an open attic just above the saloon. It was a warm summer night, and a he-goat walked up the staircase to see what he might see. The goat stood in the doorway looking at the drunk minister just as he was coming out of his stupor. Immediately the man thought his visitor was none other than Satan come to claim his eternal soul for the pit. He sobered up immediately and was gloriously converted then and there. At his morning service he pictured Hell so vividly that hundreds were saved.

And what shall we say of the myriads of conversions, dramatic and undramatic, which constitute the ongoing miracle of divine grace in human experience through the centuries? This is accomplished "by my Spirit, says the Lord Almighty" (Zechariah 4:6).

THE HOLY SPIRIT AND PRE-EVANGELISM

The late Halford Luccock spoke of the "the human network in Paul's conversion," referring to the complex web of circumstances and personalities employed by the Lord to bring the persecutor to the Damascus Road confrontation. "It is hard for you to kick against the goads," Christ told Paul on that day (Acts 26:14). God breaks up the fallow ground of human souls and plants seeds.

We have already spoken of the preparation for conversion in common or prevenient grace (see Chapter 3), but here we want to explore the indispensable superintendence of the Holy Spirit in opening hearts to the saving Word. There is a divine "prior" to any positive human response. "He chose to give us birth through the word of truth," James says (1:18) and then urges us to "humbly accept the word planted in you, which can save you" (1:21).

Cornelius the centurion is another case in point (see Acts 10:1, 2, 34, 35). God was at work in this man's life long before he heard "the message God sent to the people of Israel, telling the good news of peace through Jesus Christ, who is Lord of all" (v. 36). Soon Cornelius found himself at a gospel meeting arranged by the Lord where Peter stated, "We are witnesses ... He commanded us to preach" (vv. 39, 42). "While Peter was still speaking these words, the Holy Spirit came on all who heard the message" (v. 44). As Peter later testified: "As I began to speak, the Holy Spirit came on them as he had come on us at the beginning" (11:15). Here we see the power source of the work of evangelism.

Later in Acts we read about Lydia in Philippi: "The Lord opened her heart to respond to Paul's message" (16:14). Without this beautiful work of the Holy Spirit, without His orchestrating the proclamation and the response of faith, there would be no results because "The man without the Spirit does not accept the things that come from the Spirit of God, for they are foolishness to him, and he cannot understand them, because they are spiritually discerned" (1 Corinthians 2:14).

The Holy Spirit employs human beings to articulate the message. As Peter stated so clearly: "We are witnesses of these things, and so is the Holy Spirit, whom God has given to those who obey him" (Acts 5:32). Here we have the three components in the equation of effective evangelistic preaching: human witness, divine witness, and human responsibility. Repentance and faith are spoken of in Scripture as gifts from God, as are all good things (James 1:17); but gifts must be received or they are of no use to us. Water is a gift of God, but it must be drunk; air is a gift of God, but it must be breathed; the Word of God is a gift, but it must be read and believed and lived.

Friendship evangelism (to be discussed more fully in Chapter 13, which deals with the overall strategy of evangelism) is often pre-evangelistic. We never know what role our contact and contribution will play in the Spirit's preparatory work. When we pray for an unsaved individual, we are working with the Spirit of God in the earnest desire that some witness will come this day to jar the remembrance of that person and bring to conscious awareness germane thoughts and considerations in relation to Christ.

It is exciting to ponder how extensive this work of pre-evangelism by the Spirit may indeed be. Reports persist of tribes and remote people who have been told in dreams and visions of the coming of a special messenger who would tell them of the true and living God. Don Richardson has movingly argued that redemptive analogies exist in the most primitive cultures which can only be understood as parts of an overall divine strategy to bring the gospel to those who have never heard.[2] This may help us understand some of the utterances of longing from the Egyptian prophet Ipu-wer (c. 2100 B.C.) or Plato's cry for a divine shepherd or Virgil's messianic fourth ecologue. "The Lord of the harvest" (Matthew 9:36) is in charge of our areas of ministry, which we need to be reminded again and again are all "the work of the Lord" (1 Corinthians 15:58; 16:10).

THE HOLY SPIRIT AND POWER IN THE PROCESS

Everything which we assert with respect to the ministry of the Holy Spirit is predicated on the orthodox understanding that the Holy Spirit is a person and is Deity.[3] One of the most helpful studies of the ministry of the Holy Spirit in this age, in my judgment, is that of F. Dale Bruner, who argues convincingly that the fundamental truth of the experience of Pentecost is that the Holy Spirit has come personally, permanently, and plenarily.[4] An important facet of the baptizing work of the Holy Spirit as seen in Acts 2 is Christian preaching. The sermon quoted there ranges from the Holy Spirit's coming to the sufficiency of Jesus Christ (vv. 14-36) and on to faith in Christ and baptism (vv. 38, 39). This is all accomplished through the work of the Holy Spirit. Paul's description of early Christian experience is expressed in the simple phrase "beginning with the Spirit" (Galatians 3:3). The more particularized description of the Spirit's work in applying the benefits of Christ's atonement has three primary foci.

The Holy Spirit in Conviction

Henry Alford well observes of our Lord's dialogue with the woman at the well in John 4: "The first work of the Spirit of God, and Him who spoke here in the fulness of that Spirit, is, to convince of sin . . . the heart must first be laid bare before the wisdom of God: the secret sins set in the light of his countenance; and this our Lord does here."[5] We see this work of conviction proceeding in Acts: "they were cut to the heart" (2:37); "when they heard this, they were cut asunder" (literal translation, 5:33; same in 7:54). This is a deep, drastic work of the Holy Spirit in human hearts through the Word of God.

In our day of upbeat Christianity and pulpit chitchat, we seem to see precious little conviction of sin. Conventional pick-me-ups do not meet man's need; nor does rhetorical brinkmanship. Only the Holy Spirit convicts of sin and brings men and women to salvation in Christ. This convicting work is set forth in John 16:8-11. The word "convict" is a legal term. B. F. Westcott found that the word had four shades of meaning, all of which need to be considered: an authoritative examination of the facts, unquestionable proof, decisive judgment, and punitive power. The Holy Spirit is intent on convincing humankind of sin and guilt before a holy God. As George Smeaton observes, "He sets forth truth to the mind, and maintains it against every prepossession or contrary opinion." The three themes of the Spirit's convicting power are:

1) The criminality of unbelief—"because men do not believe in me."

2) The availability of righteousness—"because I am going to the Father."

3) The finality of Satan's defeat—"because the prince of this world now stands condemned."[6]

This is the faithful ministry of the Spirit of God. Are we in harmony with His message? Bishop Moule said even in his day: "A full strong current of opinion in the professing Church of Christ runs at the present day directly against a grave, thorough-going doctrine of sin and its correlative truths of eternal judgment, and of the unspeakable need of the atoning blood, and of living personal faith in the Crucified and Risen One, 'according to the Scriptures.'"[7] The old Moravians always contended, "The Spirit always answers to the blood." We must do likewise.

The Holy Spirit in Conversion

The Holy Spirit is the agent of the new birth (John 3:5; cf. 1 Corinthians 6:11; Titus 3:4-7). To be baptized in the Spirit is to become Christ's. The baptism in the Spirit and water baptism are so closely coincident in time in the New Testament as to virtually be indistinguishable ("the one baptism" of Ephesians 4:5). "The pangs of the new birth," as Increase Mather described them, speak of "the long struggle and intense turmoil" normatized by the Puritans. This may well be the experience of some who come to Christ (particularly in later life or out of the deep troughs of gross sin), but we have no Biblical justification for requiring it. Christian workers are like midwives in this sense (cf. Galatians 4:19). There is agony and pain in this birth, though not always identical in degree or detail.

The new birth is the impartation of spiritual life—eternal, divine life brought to the soul. This life comes to us in the person of the Holy Spirit (Romans 8:9; cf. 1 Corinthians 6:19). The presence of the Spirit is the divine mark that we belong to God. While indwelling is not synonymous with infilling, nevertheless at conversion "we have all been saturated with one Spirit" (1 Corinthians 12:13, Goodspeed's translation). James Denney used to say that at its simplest the task of Christianity is to make bad men good—and that is exactly what the Holy Spirit does. As E. F. Kevan put it: "Just as there can be no one saved without the shedding of the blood of Christ, so there can be no one saved apart from the regenerating work of the Holy Spirit. It is this which preserves the Gospel from being a matter of mere head knowledge."[8] Chadwick expressed it this way: "The indwelling is that of a real, personal, spiritual presence . . . a personal Spirit that indwells another personality; a personality within a personality by which the Spirit becomes the life of my life, the soul of my soul; an indwelling that secures identity without confusion and possession without absorption."[9]

Is ours to ever be the torment of the unattained ideal? Does Christianity give us precept without power? Immanuel Kant conceded that humans needed the equivalent of the new birth as described in John 3 (but sadly Kant's system had no Holy Spirit).[10] The Biblical picture of the genuine believer relying on the Spirit depicts much more than memorizing statements about faith and using them mantra-like three times every morning as Norman Vincent Peale advocates. Such a view equates faith with self-confidence and gives God a small role in the process.[11] The Bible talks of nothing less than a divine miracle *ab extra*—that is, from beyond ourselves and our own energies—being quickened by the life-giving Spirit (John 6:63). Praise be to God!

The Holy Spirit in Confirmation

Immediately upon conversion the believer is sealed with the Holy Spirit (2 Corinthians 1:22; Ephesians 1:13, 14; 4:30). The sealing of the Spirit has to do with our assurance of salvation. It authenticates the birthright of all of us who are believers in Christ and our right relationship with Him as witnessed by the Holy Spirit (Romans 8:16, 17). Walvoord argues that the sealing is not experience-oriented, while Lloyd-Jones stoutly maintains that it is.[12] Clearly many believers do not live in the enjoyment and blessing of this certainty. The sealing takes place at conversion, but individual believers may not enter into the freedom and delight of this reality until sometime later in their experience. But one thing is sure—as we yield to the Spirit, we find Him to be, as one of the early Roman Christians wrote, "a cheerful Spirit."[13] But if we grieve Him or quench Him or resist Him, we find ourselves in struggle and turmoil (cf. James 4:5). What lovely ministry the Holy Spirit conducts within the believer's mind and life.

THE HOLY SPIRIT AND PASSIONATE PREACHING

As soon as the Holy Spirit was poured out in the Pentecostal effusion, Christ's own commenced to speak of "the wonders of God" (Acts 2:11) to those from every nation. As Roland Allen speaks of it: "The Holy Ghost was given: forthwith the apostles began to preach Christ. They began to preach Christ to those who did not believe."[14] The dynamic of the Holy Spirit is absolutely pivotal in all of this. In fact, the paucity of the imperative mood in the various versions of the Great Commission may well point to the fact that the outward movement will inevitably follow upon the fullness of the Holy Spirit (see Acts 1:8). One interpreter of Paul's missionary theology described it as involving spontaneity (i.e., it is an unfettered gospel), spirituality (i.e., it is under the sovereign direction of the Spirit), indigeneity (which bears marked contrast with western cultural imperialism), and universality (the whole world is the theater of operations, since the gospel is intended and provided for all persons).[15] Proper contemplation of our communications task apart from the person and work of the Holy Spirit is inconceivable.

Archbishop Coggan spoke of some sermons he had heard as being like the psalmist's description of the Almighty on a chilly day: "He casteth forth His ice like morsels: who is able to abide His frost?" Needless to say, that old English rendering may not be understandable to all of our twentieth-century hearers. As Christ-commissioned evangelistic preachers we are responsible to decode the message of Scripture and encode it into the vernacular of our listeners. Our objective is first to inform and then to inflame. In this process we experience the paradox of preaching which is: I, but not I (cf. Galatians 2:20). To serve faithfully and fruitfully in this venture we must have the unction of the

Holy Spirit throughout every step of preparation, presentation, and perseverance.

Ours must be a concern to preach a converting gospel. Lloyd-Jones decried modern-day expectations of preaching: "Preaching should always give men what they want rather than what they need. There is the feeling that men have a right to demand certain things of the messengers of God. That is a popular view of preaching, and I have no doubt that it accounts very largely for the state of the world today."[16] Whitefield preached what he called "a felt Christ." We should take one eminent preacher's words to heart: "With so many preaching to the times, there should be some who are preaching to the eternities."

But this cannot transpire if the Spirit's anointing is not upon us. In Buechner's *Book of Bebb* Brownie says, "I can't preach 'faith of our fathers living still' when my own faith is curled up inside me and died."[17] We are deputized to "cast [our] bread upon the waters" (Ecclesiastes 11:1a). We are not to watch the wind or look at the clouds because then we will not plant or reap (Ecclesiastes 11:4). We are to be "sowing [our] seed by every stream" (Isaiah 32:20). All of this carries with it the privilege of offering a juicy apple to someone who is hungry and cool water to those who thirst, as Bonhoeffer reminds us. A person listens intently as a relative's will is read, and a guilty man certainly listens as his sentence is pronounced by the judge. What we have to share has eternal importance; how dare we be impassionate or slothful in our utterance?

"The preaching of conquest must return to the pulpit," it has been said. We need warm preaching, compassionate preaching—proclamation replete with triumph and transcendence and *life*. How are we to break the pattern of what Joseph Parker has called "middle zones, graded lines, light compounded with shadow in a graceful exercise of give and take"? How are we to challenge the prevailing passivity of our times? How are we to lead people beyond religion as recreation? How can we shake loose from the mania for entertainment which is smothering our culture *and our churches*?

We deeply need a recognition that the arm of flesh will fail us. We need what our forebears called "a sensible awareness of God," "the Lord come down in power," "an awakening ministry," "the authority"—what Jonathan Edwards termed "an outpouring of the Holy Spirit." We need to lay hold of God and to be embraced by Him. We need a fresh baptism of power that will cause us to preach and proclaim with heart and heat. Jonathan Edwards's great and epochal sermon "Sinners in the Hands of an Angry God" was preceded by three days in which Edwards did not eat and three nights in which he did not close his eyes in sleep. Repeatedly he was heard to pray, "O Lord, give me New England!" We read that when he came into his pulpit on that Lord's Day, "he looked as if he had been gazing straight into the face of God. Even before he began to speak, tremendous conviction fell upon his audience."

R. W. Dale of Birmingham identified what drew him to D. L. Moody and support of the meetings in England: "The thing that drew me to D. L. Moody was that he never spoke about lost souls without tears in his eyes." This need for enduement for the preaching task is represented also by Richard Baxter in his *Reformed Pastor*:

> I marvel how I can preach . . . slightly and coldly; how I can let men alone in their sins and that I do not go to them and beseech them for the Lord's sake to repent, however they take it and whatever pains or troubles it should cost me. I seldom come out of the pulpit but my conscience smiteth me that I have been no more serious and fervent. It acccuseth me not so much for want of human ornaments or elegance, nor for letting fall an uncomely word; but it asketh me: How couldest thou speak of life and death with such a heart? Shouldst thou not weep over such a people, and should not their tears interrupt thy words? Shouldst not thou cry aloud and show them their transgressions and entreat and beseech them as for life and death?[18]

Thus the gospel preacher must be totally dependent upon the faithful and reliable work of the Holy Spirit of God. Thus with Spurgeon, "We must see souls born unto God. If we do not, our cry should be that of Rachel 'Give me children or I die.'"[19]

Several stanzas of H. A. W. Meyer's great poem "Saint Paul" pinpoint the passion the gospel messenger shares with the Spirit:

> *Oft when the Word is on me to deliver,*
> *Lifts the illusion, and the truth lies bare;*
> *Desert or throng, the city or the river*
> *Melts in a lucid paradise of air.*
>
> *Only like souls I see the men thereunder,*
> *Bound who should conquer, slaves who should be kings,*
> *Hearing their one hope with an empty wonder,*
> *Sadly contented with a show of things.*
>
> *Then with a rush, th' intolerable craving*
> *Shivers throughout me, like a trumpet call,*
> *Oh, to save these, to perish for their saving,*
> *Die for their life, be offered for them all.*

11

A Survey of the Contemporary Evangelistic Scene

But even if we or an angel from heaven should preach a gospel other than the one we preached to you, let him be eternally condemned! As we have already said, so now I say again: If anybody is preaching to you a gospel other than what you accepted, let him be eternally condemned!

(Galatians 1:8, 9)

But when God, who set me apart from birth and called me by his grace, was pleased to reveal his Son in me so that I might preach him among the Gentiles, I did not consult any man. . . .

(Galatians 1:15, 16)

They only heard the report: "The man who formerly persecuted us is now preaching the faith he once tried to destroy."

(Galatians 1:23)

Salvation must not be confused with humanization or rehabilitation, as sociologists understand these terms. Rather it should be equated with justification and sanctification, and this means that it primarily concerns man's relationship not to society, but to God. We must speak of our salvation as spiritual rather than temporal or secular if we are to do justice to the Biblical witness.

(Donald G. Bloesch, *The Crisis of Piety*)

We have attempted to delineate the priority of evangelism and the nature and necessity of spiritual conversion. In view of what the Biblical documents assert and in the light of two thousand years of church history, we have sought to understand what evangelistic preaching is, both in terms of its message and regarding essential method. We have wrestled with the hot-button issues of the content of the appeal to the lost and the use of the public invitation in our time, all within the scope of the ongoing supernatural superintendence of the Holy Spirit of God.

We must now turn our attention to just how evangelistic preaching is doing and what place it should occupy in the overall strategization of winning men and women everywhere to Christ. This requires grappling with basic ecclesiology (the doctrine of the church) and the ancillary issues of approach and apologetics, as well as the relationship of evangelism to the phenomenon of revival as we understand it Biblically, theologically, and historically.

The focus which must control all of our discussion is love for and loyalty to the gospel of Christ. Such a commandeering commitment is always seen at the center of the Apostle Paul's vision and ministry. "[P]artnership in the gospel from the first day until now" described his relationship with the church at Philippi (Philippians 1:5). That church included in its membership Lydia (a business woman), a young girl freed from a demon, and the jailer and his household and was a thriving, typical first-century congregation.

Paul's overmastering objective was "to advance the gospel" (Philippians 1:12). Paul was deeply concerned "for the defense of the gospel" (Philippians 1:16) and commended those women "who have contended at my side in the cause of the gospel, along with Clement and the rest of my fellow workers, whose names are in the book of life" (Philippians 4:3). Living a life "worthy of the gospel" and "contending . . . for the faith of the gospel" (Philippians 1:27) constrained Paul to even rejoice when the gospel was preached by those who did not agree with him on every fine point and who actually opposed him (Philippians 1:15-18). The main thing is that "Christ is preached" (v. 18). As D. L. Moody used to say: the main thing is to keep the main thing the main thing.

How are we doing in regard to proclaiming the gospel through evangelistic preaching? We cannot intelligently discuss where we ought to go until we know where we are.

THE TIMES

> Although I am less than the least of all God's people, this grace was given me: to preach to the Gentiles the unsearchable riches of Christ. (Ephesians 3:8)

The fact is, we are living in the time of the greatest gospel harvest in the history of the Christian church. As we look at what God is doing in Central and South America, in sub-Sahara Africa, on the rim of the Pacific (with Korea almost one-third Christian), and in eastern Europe and the Soviet Union, we see a volcanic move of the Spirit, a veritable tidal wave in which thirty-five hundred new churches are being planted every week.

All of this is set against a population explosion which brings an annual net increase in population from between ninety million to one hundred million persons. Half of the world's population is poor, and half a billion are on the edge of starvation. The massive problems attendant to this growth—social, environmental, economic, moral, and spiritual—boggle the mind. In 1900 84 percent of the Christians were in the West;[1] by the end of this century 29 percent will be in the West. Soon there will be more missionaries from the Two-thirds World than from the West. The staggering implications of urbanization and the lack of leaders abroad are sobering. Hiebert has made an important observation bearing on the communication of the gospel in this setting:

> There are dangers in depending too much on mass media to evangelize the world. They have been particularly effective in spreading information. They have been less effective in leading people to personal commitments to Christ and least effective in bringing converts together into assemblies of believers. Media cannot substitute for personal witness based on relationships of love and trust.[2]

There is much to encourage and inspire Christ's church today. The crisis in the Persian Gulf opened new doors and extraordinary opportunities. Protestant churches have grown 500 to 700 percent in Argentina since the early eighties. Indonesia may now be 25 percent Christian. A Billy Graham School of Evangelism was recently held in the Soviet Union, attracting five thousand pastors and laypersons. The Russian Orthodox Church has asked for twenty million Bibles. The first conversions have been reported from Mongolia. "Unprecedented numbers of Chinese intellectuals have become Christians" since the Tiananmen Square massacre, on a scale which "has no historical parallel in Chinese history."[3] Albania has opened up to the gospel. What a marvelous time in which to be alive and to preach the gospel of Christ!

But we must recognize that the cults are relentlessly active and old religions are stirring. (For example, in India Hindu fundamentalism is claiming converts from Christianity faster than Christianity is making converts.) The National Association of Evangelicals has given itself a new emphasis on evangelism in this country under the theme "Proclaiming Jesus Christ . . . Together," but the Vatican has launched Evangelization 2000, a decade of emphasis on evangelism in which clergy will be the first target. Evangelical inroads are at risk and must be protected.

The North American church in general is resting in a morass of passivity. Andre Malraux has undeniably asserted, "The death of Europe is the fact of our times," and in North America we are seeing the Europeanization of the church. There are a hundred and thirty-five million unchurched people in the U.S., making our country the fifth largest unchurched country in the world (behind China, Russia, India, and Indonesia). The Barna Research Group reports that only 34 percent of U.S. citizens who claim to be Christians worship God at least once a week. Ninety percent of the people in Alaska are unchurched and 70 percent in Hawaii, with California, Oregon and Washington leading the lower forty-eight states.

Here is an overview of the situation we face in gospel proclamation: a massive moral and spiritual collapse in our society; severely acculturated Christianity (murderous losses and great restlessness in the mainline denominations, but serious plateauing and passivity among evangelicals; the Mormons are growing the fastest of all religious groups—6 percent annually); the television age and a move to an entertainment paradigm, precipitating fierce competition for listeners; great psychological turmoil over male authority throughout our culture. There is never a book about God or faith on the *New York Times* Book Review Bestsellers list (apart from Kushner's *Why Bad Things Happen to Good People*, which sadly opts for a finite deity). Christian concerns are marginalized by the world and are even often trivialized among us.

The United States, Brazil, and the Ivory Coast accounted for the biggest increase in AIDS cases in 1991, according to the World Health Organization. The largest number of reported AIDS cases is still found in the Western world. Our large cities are decaying, and our infrastructures are falling apart. We are seeing fast-moving change with tremendous opportunity for evangelism in our time, but Bible-believing Christians seem numb and unstirred. James Spencer has not overstated the need for Christians to mount a "countervailing witness to the destructive forces of secularism, occultism and cultism."[4] The challenge before us is the struggle for the souls of an entire generation.

In the short range we can reasonably be only pessimistic. Carl F. H. Henry is more on target with his dire warnings of Western civilization on the brink of a new Dark Ages with a return to paganism and spiritual chaos[5] than is Ben Wattenberg's rather euphoric prediction of a surging America in the nineties, although even Wattenberg has his qualms about "western flaccidity."[6] However, in the long term believers in Christ are optimistic (because in a real sense our theology is eschatological, centered on the hope of Christ's future return and reign).

The danger we face is epitomized in the example of John R. Mott (1865-1955). Mott, converted in a revival, quickly became interested in evangelism. Associated with Moody, James Brookes, A. T. Pierson, and others, he led the way in the Student Volunteer Movement to proclaim "the evangelization of the world in this generation." However, his associations became increasingly ecumenical, and the YMCA, in which he was a prime mover, displays the dilution of the gospel and the denial of the supernatural seen everywhere today. While his friend Robert Speer contributed to *The Fundamentals*, Mott did not. Speer stayed steady; Mott accommodated. Though having many moving and beautiful qualities, this man's course is a warning as to what can happen in the swirling vortex of our times.[7] His legacy is feeble and flawed.

TYPES OF EVANGELISM

> For the Son of God, Jesus Christ, who was preached among you by me and Silas and Timothy, was not "Yes" and "No," but in him it has always been "Yes." (2 Corinthians 1:19)

The message we preach is Jesus Christ, but five basic types of evangelistic involvement are operative with varying degrees of effectiveness on the current evangelical scene.

Personal Evangelism

From the beginning personal witness has been an essential component of Christian service. To be sure there have always been especially gifted individuals such as Dr. Walter Wilson of Kansas City or Dr. William McCarrell of Cicero, Illinois, founder of the Fisherman's Clubs and a man who could turn the conversation from the rubber eraser on a pencil to a discussion of human mistakes and sin with marked facility.

But I am afraid that E. Stanley Jones is correct when he argues that "the vast majority of Christians are not committed to evangelism."[8] The reality of the situation seems to be that even fewer pastors are soul-winners. Packer is right in stressing Richard Baxter's formula, "Every pastor an evangelist." As Baxter insisted, "Every pastor must study the difficult art of winning souls."[9] The case here is very much like Andrew Murray's *The Key to the Missionary Problem*, in which the point is soundly made that unless the pastor has the passion and the burden, it is most unlikely anyone else will either.

The widespread recognition of the positive contribution of incarnational or lifestyle evangelism may be partly responsible for the decline of confrontational evangelism in our day. (This is not to say that lifestyle or friendship witness is of no value, but only that we can retain the one without discarding or neglecting the other.) Also, as we have become more upwardly mobile we have been beguiled by society's maxim: polite people don't discuss politics or religion in public. The days when we conducted seminars in personal soul-winning have faded, and books such as L. R. Scarborough's *With Christ After the Lost* or R. A. Torrey's *How to Bring Men to Christ* or John R. Rice's *The Soulwinner's Fire* are not as popular now as they once were. Nonetheless, Paul Little's *How to Give Away Your Faith*, Bill Bright's *Witnessing Without Fear*, Mark McCloskey's *Tell It Often, Tell It Well*, and Rebecca Pippert's *Out of the Saltshaker and into the World* effectively blend confrontational and lifestyle approaches.

Parish Evangelism

While there are some stellar exceptions, generally the waters of the baptistery are less used in our time. In this age of the megachurch, much of the growth is transfer or biological growth, with little convert growth. Some megachurches are so crowded that their evangelistic outreach has been hamstrung just by virtue of logistical considerations such as parking space or seating capacity.

Particularly in the sixties and seventies we went through a phase in many circles in which the pulpit became a lectern and the sanctuary a classroom. The prevailing idea was that the church was only for the saints, who would then go out and do evangelism. Gradually it has dawned on us that there are unconverted people in our services who also need to be addressed. If we rely on the traditional evening service as the evangelistic service (as was once appropriate and effective), we will perhaps be preaching only to the converted. In one congregation I served, I was always free to address the unconverted whenever the text was kerygmatic in nature; but it was always understood that on the third

Lord's Day of every month the message would especially focus on the way of salvation, and a public invitation would be given. A steady stream of new converts provided immense encouragement and challenge for this local church and brought much praise to God. Clearly this is not an either/or but a both/and situation.

Movements such as Churches Alive, Lay Witness Movement, and Evangelism Explosion have often brought a quickening of the evangelistic pulse. Though not everyone is comfortable with the more vigorous "button-holing" of Evangelism Explosion, thousands in this country and abroad can testify that it has provided a most helpful and practical vehicle for witness.[10] Evangelism Explosion, with some seventy-five believers going out weekly, was one of the most exciting things I saw happen in one church I pastored, a church in which evangelism had been chiefly the function of the preaching pastor. So many persons with addictive patterns came to know the Savior that a homogeneous subgroup, which we called the Garden Class, came into being. The Evangelism Explosion method can be adapted to varying local situations, but again the pastor must be involved or the program will be severely limited.

George Peters has given us a significant study entitled *Saturation Evangelism*, by which he means the total mobilization of the local church in concert with other churches to impact an entire community for Christ.[11] This is based on the Evangelism in Depth approach first used by the Latin American Mission.[12] The key here is, every believer is responsible for the spiritual well-being of his or her neighbor. "[T]he successful expansion of any movement is in direct proportion to its success in mobilizing and occupying its total membership in constant propagation of its beliefs." Peters traces the results of this approach both in Latin America and through its counterpart, New Life for All, in Nigeria.[13] We shall develop in Chapter 13 something more of the range of possibilities in the local church for using film evangelism, outdoor evangelism, etc. The more recent adaptation of these principles in a Christ for the City campaign saw the evangelical church in Barranquilla, Colombia increase by 35 percent, with six thousand new Christians.[14] This program is based on cooperation rather than competition among the churches and focuses heavily on prayer and spiritual warfare.

An early prototype of this kind of local church mobilization was provided in the Tell Scotland movement of which Pastor Tom Allan was the field organizer. In his seminal work *The Face of My Parish*, he shares the vision which made a substantial impact on his congregation in suburban Glasgow.[15] The four phases were: 1) visitation by lay persons of

1,854 homes within ten days; 2) person-to-person follow-up and wit-nessing with literature; 3) the organization of Bible study classes to answer the questions of new believers and others; and 4) the formation of small groups for spiritual fellowship and sharing similar to the 2:7 or shepherding groups more recently developed in this country.

The urgency of the local congregation's seeing its central task to be the communication of the gospel has in large part been diminishing in American church life.[16] Martin P. Marty has stated that evangelicalism is now the cultural religion of America; as we have bowed to the pre-vailing cultural currents, we have lost our first love. The necessity for authentic evangelistic vitality is both theological and practical.

Parachurch Evangelism

The proliferation of organizations outside the local church to address varying aspects of the evangelistic mandate is one of the striking devel-opments of our time. This phenomenon is in a sense a judgment on the local church for its tardiness and sluggishness, but it is also an indica-tion of the increasing complexity of the task which the church faces. Organizations such as Campus Crusade for Christ, Intervarsity Christian Fellowship, the Navigators, Child Evangelism Fellowship, the Gideons, Bible Study Fellowship, Christian Women's Clubs, etc. have all vigorously enhanced the church's effort to obey the Great Commission of our risen Lord.

Jerry White in an otherwise helpful treatment seeks to argue that anything outside the local church is parachurch, including confer-ence/district and denominational activity.[17] Inherent in all of these asso-ciations is the recognition that a local church cannot perform every function alone but can join with others in very practical and profitable joint efforts. But Paul Rees correctly points out that denominational or synodical functions owe their existence to the church and are account-able to the church in a way in which the parachurch does not.[18] White's contention that Paul's missionary band is the prototype of the para-church overlooks the organic bonding of the missionary bands to the sending local assembly (cf. Acts 13:1ff.).[19] To use such terminology as para-local church does not seem particularly helpful.

Beyond question, the church which Jesus Christ is building has learned new methods, has obtained new tools, and has been cross-fer-tilized by new concepts through the parachurch. Certainly there should be cooperation between the two. John Stott is right in seeing the insti-tutional church as being in danger of quenching the Spirit and the para-church as being in danger of ignoring the body. Thank God for specialized ministries and for every method and means for the *bona fide* proclamation of the gospel. This must be acknowledged and received in the spirit of the apostle whose primary and passionate desire was "to win as many as possible" (1 Corinthians 9:19).

The church of Jesus Christ is unique, for it is the church Christ established. But the view that all ministry must be conducted under the aegis of a local body of believers or an association of churches is an unattractive and petulant narrowness. At significant points the local church must recognize the reality and the relevance of the universal church. A most helpful treatment of a wise and balanced symbiotic relationship between the church and the parachurch is to be found in Frank Tillapaugh's *The Church Unleashed*.[20]

Planting Evangelism
Beyond question, the planting of new churches is one of the ways in which evangelism is being done today. The whole church growth movement has come of age with maturity and balance. We shall deal more specifically with church planting as a means of evangelism in Chapter 13.

Pulpit Evangelism
Pulpit evangelism continues to be a very crucial ingredient in all parts of the evangelistic mix. Historically pulpit proclamation has played an important role on the evangelism scene—and will continue to do so because evangelistic preaching is part of God's plan (cf. 1 Corinthians 1:21). To the degree that preachers are narcotized by the spirit of this age, our evangelistic preaching will be negligible in its power or impact. If we are only the high priests of the evangelical establishment, put a fork through us—we're done. Soft-soap preaching intent on disturbing no one will accomplish nothing.[21]

Crusade evangelism is not as common in local churches but can still have viability when careful preparation is made. Cooperative evangelism with several churches or in a city-wide campaign has been mightily blessed of God in our time. With the demise of Billy Sunday and the tragedy of B. Faye Mills, many thought the day of mass evangelism was over. Then God raised up Billy Graham.[22]

Billy Graham's focus on the gospel and his faithful loyalty to Scripture explain why even in his seventies his ministry in Hong Kong and Scotland through satellite and video technology have reached out to additional millions of people. (In the Hong Kong crusade over one hundred million people in thirty-three countries shared in the services.)

And beyond the crusades themselves have come the "Hour of Decision" radio broadcast, *Decision* magazine, Operation Andrew, Worldwide Pictures, the Congresses on Evangelism at Lausanne, Amsterdam, etc., the School of Evangelism, the Billy Graham Center at Wheaton College, etc. The two Congresses for Itinerant Evangelists in Amsterdam each drew sixteen thousand believers from many countries. The fruit from all this is astounding.

The fact is, the gospel of Christ and the centrality of the cross have been faithfully proclaimed and used by God in our generation through His servant Billy Graham and many others like him. John Gerstner dismisses Graham as "the most famous dispensationalist" (which to Gerstner means he is "a dubious evangelical,"[23] a perfectionist, one who fails to glorify God or His attributes, one who mistakenly considers his theology Christian) and who on top of that is an Arminian (and therefore not entitled to wear the label "evangelical"). But we may be of good cheer, for Gerstner also does not find acceptable C. I. Scofield, H. A. Ironside, Donald Grey Barnhouse, James Montgomery Boice, R. B. Kuiper, J. Oliver Buswell, and the Westminster faculty including John Murray, Ned Stonehouse, Cornelius Van Til, John Frame, etc. Gerstner's diatribe must be answered point by point, but is it not curious that the only group he can cite which holds to his views is the Protestant Reformed Church and that his particular brand of high Calvinism has not given us an evangelist in this century?

THE TRENDS

> . . . the faith and love that spring from the hope that is stored up for you in heaven and that you have already heard about in the word of truth, the gospel that has come to you. All over the world this gospel is bearing fruit and growing, just as it has been doing among you since the day you heard it and understood God's grace in all its truth. (Colossians 1:5, 6)

Since God's gracious and sovereign purpose is the salvation of sinners, we are not surprised to see His faithful work around the globe, nor are we shocked to see new and striking testimonies raised up even in the torpor of our own culture. While the model of Willow Creek Church in the Chicago area, pastored by Bill Hybels, will not appeal to many, and while in the main it is not transferable to other contexts, here is a model of ministry which God is using to bring salvation to many. The Saturday night service and the two Sunday services are explicitly services for seekers and are designed to appeal to the non-churched (these weekly services attract upwards of twelve thousand persons). The Wednesday and

Thursday night services are directed to believers and feature solid Bible teaching, Communion, and worship (these attract upwards of five thousand to seven thousand). A networking of small groups further nurtures the life of the body. The appeal of this model—its non-traditional approach, its music, its drama segment—has become extensive. It does not frankly reach me or my understanding of the priority of divine worship. To me, it caters to spectatorism. I prefer expository preaching. But unquestionably those who have attended Willow Creek and have heard or know or have seriously read Bill Hybels realize that he is a believer in Christ who ascribes to inerrancy and is true to the gospel of God's saving grace.[24] Hundreds are baptized annually through that ministry.

Opinions and tastes differ. Willow Creek's ministry style is not everyone's cup of tea; the user-friendly philosophy walks the line at times. Yet it would seem that John MacArthur's recent assault on this work is overdone and unfair. MacArthur includes this ministry in his trio of deadly influences undermining the spiritual life[25] and accuses Hybels of "prostituting the ministry" and being in opposition to God. This is extreme. The marginalization of Scripture in evangelism must ever be a serious concern, but matters of form and format are not touchstones of orthodoxy. Rather, our overwhelming concern ought to be:

> *Spread, O spread, thou mighty word,*
> *Spread the kingdom of our Lord,*
> *That to earth's remotest bound*
> *All may heed the Joyful sound.*
>
> (Jonathan F. Bahnmaier)

12

Our Ecclesiology and Evangelism

[W]e know that he has chosen you, because our gospel came to you not simply with words, but also with power, with the Holy Spirit and with deep conviction. You know how we lived among you for your sake . . . you welcomed the message with the joy given by the Holy Spirit. And so you became a model to all the believers. . . . The Lord's message rang out from you . . . your faith in God has become known everywhere.

(1 Thessalonians 1:4, 5, 6b-8a)

I felt how decent English Protestants, or the sons of such, might with zealous affection like to assemble once a week and remind themselves of English purities and decencies and Gospel ordinances, in the midst of a black howling Babel of superstitious savagery, like the Hebrews sitting by the streams of Babel. But I feel more clearly than ever how impossible it was that an extraneous son of Adam, first seized by the terrible conviction that he had a soul to be saved or damned, that he might read the riddle of this universe or go to perdition everlastingly, could for a moment think of taking this respectable 'performance' as the solution of the mystery for him! Oh, heaven! Never in the world! Weep ye by the stream, Babel, decent, clean English-Irish; weep, for there is cause, till you can do something better than weep; but expect no Babylonian or any other mortal to concern himself with that affair of yours.

(Thomas Carlyle, in 1849, writing of a visit to Ireland)[1]

And the Lord added to their number daily those who were being saved.

(Acts 2:47b)

What the church should be and do with respect to evangelism must be governed and guided by our ecclesiology—our doctrine and theology of the church.[2] American pragmatism's fixation on what works and what works well must not be the determinative. The corrective function of Scripture must relentlessly be applied to our praxis, for narcissism even in the spiritual realm is essentially a regressive phenomenon. Constant navel-gazing means death, and thus Moltmann is right in saying, "The church's first word is not church, but Christ."[3]

We are not looking here at church work per se; we are looking at the work of the church. We have in our purview both the universal and the visible church, as well as the ideal and the real. Dorothy Sayers well observed that God's great self-humiliation is seen not only in the self-emptying of the incarnation and in His being "obedient to death—even death on a cross!" (Philippians 2:8), but in His involvement and intimacy with the church. Many have felt that in choosing a bride Christ married too far beneath His station. Swinburne spoke for more than himself when he asserted, "I think I could worship the crucified were it not for His leprous bride." Yet, as Howard Snyder ably contends, "The church is God's agent of evangelism."[4] He is less successful in urging a charismatic model for the church as over against an institutional one. No one would deny his basic point, but the institutional aspect of the common life of all in the body is an inescapable given.

The church's essential problems in our time display the pervasive effects of secularism, a situation potently argued by Os Guiness in *The Gravedigger Files* and by Kenneth Hamilton in his *Earthly Good: The Churches and the Betterment of Human Existence*, in which Hamilton severely criticizes the church for "commending the gospel primarily on the grounds of the personal and social good it can bring about on this earth."[5] This is the ultimate tragedy of our acculturation.

The local church is a gathering of believers among whom the Word of God is preached, the sacraments administered, and mutual discipline experienced. Thus the church, a visible community, is the essential vehicle God has chosen to accomplish world evangelization. Every local church is meant to be evangelistic; we have our divine marching orders. The pattern for this is seen in three Greek words translated "preach," "foundation," and "build" in Romans 15:20. The task begins with preaching the gospel; it involves a foundation, the work of teaching new converts; and it entails building, developing a strong congregation. A vital, virile local congregation is essential.[6] You can't put live chicks under a dead hen. Or as Joe Aldrich puts it: "God is not in the business of putting healthy babies in sick incubators."[7] What, then, ought to characterize a local congregation which yearns to fulfill its call to be a birth matrix and a growth context for precious souls?

THE CHURCH MUST BE A COMMUNITY OF CREDIBLE WITNESS

A witness is a person whose life and faith are so completely one that when the challenge comes to step out and testify for his faith he does so, disregarding all risks, accepting all consequences. (Whittaker Chambers in *Witness*)

The living Christ laid it out thus: "[Y]ou will be my witnesses" (Acts 1:8). The Greek word translated "witness" is the root from which we derive our word *martyr*. In English, *witness* comes from "to wit (to know)." We sometimes speak of "the hermeneutics of testimony," the reasons we pay attention when certain people speak. In this regard Martin Marty quotes Paul Ricoeur as saying, "The term testimony should be applied to words, works, actions, and to lives which attest to an intention, an inspiration, an idea at the heart of experience and history which nonetheless transcends experience and history."[8] Bravo!

We have already taken a position that *presence witness* is crucial but is not fully Christian unless complemented by *proclamation witness*. Church growth people led by Peter Wagner press us to what they call *persuasion witness* and an accompanying concern to register a positive response of commitment and discipleship. I could not agree more but would include that in my understanding of proclamation.

The authentication of verbal witness by genuine life and character—that is God's plan (cf. Matthew 5:16). For example, John Wesley was greatly drawn to the testimony of the Moravians on board ship as he marveled at their fearlessness and poise during a raging storm. Who can calculate the consequences of "good deeds" of love and mercy. Our reactions to provocation can make or break our credibility as witnesses (cf. Paul's calm during a storm in Philippians 1:27-30).

Certainly as bearers of the gospel we want to bring just that—good news—to our hearers. We do not want to create spiritual masochists. We want to pitch the truth positively and attractively. Yet we must be true to our message. There is a scandal and a stumbling-block in Christ's gospel which we cannot sanitize (cf. 1 Corinthians 1:18-29). We offer more than a spiritual salad bar where people are free to take only what appeals to them. In fact, the gospel dislocates in order to relocate; it disorients in order to reorient. This is why Charles H. Spurgeon bore a cross of controversy in "the Downgrade movement" among British Baptists in the last century. He saw "a chasm opening" between those who believed the Scripture and those who did not. He was censured by a vote of 2,000 to 7, but he stood firm. An essential dynamism of our corporate life must be unyielding fidelity to Christ and the Word. The church is a herald, and a herald must proclaim the message he has been given!

> *So let our lips and lives express*
> *The holy Gospel we profess;*
> *So let our works and virtues shine,*
> *To prove the doctrines all divine.*

THE CHURCH MUST BE A COMMUNITY OF FAITHFUL PRAYER

Prayer is the forgotten force in evangelism today. Few witness training courses devote major emphasis to the necessity of prayer for fruitfulness in witnessing. Yet, all evangelism must begin with prayer. Unless the role of prayer in evangelism is recaptured, the church will only plod along in a world racing swiftly toward hell. Prayer is our greatest need. (Joe Ford and Robert Saul in *How to Witness*)[9]

No one has written more clearly or more compellingly about the paramount place of intercessory prayer in winning the lost than the late Lewis Sperry Chafer. Since the unveiling of the gospel by the Spirit is of the very essence of evangelism, Chafer does not put it too strongly when he writes, "The Spirit must wield His mighty Sword and that work of the Spirit, to a large extent it would seem, is subject to believing prayer."[10] Curtis Mitchell has challenged the emphasis on praying for the lost, maintaining that our prayers should be for the saints rather than for sinners.[11] Surely we should pray for the growth and renewing of the church, for the New Testament gives us instances of praying for individual Christians. But do not Matthew 7:7 and Philippians 4:6 open the door for earnest intercession for those who do not know the Savior? What matter would be better to pray for and to seek God's face about?

We know without a doubt that we are praying in accordance with the will of God when we pray for the conversion of sinners (cf. 1 Timothy 2:3, 4; 2 Peter 3:9).

If the church is to visually and verbally communicate Christ, it needs sensitivity regarding the privilege of the saved and the desperate need of the lost. There needs to be an atmosphere of concern which is born of prayer. For too many of us late-twentieth-century Christians, prayer is like a foreign country in which we are visitors and tourists but are never really at home. Matthew Henry used to say that prayer is like the boat-man's hook—it is not meant to bring the shore to the boat but the boat to the shore. The praying church will more certainly be in alignment with what God wants to do through it.

Armin Gesswein used to tell of a missionary traveling through India to trace the genesis of a mighty moving of God's Spirit which led to the conversion of thousands. He followed the action to a believer whose prayers had been answered after long vigils of intercession. That man was John Hyde, or "Praying Hyde" as he came to be known. Similarly, David Brainerd's *Prayer Journal* was like molten lava; it powerfully impacted William Carey, Henry Martyn, and Robert Murray McCheyne, men through whom God poured out incredible showers of blessing. St. Peter's in Dundee, which McCheyne pastored, had thirty-five prayer meetings weekly, of which five were children's prayer meetings. Most heartening just recently in our own country have been the Concerts of Prayer and evidences both from New England and the Pacific Northwest of potent stirrings of the Spirit. Vigorous evangelism is inextricably linked to a strategy of prayer.

THE CHRISTIAN CHURCH MUST BE A COMMUNITY OF SPIRITUAL NURTURE

> At the end of the service there was always what we knew as 'the after-meeting.' It was held to give the opportunity to those who wished to come into the full membership and fellowship of the church, to indicate that desire. There was no pressure made, but that night when the invitation was given, a trembling hand went up from Staffordshire Bill's corner and a murmur of joy and delight from all the rest of us. The Doctor said, 'Stand up Mr. Thomas, and let them see the latest monument to the grace of God'; and he stood and joined us, a very 'elderly babe' in Christ, but as precious to all the church as any new baby in a natural family. (Mrs. Bethan Lloyd-Jones, in *Memories of Sandfields*)[12]

New converts are like newborn babies. They immediately need nurturing and sustaining relationships which will foster and sustain healthy growth and development. Gene Getz rightly insists, "It is important to emphasize—and to emphasize emphatically—that outside the context of the church and the experience of drawing upon other members of the body, a new babe in Christ will not grow into a mature, responsible disciple of Jesus Christ."[13] Much traditional evangelistic effort has been woefully weak in follow-up. Jesus was dedicated to assimilation, as were the apostles and the early church.

Robert Coleman is on the mark in *The Master Plan of Evangelism*, and Bill Hull's work on discipleship points us in the direction we need to go as well.[14] While the "discipleship" vocabulary itself is not particularly found in Acts or in the epistles, the phenomenon of discipleship is emblazoned large (cf. 2 Timothy 2:2). Surely we need new believers' classes and converts' classes and growth groups, but we probably need something more. Each new believer should be discipled by a more mature Christian and encouraged in an accountability relationship to take those critically important steps in the formative stages until he or she is ready to disciple someone else. Excellent materials are available from the Navigators or Campus Crusade for Christ.[15] Both of these organizations, along with others, have been immensely helpful to the church in focusing concern on reducing "the follow-up gap" or "the baptism gap."

The fading of believers' commitments vexes those who shepherd souls (cf. Matthew 13:1-23) but does not persuade them to cease their discipling. James Gilmour of Mongolia, commenting on Galatians 4:19, observed: "It is a carrying of men and women in prayer until the image of Christ be formed in them, and how many of them prove abortions." There are many perils and crises for new believers, but how thrilling it is to see them grow and develop. We are duty-bound to decrease the dropout rate and improve quality control through the power of the Holy Spirit. The vitality and testimony of the church depends on it.

THE CHURCH MUST BE A COMMUNITY OF JOYFUL ASSURANCE

Now it is God who makes both us and you stand firm in Christ. He anointed us, set His seal of ownership on us, and put his Spirit in our hearts as a deposit, guaranteeing what is to come. (2 Corinthians 1:21, 22)

The first epistle of John was expressly written to believers "that you may know that you have eternal life" (1 John 5:13). We have a "know so" salvation. Since God at our conversion makes us new creatures in Christ through His Holy Spirit, it is not presumptuous of us on the basis of Scripture to expect to *know* beyond the shadow of a doubt that we have been born again. We are not to rely on fickle feelings or emotional undulation. Rather, on the basis of the sure Word of God we can, as Calvin said, "presume on God's veracity." The believer who lacks assurance cannot experience all God intends in Christian witness and joy.

Many of the Puritans and various Reformed Christians today do not consider assurance essential to faith, believing that "Assurance is not normally enjoyed except by those who have first labored for it and sought it, and served God faithfully and patiently for some time without it."[16] The danger of this teaching is that it may lead Christians to rely upon their own good works for assurance (a view which conflicts with Galatians 3:3). Interestingly, Kuyper, Bavinck, Vos and Berkhof held to the contrary—namely, that "True faith, as including trust, carries with it a sense of security, which may vary in degree. There is also an assurance of faith, however, that is the fruit of reflection."[17] It would seem there is Biblical warrant for an initial and immediate assurance of a right relationship with God and sins forgiven (associated in Scripture with the proper administration of the keys of the kingdom—cf. Matthew 16:19 and John 20:23); such assurance comes from the Holy Spirit through the Word of God (Romans 8:16). There is also a more ripened and reflective assurance, featured in 1 John as birth marks of all who are in the family of God, inevitable evidences in the life of real Christians—obedience to Christ, love for brothers and sisters in the faith, victory over besetting sin, etc.

John Wesley struggled much with the issue of assurance—was he really among those who belonged to Christ? (Many can identify with him because of the system of teaching under which they were reared or personal temperament or their experience in life's primary relationships.) In his *Journal* Wesley comments, "Being again at St. Paul's in the afternoon, I could taste the good Word of God in the anthem which began: 'My song shall be always of the lovingkindness of the Lord: with my mouth will I ever be showing forth Thy truth from one generation to another.' Yet the enemy injected a fear: 'If thou dost believe, why is there not a more sensible change?' I answered, (yet not I,) 'That I know not. But this I know, I have now peace with God.'" This is like the testimony of the man born blind: "One thing I do know. I was blind but now I see!" (John 9:25). The fact that we can't and don't know everything doesn't mean we can't know anything. The full assurance of faith is part of the believer's birthright; the local representation of Christ's great body sings joyfully as those who know they have eternal life because they have Christ!

THE CHURCH MUST BE A COMMUNITY OF BIBLICAL WORSHIP

> The first and central act of religion is adoration. (Baron Von Hugel)

The true worship and praise of our God is not a side issue or an incidental aspect of our common life in the body of Christ. Heart worship is a reality for the true believer until the return of Christ, when we will praise Him face to face. As Kierkegaard put it, in worship God is the audience and the worshipers are the actors (not, of course, in the sense of pretending but of actively offering adoration to God). The preacher in this scenario is the prompter in the wings assisting and aiding believers in this extraordinary encounter with the Most High God.

Those of us with more low-church, free-liturgy propensities can only express elation that among the more liturgical (which has sometimes meant a deemphasis on evangelism) there has arisen a sharply focused interest in relating worship liturgy to evangelism. This has been called "liturgical evangelism."[18] While some of us may not be comfortable with such nuancing, we can again but express euphoria and gratitude that the authentic gospel of Christ can be expressed within a wide variety of forms. In view of the fact that there is no evidence of a uniform liturgy in the early church, we can only conclude that the Holy Spirit in His gracious sovereignty deigns to meet and bless the people of God in varied situations. All praise be to God.

THE CHURCH MUST BE A COMMUNITY OF FAMILIAL FELLOWSHIP

> They devoted themselves to the apostles' teaching and to the fellowship, to the breaking of bread and to prayer. . . . Every day they continued to meet together in the temple courts. They broke bread in their homes and ate together with glad and sincere hearts. (Acts 2:42, 46)

The vitality of the early church and the vigor of the church of the catacombs are not entirely absent in the contemporary church. The Christian church is to ever be an island of caring in an increasingly impersonal and affectively starved world. The megachurch is one of the major phenomena of social change in our times, but we must beware of a danger in this exceptional model; namely, it is easy to get lost in the large church, even with its sub-groupings. Most Americans are still most comfortable in an average-sized or smaller church. Every congregation—whatever its size—has exciting opportunities to express Christian concern and caring to the lonely, the lost, the estranged, the disenfranchised.

A friendly church is not always easy to find. Some congregations drag their feet on any evangelistic innovation because quite frankly they are content with the current mix. A sister in Christ told me years ago, "I don't like our church any more—I don't know all of these new people." However, satisfaction with the status quo and a desire to be a MAS (Mutual Admiration Society) spell certain spiritual demise.

In Genesis 11 we find the story of the Tower of Babel, a historical picture of mankind's effort to build community around an instrument of its own creation. In contrast, in Acts 2 we see the picture of God's community in action. The Donner expedition was destroyed because its members refused to exercise sharing and community on their westward trek. The truth is, we are interdependent; we very much need other (1 Corinthians 12 is a remarkable treatise on this truth as it relates to the church). As Francois Mauriac so beautifully portrays in his stories, "The marks left by one individual on another are eternal, and not with impunity can some other's destiny cross our own."

A few years ago a hundred and fifty reporters, one billion viewers, and twenty-six countries willing to spend six million dollars were concerned about three whales trapped in the Arctic ice off Barrow, Alaska. What about the millions who are outside of Christ just beyond our doorsteps and our church porch? Of how much greater value they are than those unfortunate whales. Francis Asbury, the great itinerant Methodist preacher in the early years of our nation's history, exemplified the ethic of self-sacrifice, the core of all true community. He did away with the liturgical/sacramental means familiar to the Wesleys and those who followed after them; he did away with clerical dress, inviting men to a hazardous itinerant ministry instead.[19] True gospel preaching is willing to pay a price for the sake of Christ and those who need Him. This ethic of sacrifice must inform our approach as to what direction the church should take in our day. Samuel Rutherford reflects this marvelous spirit:

> *If one soul from Anworth*
> *Meets me at God's right hand,*
> *My Heaven would be two Heavens*
> *In Immanuel's land.*

THE CHURCH MUST BE A COMMUNITY OF FORCEFUL PROCLAMATION

Decline of spiritual life activity in the churches is commonly accompanied by a lifeless, formal, unfruitful preaching, and this partly as cause, partly as effect. On the other hand, the great revivals of Christian history can most usually be traced to the work of the pulpit. (E. C. Dargan, *History of Preaching*)

Preaching is the lifeblood of the Christian church. C. H. Spurgeon expressed the excitement of preaching when he said: "Give me the Bible and the Holy Ghost and I can go on preaching forever." I am not speaking of the indolent repetition of old phrases but of the reverent, skillful, systematic, Spirit-led opening of the Word of God for the people. Proper exegesis of Scripture is the cracking of the lock to get at the treasure.

Many are in spiritual famine and desperately need to hear the Word of God. As Milton said in *Lycidas*:

> *The hungry sheep look up, and are not fed*
> *But swollen with the wind, and the rank mist they draw,*
> *Rot inwardly. . . .*

The only sufficient answer for such need is the Word of God with its life-giving message for the unsaved and its nourishing diet for believers at every stage of their spiritual pilgrimage. William Willimon in a brilliant essay in *The Christian Century* divides the issue in this way: preaching, entertainment, or exposition? Shall we succumb to the sound-bite approach to sermonizing? Shall we thus compromise the integrity of the preached Word?

This issue of loyalty to the Word was something the young Billy Graham had to face early on when his brilliant early associate in Youth for Christ, Chuck Templeton, counseled Graham to follow him into modern scholarship. When Graham refused, Templeton predicted, "He'll never do anything for God. He'll be circumscribed to a small little narrow interpretation of the Bible."[20] Graham has never been ashamed of saying, "The Bible says." Neither should we, come what may. Luther was right—when we preach the truth, the dogs will begin to bark. So what? Let them bark.

The church is often frighteningly frail—but it will last forever (see Matthew 16:13-20). We should desire to strengthen the church; we will not rescue the perishing by ignoring or attacking the lifeboat. Luther was right in his projection that as this age draws toward a conclusion there will be two churches—the church of Jesus Christ and the church of the Anti-Christ. We should want to cultivate and strengthen throughout these days the marks of the true church: namely, unity, purity, catholicity, and apostolicity. Considering the toxicity of our culture, this is an immense undertaking. "But if [or, since] God is for us, who can be against us?" (Romans 8:31).

We shall turn in the next chapter to a specific evangelistic strategy for the local church in our day.

13

A Strategy for All-out Evangelization

You, however, did not come to know Christ that way. Surely you heard of him and were taught in him in accordance with the truth that is in Jesus.

(Ephesians 4:20, 21)

This is the gospel that you heard and that has been proclaimed to every creature under heaven. . . . We proclaim him, admonishing and teaching everyone with all wisdom, so that we may present everyone perfect in Christ.

(Colossians 1:23, 28)

We loved you so much that we were delighted to share with you not only the gospel of God but our lives as well . . . we preached the gospel of God to you. . . . And we also thank God continually because, when you received the word of God, which you heard from us, you accepted it not as the word of men, but as it actually is, the word of God, which is at work in you who believe.

(1 Thessalonians 2:8, 9, 13)

The dimensions of world evangelism are so awesome that only the whole church throughout the world, working in proper partnership, can get the task done. How to work together as full partners, that is the question.

(Isabelo Magalit, at Urbana, 1979)

*My right flank is retreating. The centre is giving way. The
situation is excellent: I will attack.*

> (Marshall Foch, French general in
> World War I)

The Christian response to the spiritual need of the world cannot be
casual or haphazard. We have attempted to survey something of the
present situation and to suggest the general contour of what the church
ought to be and where the church should be going. Now we will address
how we get from where we are to where we ought to be. Our purpose
here is to project an evangelistic strategy for the local church or for an
association of churches and to see the integral role evangelistic preaching plays in such an overall strategization.

The familiar adage is correct: if we fail to plan, we plan to fail. It
goes without saying that local churches need to set goals, and a special
emphasis on evangelism is consistent with proper prioritization in the
local church.[1] Donald Bloesch has spoken of "the gift of battle" as one
of the Holy Spirit's rich endowments. Victory in spiritual warfare
requires strategization as surely as does any military campaign. Lidell
Hart, the foremost student of military strategization in this century,
quotes Napoleon's axiom: "The whole art of war consists of a well-rea-
soned and extremely circumspect defensive, followed by rapid and
audacious attack." Napoleon further urged: "The art of war lies in
becoming master of the lines of communication." Strategic penetration
of enemy lines is key.[2]

In Nigel Hamilton's classic study of Montgomery of Alamein we
learn of this heroic Christian general's basic strategy: strength through
concentration and mobility. Effective strategization is the result of careful analysis of the enemy, tactical vision, and the courageous overcom-
ing of fear. Montgomery found it difficult to change his plans but would
do so when appropriate, recognizing that flexibility and mobility are
essential. Leaders in business and industry are increasingly using
"visioning"—i.e., working together to envision what an organization
can be like in five to ten years. "A vision is an exciting picture—an end
state—of what an organization wants to be. It not only appears to people's minds but also to their hearts and spirits."[3]

Visioning and strategic planning not only need to be done on a
broad scale but more specifically in each local church.[4] Jim Peterson of
the Navigators and Donald Posterski of Intervarsity have both given us

helpful pieces calculated to develop an evangelistic strategy which takes us beyond our comfort zones.[5] What kind of overall strategy is needed?

OUR STRATEGY MUST BE INCLUSIVE

It is quite impossible to be "in Christ" and not participate in Christ's mission to the world. (Dr. James Stewart, *Thine Is the Kingdom*)

Every Christian is involved in getting the gospel out to every person! No special call is given to Christians to become part of the Christian world task. There is a division of labor, to be sure, as the Antiochian pattern in Acts 13:1-3 clearly shows. First evangelized by anonymous evangelists, the church at Antioch was built up and nurtured by able teachers and leaders. In response to the Holy Spirit's nudging, the church sent out emissaries "for the work to which I [the Spirit] have called them" (Acts 13:2).

The target of Christian witness is the whole world. "The world is my parish," cried John Wesley. This contrasts sharply with the puzzling absence of missionary zeal among the Puritans of the sixteenth and seventeenth centuries. Dr. David Bebbington suggests this was due in large part to Puritan spirituality with its lack of assurance of salvation and the resultant introspective piety.[6]

John 3:16 portrays the whole world and every person in it as the objects of God's love and thus of our testimony. Thus prayer for all people parallels God's desire for all to be saved (1 Timothy 2:1-4; cf. 2 Peter 3:9 and 2:1, which says the Lord has "bought" everyone). Each congregation should identify people groups and then build bridges of outreach to them. Every congregation is in the middle of a mission field. Even smaller, more rural churches can target persons God wants them to reach with the gospel—migrant workers, people at the county fair or the community parade, etc.

Our witness needs to extend even to resistant persons and groups, though we are well advised to "identify receptive people"—i.e., to especially make use of those circumstances that make people more open to the claims of Christ. George Hunter lists a number of "indicators" of receptivity: unchurched people who have some kinship or friendship link with believers; people who need a particular kind of ministry (support groups for single parents, the addicted, etc.); people who have recently moved and are facing change and adjustment (a Christian "Welcome Wagon"); people in significant life-transition (retirees, etc.).[7] "The field is the world" (Matthew 13:38), and our strategy for evangelism must encompass all and exclude none.

The sheer enormity of the task requires total mobilization, and this begins with the pastor or other spiritual leaders. Kenneth Callahan well argues that often today "we wrongly focus more on membership than on salvation, more on institutional maintenance than on societal outreach, more on concerns for lost dollars of giving than on mission with specific human hurts and hopes."[8] The church is to be a mission outpost. To fulfill this calling, we must move away from a maintenance mode in the local church. Such a turn-about has to begin in the pastor's own heart and mind and life. A spate of immensely practical books help the pastor redefine his role in more evangelistic terms.[9] George Peters observed some time ago that "European churches and their leaders have never seen the connection between evangelism and pastoral ministry." Though this is not altogether true in the North American church, the pastoral leadership team must employ bold and creative strategization or we shall continue to atrophy.

Preaching, counseling, visitation, pastoral function in all of the passages of life, community involvement, radio and television ministry all afford the pastor opportunities for evangelism. I like Vincent Taylor's test of any theologian: can he write a tract? The same goes for the pastor. Willingness and ability to concisely and effectively communicate the gospel is paramount.

Church leaders and laypersons all equally need to care for the lost. We are thinking here of more than happy and enthusiastic programs for outreach; we are focusing on "foundational life searches," as Callahan puts it. Callahan makes an important point when he says the church is not to become the center of people's lives but is rather to be in the center of people's lives. That is, we must beware of allowing the church to become an activity trap that consumes people's lives. Christians are rather to be meaning makers, personalizing their faith in every context of existence.

OUR STRATEGY MUST BE COMPREHENSIVE

You blame me for weeping, but how can I help it when you will not weep for yourselves, though your immortal souls are on the verge of destruction, and for aught you know, you are hearing your last sermon, and may never more have an opportunity to have Christ offered to you. (George Whitefield)

Not only should every believer be involved in an outreach strategy in some way consistent with his or her spiritual gifts, but every Christian organization and program should be participating in the implementa-

tion of an evangelistic strategy in a local body of believers. Special seekers' services should be part of the ministry of every local church. The
way of salvation needs to be made clear in all services; kerygmatic texts
should be expounded and appropriate invitations extended. The tone is
set by the prayers and concerns emanating from the hearts of those who
lead and participate in the public services.

Granted, the services of the church are above all intended to pro-
mote the worship of God. Kierkegaard rightly insisted that "If you have
not felt that God is present here, and that you are before God, then your
visit to God's house has been in vain." But the God before whom we
appear is a judging and a forgiving God, and no one should sit through
a service without experiencing a vivid awareness of the divine offer of
saving grace.

Though advocating that the church be a potent evangelistic force,
Dr. D. Martyn Lloyd-Jones also approvingly quoted John Owen's definition of a gospel church:

> What is an instituted church of the gospel? A society of persons
> called out of the world, or their natural worldly state, by the admin-
> istration of the word and Spirit, unto the obedience of the faith, or
> the knowledge and worship of God in Christ, joined together in a
> holy band, or by special agreement, for the exercise of the commu-
> nion of saints in the due observation of all the ordinances of the
> gospel.[10]

This is an admirable statement in many respects, but it falls short in that
it lacks a clear sense of the mission of the church in evangelization and
outreach. We need to do more than imply or assume evangelistic outreach. It must be a stated and visible goal and action on the part of the
church at large and of each local congregation. Let us elaborate on this
point.

Every department in the church should have clear evangelistic focus.
Every Sunday school department needs to have regular training sessions
on how to lead children, youth, and adults to Christ. Daily vacation
Bible schools and Christian day camps should have "decision" days
when prayerful and concerted emphasis is placed on making the way to
Christ clear and compelling. Bible camps have always been a most fruitful open door. (A survey at Moody Bible Institute revealed that 85 percent of the students had made their initial commitment to Christ at a
summer camp.) In all of this, follow-up is exceedingly important.
Moreover, none of these outreaches should supplant the witness of the
Christian home but should rather build on it. Parents should be encour-

aged to read good literature on leading their own children to Christ and nurturing them in a growing knowledge of the Lord (cf. Ephesians 6:4).[11] Special evangelistic meetings in the local church or in the community, or special children's evangelistic services, also reap a rich harvest. "Uncle Win" in earlier days and Willard and Margaret Grant and other skilled gospel servants have been mightily used to bring children into the kingdom.

A growing missionary program in the local church raises the threshold of awareness concerning world need and universal church responsibility. Praying for missions, giving for missions, receiving news from various fields, life-commitment times, powerful missions conferences, weekly missionary moments in Sunday morning services, programs for faith-promises and increased understanding of what Christian stewardship is all about—all this can help us move us out of the privatization of our faith and away from general passivity.

Ministry in jails and prisons, outdoor services in parks, street meetings, regular meetings conducted in skid-row missions, and services in nursing homes and retirement centers all afford opportunity for the utilization of God-given talents by gospel teams. Trained personal workers have special open doors. Every congregation should have home visitation teams, whether they are of the Evangelism Explosion type or not. Bus ministry is still viable but should be supplemented by outreach into homes. Loving perseverance in all this is of utmost importance. A survey done by the National Retail Dry Goods Association has shown that 88 percent of the salesmen surveyed quit after three calls or less, while 12 percent of the sales force keep on calling—and the 12 percent do 80 percent of the business. Various ongoing contacts with people bring endless opportunities for acts of kindness, seeds which may bear much fruit (Psalm 126:6). Various means of making use of these opportunities should be evaluated carefully. The building of a cradle roll department by using mothers of newborns still works. The overuse of telemarketing and strong resistance to phone solicitation may indicate not using this method just now. Crisis hot lines, well advertised and manned with trained personnel, present valuable opportunities to address problems of chemical dependency, crisis pregnancy, sexual abuse, suicidal impulses, beatings, etc. (The work of Youth Development, Inc. [YDI] is one good source for this type of outreach.) Every local situation must be carefully analyzed.[12] What works in one location may not work elsewhere. Those who are skeptical about how an evangelistic strategy will work in a small town need to be encouraged to see that there is a way.[13]

A certain small church in an area with dwindling population was not experiencing numerical growth. In fact, after sixty years and seventeen pastors the church was about the same size. Yet in those years twenty-five people from that congregation entered state-side or overseas ministry full-time. Consider the influence of that local church—that is genuine church growth!

The multiplication of small-group Bible studies in recent years has been a great blessing in many congregations.[14] Fellowship groups and friendship groups and the fostering of lifestyle evangelism by these means can be immensely productive. In addition, every church should have a well-stocked library with well-chosen current releases which inform and inspire readers with what God is doing in our world today and help them to see their own place of ministry in relation to the larger picture. Every church and every believer should also be well-stocked with attractive literature for distribution as opportunities come. Who knows what fruit God will bring from a timely tract.[15]

Specialized ministries to the deaf, the blind, and the physically and mentally handicapped should not be overlooked in framing a local strategy for outreach. Ministries to students by churches adjacent to colleges or universities can present awesome challenges as well. Hospitals, business centers open for special noon luncheons, Lenten noon services, concert series, day-care centers, and much more are examples of outreach ministries which are appropriate and possible in various locations. And finally, no local church outreach is complete without some participation in Jewish evangelism, for the gospel was given "first for the Jew" (Romans 1:16). Oh, what opportunities exist. Each local congregation faces the challenge and unequalled privilege of formulating a strategy for its own situation and community.

OUR STRATEGY MUST BE INNOVATIVE

> Proud man has a desire to preach new doctrine, to set up a new church, to be an original thinker, to judge and consider and do anything but obey. (Charles Haddon Spurgeon)

Dr. David Bebbington has insightfully described four characteristics of evangelicalism: conversionism, Biblicism, crucicentrism (cross-centeredness), and activism (i.e., the use of a variety of efforts for the welfare of others' souls).[16] The message of the gospel is a constant, but the methods may and *must* adapt to changing situations. Finney's "new measures" were much opposed but subsequently became widely used. D. L. Moody himself was called "Crazy Moody" because of some of his unorthodox ways. The Duke of Wellington used to say, "They came on in the same old way and we stopped them in the same old way." Sadly, some pastors and churches know little more than the "same old way." I am not advocating ridiculous and unseemly innovations—a preacher swinging out of the balcony with a rose in his mouth or a jazz guitarist playing "Someday My Prince Will Come" on the first Sunday in Advent. I am not recommending that preachers follow the lead of the clergyman who preached while strapped to the steeple because his congregation met his challenge to have a hundred and fifty people in Sunday school. The dignity and standards of gospel preaching as it is presented in the Scriptures must be maintained.

Yes, we must be willing to proclaim Christ's message in daring and sometimes disputed ways—at all times and in all ways being obedient and faithful to the heavenly vision (cf. Acts 26:19). We should never seek novelty for novelty's sake but should rather use innovation carefully and prayerfully. We should thoroughly understand present practice and sensitively explain proposed changes. Never be a Lone Ranger; remember, "we are all members of one body" (Ephesians 4:25). Listen to the suggestions and comments of others, and use or modify them as seems best. But do not turn back simply because of criticism either. Industry and business do not take "no" for an answer; why should the work of the Lord? A radical recasting of current ministries, sharing facilities and staff, developing an AIDS outreach ministry, and whatever else we believe God is leading us into should not be unthinkable, for we worship and serve a God who says, "I make all things new." Half of the churches in America now use personal computers. This was unthinkable just a few years back.

In Mexico, where government regulations regarding worship and evangelism are very stringent, resourceful and creative Christians are finding ways that work. For example, Pastor Ruben Ramirez Meyer began a fledgling church and has since then founded 350 new churches in the Vera Cruz area while himself pastoring a congregation of five thousand. He has also started a Bible institute that maintains a strong emphasis on experience in ministry.[17] If we are to proclaim and spread the good news of Jesus Christ fruitfully, we must break away from traditional but ineffective patterns, taking risks and engaging in bold evangelism. One dedicated group of young men in a congregation I served picked up draftees the night before they were to be shipped out and gave them a wonderful time of recreation, good food, and invigorating gospel testimonies. A steady stream of decisions for Christ resulted.

Lyle Schaller skillfully argues that building new facilities for a church should be dovetailed into the evangelistic purpose of the congregation. The physical structures of the church should express not only our theology but our concern for newcomers and a gracious welcome. "Does the design reinforce values and goals?" is a pertinent question.[18]

Church planting could be one of the bold new approaches to evangelism in the near future, for in the next few years one hundred thousand churches are expected to close in the United States. This calls for courageous witness and creative evangelism! A *Christianity Today* article on the church growth movement, entitled "Church Growth Fine Tunes Its Formulas," quotes Dr. John Stackhouse as saying:

> The history of evangelicalism in North America shows that it is quite technique-oriented. Evangelicals are willing to innovate in a way that surprises Christians of other stripes, who tend to see evangelicals as conservative in every respect. In fact, they are not at all conservative when it comes to the practice of Christianity, and especially evangelism.[19]

C. Peter Wagner's *Church Planting for a Greater Harvest: A Comprehensive Guide* is a most practical and helpful guidebook.[20] Instead of getting larger and larger, perhaps a congregation should plant a daughter church. Rather than spending a small fortune on relocation, the planting of a new church in an advantageous location may be God's plan. In all of this there is a call for risk-taking akin to C. T. Studd's convicting poem:

> *Some wish to live within the sound*
> *Of church or chapel bell;*
> *I want to run a rescue shop*
> *Within a yard of hell.*

OUR STRATEGY MUST BE COOPERATIVE

> Ours is but an inch of time in which to stand and preach Christ, then the endless roll of eternal years. (Robert Murray McCheyne)

The scope and urgency of our task summon us out of competition with one another into cooperation with all who have the same precious faith in Christ. The old denominational distinctives have receded in significance for most people. Now when they move into a new community they look for a vital fellowship with sound Bible preaching and an effective program for their children and youth. The fact is, none of us can do the job alone. We need cooperation in undertaking evangelism both on the larger scale and in providing local churches with the training needed to complete the task.

Spener maintained that the church is "a school of the Holy Spirit," and Franke described the church as "a seat of wisdom and piety." The issues are too momentous and the time too short for us to be ingrown and cantankerous with one another. Picture a marching band. As the musicians move through a snappy routine, the trumpet players incredibly try to trip each other. Then the percussion section begins to play so loudly, you simply cannot hear the rest of the band. The members of the clarinet section, tired of being overlooked, sit in a circle and play for themselves (which nobody notices). All the while the Drum Major is trying to restore order. This type of performance would not bring a prize in any band contest, nor would it bring respect or applause from those sitting in the grandstands. But sadly this is frequently how the witnessing church appears to others. We seem more intent on one-upmanship than on the Kingdom of God. *Evangelism must be a team effort.* Local churches need to come out of isolation and enlarge the circles of opportunity as they pray and proclaim Christ's good news together. John 13:35 describes our identification badge as Christ's disciples: "All men will know that you are my disciples if you love one another." After all, who wants to listen to or watch a quarrelsome marching band?

Some years after a certain church split, I was invited to an evangelistic crusade sponsored by the resulting two congregations. People in the community were surprised and perplexed when the meetings received good attention and, praise God, had positive results. You see, when the people of God get along and labor together in the work of God, the world will take notice and lives will be changed.

OUR STRATEGY MUST BE COMMUNICATIVE

> To preach the Gospel . . . it is a manifestation of the Incarnate Word, from the Written Word, by the spoken word. (Bernard Manning)

The effectiveness and worthiness of all evangelism is predicated on the accurate transmission of the gospel message. Whether we are talking about one-on-one witness or mass evangelism, everything hinges on fidelity to the historic Word of God given under the power and unction of the Holy Spirit. And evangelistic preaching in the local church is the key means of proclamation. Dr. Billy Graham has repeatedly asserted, "The greatest evangelistic opportunity in America is for evangelistic pastors in pulpits of local churches." Yes, the church is to feed the flock and to address the pressing issues of our times in the light of Holy Scripture (never forgetting that "Evangelism is social action").[21] But we must also affirm the undeniable importance of evangelistic preaching from the pulpits of local churches.

God has promised to bless and use this message of salvation to the conversion of souls. On one occasion Billy Graham preached in a huge stadium, but the meeting seemed dead. On returning to the hotel, Graham said to a layman accompanying him that he was troubled over the lack of life and power in the service. The layman replied, "I agree with you. There was little power in the service, and I think I know the reason. You did not preach the cross." That night Billy Graham made a resolution that he would never again preach without lifting up Christ and Christ crucified for sinners (cf. John 12:32; 1 Corinthians 1:18-23). This is a lesson none of us dare ignore or forget.

A young man mocking George Whitefield, repeating the preacher's words and mimicking his gestures, stopped abruptly when the Holy Spirit brought him under conviction. As a result that man came into salvation. A Russian actor in Moscow whose lines repeated and mocked Scripture stopped under the conviction of the Spirit and was converted right on the stage. A thief hiding under a table in a lumber camp when Stephen Grellet preached to a large empty dining hall came under conviction and was converted. When Charles Spurgeon tested the acoustics in the new Tabernacle in London and repeated John 1:29 several times, a painter finishing his work came under conviction and was saved. The spoken proclamation of Christ's gospel is indispensable in developing an evangelistic strategy.

The Minister's Prayer

I do not ask that crowds may throng the temple,
That standing room be priced;
I only ask that as I voice the message
They may see the Christ.

I do not ask for churchly pomp or pageantry,
Or music such as wealth may buy;
I only pray that as I voice the message
He might be nigh.

I do not ask that men may sound my praise
Or headlines spread my name abroad;.
I only ask that as I voice the message
Hearts may find God.

(Author unknown)

14

The Intelligibility of the Christian Truth-claim

Therefore, since through God's mercy we have this ministry, we do not lose heart. Rather, we have renounced secret and shameful ways; we do not use deception, nor do we distort the word of God. On the contrary, by setting forth the truth plainly we commend ourselves to every man's conscience in the sight of God. And even if our gospel is veiled, it is veiled to those who are perishing. The god of this age has blinded the minds of unbelievers, so that they cannot see the light of the gospel of the glory of Christ, who is the image of God. For we do not preach ourselves, but Jesus Christ as Lord, and ourselves as your servants for Jesus' sake.

(2 Corinthians 4:1-5)

Yet all the same our way isn't the way of the world. You can't go offering the truth to human beings as though it were a sort of insurance policy, or a dose of the salts.

(George Bernanos)

On the contrary, we speak as men approved by God to be entrusted with the gospel. We are not trying to please men but God, who tests our hearts.

(1 Thessalonians 2:4)

The Lord Jesus Christ "preached among the nations . . . believed on in the world" (1 Timothy 3:16)—this is the very core of the plan of God being worked out in this era and in our world. As H. H. Farmer so succinctly put it: "Here and now God's saving activity in the world in Christ once again encounters the souls of men." Notwithstanding the massive and seemingly insoluble problems besetting humankind, and in addition the tragic moral and spiritual decadence of our age, we are living in the time of the greatest gospel harvest in the history of the Christian church. This is occurring chiefly in the Two-thirds World, for the severely acculturated churches of western Europe and North America, with but few exceptions, are suffering from the spiritual blahs.

Thus Engle and Norton's probing monograph a few years back (*What's Gone Wrong with the Harvest?*) struck a responsive chord— and still does for every gospel communicator.[1] Every generation of Christians has faced the formidable task of building a bridge between the gospel message and the alien and intimidating cultures in which they found themselves. Thus the early church faced the Greco-Roman world, and every missionary today confronts complex contextualization challenges. Engle and Norton are not wide of the mark in their concern for communicational breakdown in our own situation. Many a pastor and evangelist wrestles with the question, is anyone out there listening? How can we restore the "cutting blades" of kerygmatic proclamation by the church to our culture?

The fact is, we address an idolatrous culture. We are back in Canaan, so to speak. Our hearers (and perhaps we ourselves) are being assaulted by idols to which we must not capitulate. A missionary to Indonesia while on furlough wrote: "Oh my, so many places today appear to be 'watering down the Truth' and our hearts are saddened. Since early July we've traveled 9000 miles and have not been very encouraged in our church contacts." We live in and seek to proclaim the gospel to a vast Peyton Place. Will the message be believed? Dare we hope for success in our evangelistic endeavors, considering how far gone our society is morally?

The *New York Times* has, on the front page no less, spoken of Christians as "narrow-minded and the chief road-blocks to new ideas and change in our society." Thomas Hine's new book *Facing Tomorrow* advances the premise that Americans disillusioned about the prospect of progress have withdrawn into "self-centered escapism," seeing themselves increasingly as "consumers of their own lives." How do we communicate the gospel effectively to those who hold the Marilyn Monroe philosophy of "I believe in everything . . . a little bit"? Is the everlasting gospel intelligible to a recent correspondent of *Time* magazine who wrote of Marianne Williamson and her sermons (cf. Chapter 6), "Finally someone is talking about the God that I always knew existed: the nonjudgmental God, the loving God, the God who has no requirements, no prejudices and no restrictions. Gone is the pomp and circumstance. Gone are all the scare tactics promising hell for not believing in the 'right way.' Gone are the pleas for cold cash to save your soul and build a church or school or theme park or . . . or . . . or."[2]

Even John Wesley stated in his day, "Nothing is more repugnant to capable, reasonable people than grace." Even as astute a social observer as Christopher Lasch (whose *The Culture of Narcissism* and *The Minimal Self* were most incisive analyses of contemporary culture) in his most recent volume (*The True and Only Heaven*) speaks of his own journey as "the making of a malcontent," and while pooh-poohing the idea that civilization is making any real progress really offers no solutions.[3] Truly there is "no health in us." and T. S. Eliot's haunting lines from *Murder in the Cathedral* capture it all:

> *Sweet and cloying through the dark air*
> *Falls the stifling scent of despair.*

Is our message communicable? What are the factors which must be considered in addressing the Biblically illiterate, overwhelmingly secular modern mind? The situation will not substantially improve as the age draws to a close (see 2 Timothy 3:1ff.). What can we do?

VERACITY

"I am not insane, most excellent Festus," Paul replied. "What I am saying is true and reasonable." (Acts 26:25)

The Christian truth-claim is asserted as part of the historic and orthodox Christian worldview. Now, every person has a worldview, even if it is implicit or not formally articulated. In arguing for a more forthright statement of the Christian worldview, David McKenna quotes Kenneth Boulding's three components of any worldview: 1) it must have an interpretation of human history in which we find our own role; 2) it must have a moral standard or system of values by which to judge good and evil, truth and error; 3) it must have a vision for the future that is significant.[4] Even a *Time* magazine essayist recognizes that the current clash in our culture over sexual mores is the product of differing worldviews: "What we are witnessing is in fact a clash between two earnest and articulated theological impulses. Traditionalists and innovators disagree about sex because they disagree about the universe, and about God."[5]

The fact is, a series of competitive worldviews is vying for attention and acceptance. Christianity is not "a mighty maze and quite without a plan" as some have claimed. Biblical Christianity is a coherent system of thought which (as Edward John Carnell used to argue so capably) is vertically consistent and horizontally fits the facts better than any other system. We can invite others to test the Christian gospel—we are not timorous about confrontation, for we are confident of its truth. Contrary to Karl Barth and Cornelius Van Til (who came from very different positions to a similar conclusion), I am convinced that believers share significant common ground with unbelievers and that there are a number of positive starting points in making a case for the Christian gospel. While the natural man is limited in spiritual perception (cf. 1 Corinthians 2:14), he nevertheless possesses the *imago dei* which, though defaced by sin (there are noetic effects from the Fall), has nevertheless not been totally effaced. Language communicates, and even an unconverted person can grasp the essential meaning of words. For example, E. D. Burton, an unbeliever, wrote a splendid commentary on Galatians in the old ICC. Though he believed Paul was wrong on the atonement, he understood much of what the Apostle Paul wrote.

The Christian Gospel Is Reasonable

No one has demonstrated this better than the late Christian apologist Francis Schaeffer. Evangelistic preaching must be deeply involved with apologetics, as Schaeffer so impressively pleads in his numerous books. Communication of the gospel to this generation must be given in terms they understand. "The invitation to act comes only after an adequate base of knowledge has been given."[6] Schaeffer's critical point is that God is a non-determined being, and God has made human beings as non-determined beings; i.e., they have the power to believe or not believe. Therefore, the presentation of a choice must be part of our proclamation.

In light of all this we can only deplore Barth's denial of general revelation and those who follow Barth (for example, Donald Bloesch who denies both rational consistency and empirical verification as tests of truth).[7] This is the Kantian worldview with its inevitable anti-intellectual agnosticism (review the disastrous implications of Kant's denial of objective significance for religious and moral truth in the work cited in the footnote).[8]

John Calvin began his *Institutes* with the knowledge of God. We too must begin with the God of the Bible. "Without faith it is impossible to please God, because anyone who comes to him must believe that he exists and that he rewards those who earnestly seek him" (Hebrews 11:6). Paul argued that even the pagan world has knowledge of God and His divine power (cf. Romans 1:18ff.; also see Psalm 19—where first the world of creation and then the Word of God testify to the existence and presence of God). While theistic proofs have had rough going philosophically since Kant, there is some common ground here. Taken together they present at least an intrinsic probability for the Supreme Being. Others who have argued effectively along this line include Carl F. H. Henry, Edward John Carnell, Francis Schaeffer, Elton Trueblood, Gordon Haddon Clark, and many others.[9]

The Christian Gospel Is Logical

Another strategic starting point has to do with the person and claims of the Lord Jesus Christ. This raises both the issue of the historicity of Christ (which is denied by virtually no one today) and the question of the New Testament documents.[10] Clark Pinnock's validation of the gospel basically begins by considering the uniqueness of Christ.[11] How is He to be explained? Josh McDowell, a popular apologist on college campuses, focuses extensively (and rightly) on the person of Christ. The basic argument is compelling: Is Christ a liar, or is Christ a lunatic, or did He speak the truth when He said, "I am the way and the truth and the life. No one comes to the Father except through me" (John 14:6)?[12]

Few (if any) have been a more effective witness to the skeptics over the years than C. S. Lewis, who in *Mere Christianity* makes the case from moral sense and also from the standpoint of who Christ is and what Lewis calls "first steps in the doctrine of the Trinity."[13] Wilbur M. Smith in his more classical apologetic concentrated on the epochal events in the life of our Lord and was an early pioneer in this pre-evangelistic task.[14] Occasionally the apologist must give attention to the inconsistency and shortcomings of competing systems in order to "facilitate and make possible Christian proclamation and communication."[15] The amazing thing is, notwithstanding the corrosive acids of modernity and skepticism, modern humankind cannot escape thinking about Jesus. Even a troubling modern (and blasphemous) film about Jesus triggered a cover story in *Time* magazine—"Who Was Jesus?"—which asserted with confidence the historicity of our Lord and warned the higher critics, in the words of an Anglican scholar, "If you tear up the only evidence you've got, you can say anything you like."[16]

The Christian Gospel Is Personal

While our appeal cannot legitimately be, "Come to Christ because He will satisfy all your needs" (a concession to Maslow's hierarchy of need gratification, at the apex of which is self-actualization), the fact is, Christianity is more than a system—it is reconciliation to God through the Savior. Many have been drawn to Christ because they understood that relationship with Him is so intensely personal. Indeed, what is initially propositional and factual must transmute into the personal and the relational.

Since 1917 the Soviets have sought to systematically destroy all notions of objective truth. They have not been alone in this quest. Proclaiming as vigorously as we do the objective truthfulness of the gospel representation, we must not for a moment lose sight of the need for subjective and personal verification. "Taste and see that the Lord is good" (Psalm 34:8).

Pascal was right when he said, "There is a God-shaped vacuum in the heart of every man which only God can fill through His Son, Jesus Christ." Milla Jovovich, the popular young actress and model, confesses that she sees herself as "a psycho-schizophrenic from hell" and that her greatest desire is to meet God.[17] Merrill-Lynch's "Your world should know no boundaries" campaign leaves us high and dry. The casino model leaves us empty.[18] Here is a critical point of contact, an advantageous common ground. Christianity makes sense; truth corresponds propositionally to reality. Thus we can "Always be prepared to give an answer to everyone who asks you to give the reason for the hope that you have" (1 Peter 3:15b).

VOCABULARY

Peppermint Patty says to Linus in a "Peanuts" cartoon, "I would have made a good evangelist. You know the kid who sits behind me in school? I convinced him that my religion is better than his." Linus then asks, "How did you do that?" Peppermint Patty explains, "I hit him with my lunch box."

An important element in our presentation of the gospel is our vocabulary. Preachers are wordsmiths, and words are an endless fascination for such communicators because words are their stock-in-trade. By definition, the preacher showers abundant verbiage on his hearers. Does this barrage clarify and communicate, or does it obfuscate and confuse?

Language is one of the most choice gifts of God. Gordon Clark rightly says:

If God created man in his own rational image and endowed him with the power of speech, then a purpose of language, in fact the chief purpose of language, would naturally be the revelation of truth to man and the prayers of man to God. In a theistic philosophy one ought not to say that all language has been devised in order to describe and discuss the finite objects of our sense-experience. . . . On the contrary, language was devised by God, that is, God created man rational for the purpose of theological expression.[19]

Irregardless of modern logical positivism's assault on "god-talk," humankind in our time cannot banish God from its frame of reference, even if mention of the Deity is generally found only in profanity.

So we see that words, even culturally conditioned as they are with their denotations and connotations, can carry the heavy freight of divine revelation. At the same time, just as ancient coins lose their inscriptions, words can be devalued. Some advise us that Biblical language—for example, such terms as *reconciliation* and *justification*—must be abandoned because modern man simply cannot understand them. The church is at times in danger of substituting modern psychological jargon for the Biblical frame of reference, and thus moving away from doctrinal preaching, from significant teaching, and from any effort to achieve precision in expression. We must beware, for the cultural matrix can so shape evangelism that the gospel story is lost in the process. In 1984 the late Walker Percy, a gifted writer and communicator, lamented the devaluation of the Christian vocabulary. The result is that often the believer "feels like Lancelot in search of the Holy Grail who finds himself at the end of his quest at a Tupperware Party."

The late H. A. Ironside preached a memorable series of messages in the Moody Church in Chicago years ago on "Great Gospel Words." He took the great old words such as *sanctification* and *regeneration* and expounded a key Bible passage on each one. We must not throw out the Biblical vocabulary, but should rather define Scriptural terms and develop sermons which make those terms clear and compelling for our listeners. The reiterated call for the preaching of a simple gospel can bring us onto the reefs if we are not careful. As has been wisely said before, seek simplicity but distrust it. We are dealing with the stupendous truths of the infinite God who has broken into time/space in the person of His eternally begotten Son. Slogans and clichés and hackneyed, stereotypical one-liners cannot set forth "the glorious gospel of our blessed God" (1 Timothy 1:11).

Contextualization of Biblical truth involves careful definition, cautious selection, painstaking adaptation, and meticulous application. A few years back I preached a sermon entitled "Why Did Jesus Die?," based on Romans 3:21-31. Does the forensic aspect of the atonement and our justification need to be soft-pedaled in order to communicate the "gut" of this great passage? My outline was quite simple:

    I. We are all accused.
    II. We can all be acquitted.
    III. We can all be accepted.

These forensic terms are well-known to all of us from jurisprudence. They need to be anchored in the text and then illustrated from common experience in our world today. The gospel communicator has the unparalleled opportunity of taking the timeless truths from the Holy Scriptures—truths which are "able to make you wise for salvation" (2 Timothy 3:15)—and open them up, dissect them under the tutelage of the Holy Spirit, and share them with the spiritually needy. The Word and our words—what an exciting adventure the gospel preacher enjoys.

VISIBILITY

> Evangelism that does not lead to purity of life and purity of doctrine is just as faulty and incomplete as an orthodoxy which does not lead to a concern for, and communication with, the lost. (Francis Schaeffer)

The substance of our true message and its verbal shape are not all that is needed to make our gospel communication intelligible. We as Christians are to exhibit and commend the truth of the gospel—to practice it daily. We are not only to lip the truth—we are to live the truth. This was Paul's point when he told Titus that the slaves on Crete should "show that they can be fully trusted, so that in every way they will make the teaching about God our Savior attractive" (Titus 2:10b).

Schaeffer is very telling at this point: "The final apologetic, along with the rational, logical defense and presentation, is what the world sees in the individual Christian and in our corporate relationships together."[20] He stresses the same urgent truth in his books *The Mark of the Christian* and *The Church Before the Watching World*. He appropriately presses the issue in his title *How Should We Then Live?*, his earth-shaking and momentous study of the rise and decline of western thought and culture. Schaeffer himself became a Christian in 1930 when he went forward in a tent meeting and prayed to receive Jesus Christ as his Savior and Lord. His many subsequent years of careful Christian walk and ministry confirmed the gospel truths he proclaimed and for which he stood.

The Apostle Paul reminded Timothy that his young spiritual protégé's "sincere faith . . . first lived in your grandmother Lois and in your mother Eunice and . . . now lives in you also" (2 Timothy 1:5). We are not surprised, then, to find that Paul's own life was like an open book to Timothy (cf. 2 Timothy 3:10ff.), so that he was able and obliged to say in effect, "It was my example in these things which was set before you as a guide." We are talking here about genuine, Christ-like character. Reputation is what people think we are; character is what we are. This is what lies behind George Herbert's famous maxim for ministers: "The greatest and hardest preparation is within." Paul Sangster always spoke admiringly of his father, W. E. Sangster, and his powerful preaching from the pulpit. But he said that the last three years of his father's life, when the great man of God was unable to speak, were the most powerful sermon Sangster ever preached. The quality of his life in Christ made a profound impact.

Most readers of this book would take vigorous exception to the view expressed by some missionaries quoted in an article, "The New Missionary": "In the past, we had the so-called motive of saving souls. We were convinced that if not baptized, people in the masses would go to hell. Now, thanks be to God, we believe that all people and all religions are already living in the grace and love of God and will be saved by God's mercy."[21] We may reject that view on several counts, but do our lives show that we do indeed believe people outside Christ are lost? What are we doing to win them?

A former professing Christian has recently chronicled his "revisit" to Christianity and what he experienced. Mike Bryan describes the debates and diversities in a Southern Baptist college of conservative persuasion. Interestingly, though he retained his secular viewpoint, he became quite sympathetic. He paraphrases C. S. Lewis, whom he describes as one of evangelical Christianity's most able apologists: "I am constantly surprised by the joy of Southern Baptists . . . their subtle conviction of a happiness that moves beyond its own private sphere; joy to the world!"[22]

In a rather stimulating volume, Thomas A. Reeves inquires why, despite American decadence, our people overwhelmingly disapprove of philandering Presidents or would-be presidents and of plagiarism by politicians, etc. He sees a "deeply ingrained Puritanism" in American character that cannot be eradicated.[23] We are being watched; but what is being seen?

VITALITY

When an envoy of the Pope asked Martin Luther, "Where will you be if the Pope condemns you?" Luther replied stoutly, "The same place as now—in the hands of the sovereign God!" When all is said and done, we must recognize that it is God the Holy Spirit who bears the inner witness that makes the Christian message intelligible. The endeavor and its results are in His hands. We must recognize that some persons have barricaded themselves against any overture from God. J. Sidlow Baxter is correct: "The Bible will no more speak to some minds than Christ would speak to Herod." The late Bishop James Pike told Francis Schaeffer that he had lost his faith in seminary and been left with a "handful of pebbles"; but sadly he did not seek the Lord.

The role of the Holy Spirit as the ultimate apologist is especially well portrayed by Bernard Ramm in his classic text *The Witness of the Spirit*. He elucidates John Calvin's teaching about the inner witness of the Spirit, for it is the Spirit who tells us with great assurance that the Scriptures are indeed from God. Also, both in Matthew 16:16, 17 and in 2 Corinthians 4:3-6 we see that God sends light into our hearts through Jesus Christ. The Holy Spirit is the stylus and the ink, and the message He writes on human hearts is Jesus Christ!

A man now 102 years of age has been converted and is a member of a congregation we served many years ago; two aged grandparents have prayed to receive Christ; the murderers of the slain Wycliffe missionary Chet Bitterman have become Christians; Manuel Noriega has prayed to receive Christ; Jim Murray, son of Madeline Murray O'Hair, has been converted and is preaching the gospel. Mortimer Adler, editor of *Great Books*, has professed Christ. In every wonderful story of communication and conversion, God the Holy Spirit does a supernatural work, and we have the privilege of working with Him (cf. 1 Corinthians 3:5-9).

What shall we call the story of how the brilliant atheistic philosopher in France, Emile Cailliet, who had never even seen a Bible, came so marvelously to Christ but what he called it—*Journey into Light*?[24] Abraham Kuyper was directed to the Lord while reading Yonge's novel *Heir of Redclyffe*. Watchman Nee was converted when his mother asked his forgiveness after beating him unjustly. Sadhu Sundar Singh, who fought Christianity so and burned the Christian Gospels when he was fifteen, heard a voice in Hindustani: "Why do you persecute me?" Baron Von Hugel was converted when a woman who had lost her baby threw herself on the altar. All this is the work of the Holy Spirit of God.

Wittgenstein, the eminent philosopher, had a deep sense of his own sin and was troubled that Bertrand Russell did not become a Christian. He was much taken with the resurrection and testified, "I pray a good deal. But whether in the right spirit, I do not know." He objected to Origen's belief that all ultimately would be saved.[25] Carl Sandburg said, "I went to the feet of Jesus and quit smoking," but was he saved? Mark Twain professed conversion, but there was no evidence of salvation, even though his wife influenced him greatly in that direction. There are substantiated reports that Jean-Paul Sartre prayed to receive Christ at the end of his life, and Leon Trotsky was studying the Bible and taking a correspondence course on the Bible at the time of his assassination. One source I read alleged that Charles Darwin sought Christ before he passed away. Only God knows human hearts, and "With God all things are possible" (Matthew 19:26). This is what gives us such hope in gospel ministry.

We can understand, therefore, how Samuel Zwemer, "Apostle to Islam," could say:

> I have spent sixty years thinking of the Muslim world and its problems. It began when I signed a card in 1886, expressing my interest in becoming a foreign missionary. Little did I realize all the way God would lead me into Arabia and Egypt and across the world of Islam. We must not lose faith or courage, but be earnest and steadfast and diligent until the going down of our Sun—or the rising of His Sun at His glorious appearing. I am here because my Commander-in-chief sent me and I have to stay until His command is rescinded.

As we endure in gospel proclamation, and as He continues to do His supernatural work of transformation, miracles of grace occur again and again.

15

The Corollary of Revival— Evangelism

With great power the apostles continued to testify to the resurrection of the Lord Jesus, and much grace was with them all.

(Acts 4:33)

My message and my preaching were not with wise and persuasive words, but with a demonstration of the Spirit's power. . . .

(1 Corinthians 2:4)

Revival produces an extraordinary burden of prayer, an unusual conviction of sin, an uncanny sense of the presence of God, resulting in repentance, confession, reconciliation, and restitution, with great concern for the salvation of sinners near at hand and far away.

(J. Edwin Orr)

Where the pulpit leads, there the church follows, and no matter what his or her other qualifications, if your candidate cannot preach, you will be left adrift on a glassy sea, with no wind of the Spirit to carry you forward toward God's good kingdom of life.

(Elizabeth Achtemeier)

When God promises to "provide water in the desert and streams in the wasteland, to give drink to my people" (Isaiah 43:20), we understand this to be the normal portion for the people of God. However, there are special visits of God among His people as well. *Awakening* involves God's bringing salvation to large numbers of the unconverted. *Revival* is God's doing a work of spiritual revitalization among the converted.[1] Some have thought to further distinguish between revival and renewal among the people of God, but these seem to me to be aspects of the same essential phenomenon.[2] God's special visits among the unconverted and His special visits among His own people are clearly and closely interrelated; they stand in symbiotic relationship to each other.

We human beings are cyclical creatures—physically, emotionally, and spiritually. Thus it is no surprise that periods of decay and renewal alternate in history. The resolution of this tension will not come until the Eschaton. We see this cycle very poignantly in the book of Judges, where six times we see the sequence of sin/suffering/supplication/salvation. The word "revive" (Hebrew *chayah*) occurs eleven times in the Old Testament and means "to make alive, to cause to live." The word "revive" (Greek *anazao*) is used only twice in the New Testament, though the experience is seen repeatedly. The term "continuous revival," sometimes used by well-meaning Christian believers, is an oxymoron. The whole idea of revival entails "living again," being quickened out of passivity, lethargy, and lifelessness.

No one has defined revival more aptly than Stephen Olford: "Revival is ultimately Christ Himself, seen, felt and heard in and through His body on earth."[3] Finney in his classic lectures defines revival as "the renewal of the first love of Christians resulting in the awakening and conversion of sinners to God" and "nothing else than a new beginning of obedience to God."[4] Robert Coleman emphasizes revival as a return to a true nature and purpose.[5]

The correlative nature of evangelistic awakening (when there is a stir of the Spirit and multiple conversions) and revival in a local church or on a broader area or national scale (when there is a quickening of vital pulse among believers) makes it impossible to absolutize any sequence. Sometimes one comes first; at other times the other comes first. Either way, the close connection is obvious.

The notable Cambuslang revival of 1742 in Scotland came at a low time in Christian experience in that country. Societies of Prayer (modeled after the pietistic conventicles of Philipp Spener) and the message of Henry Scougal, a professor at Aberdeen (1650-78), coupled with deep internal problems in the local parish and a dreadful storm and time of famine, all prepared a highway for the Lord. The local pastor, William McCulloch, presided, and George Whitefield made fourteen visits to Scotland. The message was chiefly one of regeneration, and even in the face of much criticism crowds came; amid uncontrolled distress, scores sought Christ and were "carried into the manse like wounded soldiers."[6] Preaching services were held at 2 P.M., 6 P.M. and 9 P.M. daily, with crowds of as much as twenty thousand gathered in the braes. Great all-day Communion services became the high-water mark of the revival. Though roundly opposed from the far left and the far right (the ultra-separatists spoke of Whitefield as "a limb of the anti-Christ" and accused him of trimming the faith), the revival spread to neighboring parishes and abroad and continued to bear fruit well into the next century. The same association is underscored by A. Skevington Wood: "Revival and conversions cannot be dissociated. They go together. Whenever the Church experiences the renewal of Pentecost, conversions invariably ensue."[7]

Though we hear of mercy-drops around the world and occasionally in the North American church, we as individuals and as local churches desperately need a spiritual quickening. The average church becomes ingrown in fourteen years. We face and must find answers for the serious crises of our decadent culture. One of the best selling books at this writing is *Final Exit*, a how-to manual on suicide. The lights have gone out in western civilization. We are witnessing the bankruptcy—the wholesale moral desensitization and disintegration—of our society, what some call "the suicide of the west." Despite the ever-deepening social and moral emergencies of our times, effective, continuing, fervent prayer is difficult to find in many churches.

We are too often anniversary Christians—always reviewing what has been, sometimes at the expense of fulfilling current responsibilities or preparing for future service. Also, as Americans we think we have some sort of most-favored nation status with God. Also, in this age of mounting indifference, when people read less, know less, and care less, we are tempted to soften the message until there is no message left. What we need above all else is that foundation of evangelism and revival on which "the Spirit is poured upon us from on high, and the desert becomes a fertile field" (Isaiah 32:15). The exploration of this reality is our subject in this concluding chapter.

IN SCRIPTURE: ORIGINALS

Lord, I have heard of your fame; I stand in awe of your deeds, O Lord. Renew them in our day, in our time make them known; in wrath remember mercy. (Habakkuk 3:2)

A recurring pattern is seen in the Biblical materials. Again and again spiritual atrophy, apathy, and apostasy are challenged and changed. Statements such as "The Lord came down in power" calmly describe divine workings which change both people and history. Thus ossified orthodoxy yields to a fresh baptism of power. God uses both visitations and withdrawings. God delights to raise up those who will exercise an awakening ministry. Wilbur M. Smith has delineated nine principal revivals in the Old Testament and seven principal revivals in the New Testament.[8] Both C. E. Autrey and Walter Kaiser have given us in-depth studies of Old Testament revivals.[9] What could be more necessary and more nourishing than for pastors and people to steep themselves in the Biblical models with all of their variety and vitality? The Biblical pattern ought to stimulate a great hungering and thirsting after the Lord in our time and in our own hearts.

The revival in the days of King Josiah is particularly significant for us because it came late in the history of Judah (cf. 2 Chronicles 34, 35). The northern kingdom had already fallen, and the southern kingdom was hurtling toward destruction. But in those days of a very young king whose father and grandfather had been infamously wicked—in those days came a refreshing and renewing visit of God which did not avert or avoid the final tragedy of judgment but apparently did defer it and gave rise to the rich ministry of Jeremiah. We see three prominent features of this special visit of God:

1) *We see a disposition to seek after the Lord.* "While he [Josiah] was still young, he began to seek the God of his father David" (34:3). The importance of such an attitude must not be underestimated. For example, the root of the spiritual stirring in Britain in the 1870s can be traced to the intercession of a severely handicapped person, Marianne Adlard, who heard of D. L. Moody and prayed earnestly, "Lord, send this man to England." He came in 1872, and the floodgates of Heaven flowed mightily through this very unlikely and unsophisticated servant of God.

The twin facets of the sovereign moving of God seem always to trace back to an individual or small cadre of individuals who have a deep spiritual burden. The Norwegian Lutheran missionary Marie Monsen was used of God to ignite a moving of the Spirit in Shantung Province in China in 1932. "Her testimony, messages and constant question to missionaries and nationals alike, 'Are you born again?' led the revival to be called 'the Born-again Revival.'"[10] The powerful stirring in East Africa began in 1929 when a missionary, Dr. Joe Church, and a national, Simeoni Nsibambi, became deeply concerned about all the nominal Christianity. Of Church's prayer it has been written: "He prayed passionately for the scattering of the mists of superstition and sin, and the shining forth of the light of the Gospel, and the site of the beautiful spreading acacia tree seemed like holy ground to be claimed for God."[11] It was in this movement that so many came to Christ, including Festo Kivengere who later became a leading bishop in the church. Similarly the Hebrides revival which began in 1949 in the parish of Barvas started with a minister and seven members of his church praying in a little wooden barn by the side of the road.

2) *We see a rediscovery of the Word of God.* These hurricanes of the Spirit always involve a return to what God has said. "I [Hilkiah] have found the Book of the Law in the temple of the Lord" (34:15). Donald Robinson cogently argues that this book found in 621 B.C. was in fact the book of Deuteronomy. Its being found led to further reforms.[12] The centrality of gospel preaching in times of revival has been widely recognized.[13] Brian Edwards quotes a missionary who observed of the moving of the Spirit in India in 1905: "At the present time, perhaps, nothing may be found to be so appropriate as the supreme importance of the Bible, the whole Bible, and fundamentally, nothing but the Bible." He also quotes an observer of the great revival in Borneo in the 1970s: "Their readiness to submit themselves to the Word was awesome."[14]

This is all the more pressing when we see the growing neglect of the Word of God in many churches today. Although far from sharing a conservative view of Scripture, James D. Smart tellingly laments that "the voice of the Scripture is falling silent in the church."[15] The fading of the Word, the recession of the Bible, and the absence of excitement about the Word are to be seen on every side. We have less and less time for exposition in depth. We settle for light treatments of Holy Scripture. Smart recognizes that in pietism and evangelical revivalism people turn back to the Word.

3) *We see dedication to doing the will of God.* In Josiah's day the Passover was reinstituted and there was a return to conscientious obedience to God's will and way. Timothy Dwight, the grandson of Jonathan Edwards, was inaugurated as president of Yale College in 1795. The school at that time was in "a most ungodly state"; indeed, there were few converted persons there. His objective as a godly man was to break the enemy's grip on Yale. He preached for the salvation of souls "in a way that is subservient to the divine glory."[16] The Holy Spirit visited Yale in a special way in 1808, 1812-13 (when a hundred students were converted as the result of prayer), and 1814-15. "The trophies of

the Cross are being multiplied," he recorded. "No weeds of infidelity throve long there." That type of turn-around—salvation and societal change—is ever the consequence of true revival. Similarly, Rochester, New York, was powerfully shaken in the revival in which God used C. G. Finney. Saloons and taverns were shut down by the dozens. Timothy Smith's now classic *Revivalism and Social Reform* gives just the tip of the iceberg.[17]

Hence we see that Biblical principles and patterns of revival show much diversity and dynamism, all based on the persistent grace and power of God. Second Chronicles 7:14 is properly the great golden text to which we return again and again: "If my people, who are called by my name, will humble themselves and pray and seek my face and turn from their wicked ways, then will I hear from heaven and will forgive their sin and will heal their land."

IN HISTORY: REPLICAS

> This is what the Lord says . . . Break up your unplowed ground and do not sow among thorns. (Jeremiah 4:3)

While there has never been an international revival, there have been national, regional, local, and individual congregational revivals with attendant conversions and waves of evangelistic outreach. Archbishop Nathan Soderblom in his Gifford Lectures in 1931 articulated the general principle well: "The yearning for salvation and the sense of God's nearness break forth at certain epochs simultaneously with over-mastering power and with effects that are felt centuries and millenniums later."

A most helpful guide in tracking the Spirit's ways has been James Burns's *Revivals: Their Laws and Leaders*.[18] Agreed, there is no uniform or rigid outline in the sequencing of revival. In speaking of Howell Harris and revival in Wales early on, Martyn Lloyd-Jones makes the important point, "The story of Howell Harris is one illustration of the fact that revival does not always come after a preliminary reformation. Revival sometimes follows reformation, but revival sometimes precedes reformation; and for us to lay it down that reformation must precede revival, and that doctrinal orthodoxy is essential to revival is simply to fly directly into the face of the facts."[19]

God does not always work in exactly the same way, but He has done a mighty work of revival again and again throughout history. We can speak of revival under Chrysostom in Constantinople, under Ambrose and Augustine, under Francis of Assisi and Bernard of Clairvaux, and under Savonarola in Florence as he fearlessly preached from the book of Revelation. The Reformation was a time of great spiritual renaissance and resurgence, with ripples under John Wycliffe, Peter Waldo, and John Hus coming beforehand as giant waves swept over Europe. John Knox in Scotland and Spener and Franke on the continent augmented the gains which had been made and renewed spiritual vision in a time when Protestant scholasticism had fossilized the church. What must encourage us most of all is God's faithfulness in the support and sustenance of His church. When His people are battered and beleaguered, fresh breezes blow from Heaven, and vitalities burst forth like spring buds after a long winter.

No historical survey or account of revivals and their leaders from the Great Awakening to the present is more balanced or encouraging or gripping than the book *An Endless Line of Splendor* by Earle E. Cairns. By studying this along with J. Edwin Orr's more fine-lined materials, the inquirer into the nature and character of spiritual movements will be satisfyingly served.[20]

Of particular interest to us here is Jonathan Edwards's involvement in the Great Awakening as he diligently served the church in Northampton, Massachusetts, in the spring of 1735. Whitefield visited Northampton and environs, and Edwards was in contact with William McCulloch of Cambuslang. Edwards wrote of that time: "There scarcely was a single person in the town, old or young, left unconcerned about the great things of the eternal world."[21] Like Whitefield, Edwards wept while he preached. The revival continued until 1742, with many converts coming into the church. Wide diversity of preaching styles and varying doctrinal emphases characterized the revival. Whitefield used a firm figure in reporting conversions, while Edwards shied away from the practice. Edwards stoutly believed one should not preach peace until the rebels lay down their arms. Edwards's godly character, "vehement longings," a strong belief in prayer as the prelude to evangelism, and his pilgrimage in preaching both in structure and toward delivery without use of a manuscript are of great practical relevance for every gospel communicator.[22]

Another local pastor's experience in revival is described in Eric Hayden's *Spurgeon on Revival*.[23] In a time of general spiritual stirring both in America and in Britain, sometimes called the Lay Prayer Revival,[24] awakening came to the Metropolitan Tabernacle in London where Charles Haddon Spurgeon pastored. The enduements of Heaven were falling on this ministry, and Spurgeon himself baptized over fifteen thousand while serving there. He reports from that time (about 1859),

"For six years the dew has never ceased to fall, and the rain has never been withheld." Corporate prayer and Biblical preaching (the book of sermons coming most typically from this period is entitled *Compel Them to Come in*) were of critical importance in what transpired. The harvest came after the anguish of the Music Hall fire in which Spurgeon almost lost his sanity. A plowing always comes before a season of refreshing from the Lord. "Make this valley full of ditches" (2 Kings 3:16) is a familiar experience to those who seek a renewal ministry. Spurgeon himself was such a man of prayer, even publicly, that it was said he would open his eyes after praying the morning prayer and be surprised to find the congregation before him.

How mercifully and graciously God has visited His people in times of great need and spiritual aridity . . . in the days of Robert Murray McCheyne and the Bonars of Scotland, of George Scott and C. O. Rosenius in Sweden (in which movement of the Spirit Jenny Lind was ultimately saved), the fifteen revivals in Wales from 1762-1862 and then the great outpouring in 1904-1906 under Evan Roberts when 110,000 were added to the churches and nineteen of twenty stayed[25] . . . the great revival which swept through China and Korea in 1906-07 chronicled by Jonathan Goforth in *By My Spirit*, which was instigated when Goforth reconciled with another missionary . . . the William Nicholson ministry in Northern Ireland in the twenties and thirties . . . the Indonesian revival of the 1970s[26] . . . the outbreaks of revival at some North American colleges in the late 1940s and 1950s[27] . . . the stirring on the prairie provinces of Canada beginning in 1972 in which the Sutera twins were much used of God and which was fueled when two estranged elders got right with each other and with God. To all of which I can cry with what Thomas Chalmers used to call "blood earnestness," *O Lord, do it again—do it again!*

IN EXPERIENCE: DEBATABLES

Oh, that you would rend the heavens and come down, that the mountains would tremble before you! (Isaiah 64:1)

Among the issues widely discussed in relation to revival, one stands above all others: From where does revival come? We long to see and experience that supernatural visitation which Scripture and history excite us to seek. To listen to Jonathan Edwards the answer seems clear: God does it! To read Charles Finney the answer seems clear: It is up to us! The Scriptures make it clear both that there are spiritual laws governing revival and that if we conform to the rules we shall experience the desire of our hearts. Each viewpoint conveys needed truth. All of us must recognize that revival lies within the sovereignty of God. God must do it! This truth preserves us from despair and an overwhelming burden when things are dry. God sees all and knows all, and hope for revival depends upon Him. But that is only one aspect of the reality. Just as we must maintain the tension between divine sovereignty and human responsibility, between the threeness and the oneness of God, between the divine and the human natures of our Lord in the hypostatic union, so we must maintain both God's divine initiative and the significance of our response to Him. Second Chronicles 7:14 does say, "If my people . . ." There are conditions for revival.

Finney exhorted: "A revival will decline and cease, unless Christians are frequently reconverted. By this I mean, that Christians, in order to keep in the spirit of revival, commonly need to be frequently convicted, and, humbled, and broken down before God, and reconverted."[28] This is the burden of Leonard Ravenhill's classic *Why Revival Tarries*.[29] Even the most ardent Calvinist preaches that prayer is necessary preparation for revival.[30] We must affirm both divine sovereignty and human responsibility in revival.

Evangelistic awakening and revival are always controversial and in that sense divisive (though not schismatic). "God often acts in a most unusual manner."[31] The interventions of God interrupt what we have customarily done and seen, and we often find this distressing. After all, when God is taking hold, we are not in control. This can be unnerving for leadership and for the congregation. What if God really did something out of the ordinary among us? Would we stand for it? Further, the phenomena of revival are upsetting. There may be shakings, weepings, cryings. All revivals have exhibited various phenomena of one kind or another. There are perceived dangers on every side.

Yes, God works in unusual ways, but at the same time strange fire and wildfire and Satanic duplication must be discerned. Our enemy would destroy the genuine through the artful use of the counterfeit. We need to remember along with Oswald Chambers that there is a paper-thin line between spirituality and sensuality. The history of revival bears ample testimony to that. Stress on irrational behavior can lead to excesses such as those seen among the Naylorites in Britain or the Camizards or French Prophets (Huguenots in the late 1680s) whose convulsions, prophecies, and tongues were very extreme. But who are we to say what God may or may not do? My counsel with regard to such phenomena is: keep the windows open, but keep the screens on (as an old preacher told me many years ago). The explosive, worldwide growth of the Pentecostal movement, much of which is conversion growth, must be considered in a similar manner.

Observably, revivals have tended to die of their own excesses. This is another reason why the idea of perennial revival is not in sync with reality. James S. Stewart indicates that the "grave danger in revival," in his opinion, is carnal and fleshly publicity.[32] Boasting and the lionization of our leaders will do us in again and again. He quotes Finney on this point: "When Christians get proud of 'our great revival,' it will cease." The Son of God is to be the attraction. As the Father told Peter when he was giving too much attention to Moses and Elijah on the Mount of Transfiguration, "This is my Son, whom I love; with him I am well pleased. Listen to *him!*" (Matthew 17:5, emphasis added). In the Welsh revival, people did not even know if Evan Roberts was going to preach or not.

Another critical caution has come from the wisdom of D. Martyn Lloyd-Jones, whose biographer puts it this way: "Truths must be held together. For this reason he was careful to warn of the danger of giving exclusive attention to the subject of revival . . . he criticised people who always talk about revival and only revival. They are only interested in the exceptional and unusual, and they tend to despise the day of small things, the regular work of the church and the regular work of the Spirit in the church."[33] This brings us to our last point.

IN OUR TIMES: HOPEFULS

Will you not revive us again, that your people may rejoice in you? (Psalm 85:6)

Olford quotes Campbell Morgan as saying, "We cannot organize revival, but we can set our sails to catch the wind from heaven when God chooses to blow upon His people once again."[34] Most believers in our congregations have never really seen revival. It has been a long time since some congregations have had much stir. We need to seek the face of God and to pray fervently for His touch upon us and upon our ministries. We had one dear brother in our fellowship who always served smaller churches and was never heralded in the annals of our denomination as being a VIP. Yet each congregation he served enjoyed a special visit from God during his tenure there. *Oh, dear Lord, grant it!*

The solemn summons of this hour is well expressed by Walter L. Duewel in his now classic *Touch the World Through Prayer*:

When God desires to do a mighty work of salvation, renewal or spiritual harvest, He calls His people to their knees. The Holy Spirit places a deep hunger for God in the heart of His children who are close enough to hear His voice. As their hearts cry out to Him, He leads them to spend more and more time with Him and to join others who share a similar prayer burden. God may lead them to add fasting to their prayer, because their heart's desire is so intense that they want to take this extra time, this more costly step, in seeking God's supernatural visitation.

But when there is no revival and the dry bones are strewn about (cf. Ezekiel 37), let us recall the apostle's admonition: "Preach the Word; be prepared in season and out of season; correct, rebuke and encourage—with great patience and careful instruction. . . . Keep your head in all situations, endure hardship, do the work of an evangelist, discharge all the duties of your ministry" (2 Timothy 4:2, 5). While hopeful and trusting for whatever the Lord God may see fit to grant us as we seek Him, may our experience of proclamation and ministry even in the most difficult circumstances be like Paul's: "But the Lord stood at my side and gave me strength, so that through me the message might be fully proclaimed and all the Gentiles might hear it. And I was delivered from the lion's mouth" (2 Timothy 4:17).

POSTSCRIPT

Before us is the most important decade in the history of civilization, a period of stunning technological innovation, unprecedented economic opportunity, surprising political reform, and great cultural rebirth. It will be a decade like none that has come before.

(John Naisbitt, *Megatrends 2000*)

And pray for us, too, that God may open a door for our message, so that we may proclaim the mystery of Christ. . . . Pray that I may proclaim it clearly, as I should. . . . Let your conversation be always full of grace, seasoned with salt, so that you may know how to answer everyone.

(Colossians 4:3, 4 ,6)

Pray also for me, that whenever I open my mouth, words may be given me so that I will fearlessly make known the mystery of the gospel. . . . Pray that I may declare it fearlessly, as I should.

(Ephesians 6:19, 20)

APPENDIX

Five Classic
Evangelistic Sermons

A SUGGESTED GUIDE FOR ANALYZING THE FOLLOWING SERMONS

1) Evaluate the title.
2) Ponder the selection and scope of the preaching portion.
3) Identify the proposition or central idea, stated or implied.
4) Analyze the development of the sermon.
5) Assess the Biblical and theological aspects of the sermon.
6) Project response to this sermon in the congregation with which you identify, or in a rescue mission, or in a community evangelistic crusade.
7) Weigh and share the following questions: Did the introduction command your attention? Did the trajectory of the sermon (emotional outline) sustain your interest? Evaluate the use of illustrative material and contemporary points of contact. Did the conclusion press for a verdict and provide a good bridge to the public invitation? Put yourself inside the mind of an unsaved person; what impressions do you get? Encapsulate whatever ideas you obtained about evangelistic preaching from this sermon.

I

Sovereignty and Salvation
By Charles H. Spurgeon

from *Spurgeon's Sermons, Memorial Library*, Volume 1
(New York: Funk and Wagnalls Company, no date)

Charles Haddon Spurgeon (1834-1892) was born in Essex, England, but was raised in the home of his grandfather, the Reverend James Spurgeon, a Congregational minister. His father, John Spurgeon, was a clerk who also served a Congregational Church in Tollesbury. After much spiritual wrestling, at age fifteen Spurgeon came to worship at the Artillary Street Primitive Methodist Church of Colchester and was converted through the ministry of a layman who used the text from Isaiah 45:22, the very text of the sermon included here. Known as "the boy preacher," Spurgeon served in Waterbeach but at age nineteen began his ministry as pastor of New Park Street Baptist Church in London, which had dwindled down to a congregation of between eighty to two hundred in attendance. God mightily blessed, and in two years a new church was built seating thirty-six hundred with standing room for an additional two thousand persons. God sent revival and used His servant throughout Britain— through the printed page, the training of young pastors, and benevolent institutions. A splendid recent biography by Arnold Dallimore is strongly recommended (*Spurgeon*, Chicago: Moody Press, 1984).

SOVEREIGNTY AND SALVATION

"Look unto me, and be ye saved, all the ends of the earth: for I am God and there is none else." Isaiah xlv:22.

Six years ago to-day, as near as possible at this very hour of the day, I was "in the gall of bitterness and in the bonds of iniquity," but had yet, by divine grace, been led to feel the bitterness of that bondage, and to cry out by reason of the soreness of its slavery. Seeking rest, and finding none, I stepped within the house of God, and sat there, afraid to look upward, lest I should be utterly cut off, and lest his fierce wrath should consume me. The minister rose in his pulpit, and, as I have done this morning, read this text, "Look unto me, and be ye saved, all the ends of the earth: for I am God, and there is none else." I looked that moment; the grace of faith was vouchsafed to me in the self-same instant; and now I think I can say with truth,

> *"Ere since by faith I saw the stream*
> *His flowing wounds supply,*
> *Redeeming love has been my theme,*
> *And shall be till I die."*

I shall never forget that day, while memory holds its place; nor can I help repeating this text whenever I remember that hour when first I knew the Lord. How strangely gracious! How wonderfully and marvelously kind, that he who heard these words so little time ago for his own soul's profit, should now address you this morning as his hearers from the same text, in the full and confident hope that some poor sinner within these walls may hear the glad tidings of salvation for himself also, and may today, on this 6th of January, be "turned from darkness to light, and from the power of Satan unto God!"

If it were within the range of human capacity to conceive a time when God dwelt alone, without his creatures, we should then have one of the grandest and most stupendous ideas of God. There was a season when as yet the sun had never run his race, nor commenced flinging his golden rays across space, to gladden the earth. There was an era when no stars sparkled in the firmament, for there was no sea of azure in which they might float. There was a time when all that we now behold of God's great universe was yet unborn, slumbering within the mind of God, as yet uncreated and non-existent; yet there was God, and he was "over all blessed for ever;" though no seraphs hymned his praises, though no strong-winged cherubs flashed like lightning to do his high behests, though he was without a retinue, yet he sat as a king on his throne, the mighty God, for ever to be worshipped—the Dread Supreme, in solemn silence dwelling by himself in vast immensity, making of the placid clouds his canopy, and the light from his own countenance forming the brightness of his glory. God was, and God is. From the beginning God was God, ere worlds had beginning, he was "from everlasting to everlasting." Now, when it pleased him to create his creatures, does it not strike you how infinitely those creatures must have been below himself? If you are potters, and you fashion upon the wheel a vessel, shall that piece of clay arrogate to itself equality with you? Nay, at what a distance will it be from you, because you have been in part its creator. So when the Almighty formed his creatures, was it not consummate impudence, that they should venture for a moment to compare themselves with him? Yet that arch traitor, that leader of rebels, Satan, sought to climb to the high throne of God, soon to find his aim too high, and hell itself not low enough wherein to escape divine vengeance. He knows that God is "God alone." Since the world was created, man has imitated Satan; the creature of a day, the ephemera of an hour, has sought to match itself with the Eternal. Hence it has ever been one of the objects of the great Jehovah, to teach mankind that he is God, and beside him there is none else. This is the lesson he has been teaching the world since it went astray from him. He has been busying himself in breaking down the high places, in exalting the valleys, in casting down imaginations and lofty looks, that all the world might

> "Know that the Lord is God alone,
> He can create, and he destroy."

This morning we shall attempt to show you, in the first place, *how God has been teaching this great lesson to the world*—that he is God, and beside him there is none else; and then, secondly, *the special way in which he designs to teach it in the matter of salvation*—"Look unto *me*, and be ye saved: *for* I am God, and there is none else."

I. First, then, how has God been teaching this lesson to mankind?

We reply, he has taught it, first of all, *to false gods, and to the idolaters who have bowed before them.* Man, in his wickedness and sin, has set up a block of wood and stone to be his maker, and has bowed before it. He hath fashioned for himself out of a goodly tree an image made unto the likeness of mortal man, or of the fishes of the sea, or of creeping things of the earth, and he has prostrated his body, and his soul too, before that creature of his own hands, calling it god, while it had neither eyes to see, nor hands to handle, nor ears to hear. But how hath God poured contempt on the ancient gods of the heathen? Where are they now? Are they so much as known? Where are those false deities before whom the multitudes of Nineveh prostrated themselves? Ask the moles and the bats, whose companions they are; or ask the mounds beneath which they are buried; or go where the idle gazer walketh through the museum—see them there as curiosities, and smile to think that men should ever bow before such gods as these. And where are the gods of Persia? Where are they? The fires are quenched, and the fire-worshipper hath almost ceased out of the earth. Where are the gods of Greece—those gods adorned with poetry, and hymned in the most sublime odes? Where are they? They are gone. Who talks of them now, but as things that were of yore? Jupiter—doth any one bow before him? and who is he that adores Saturn? They are passed away, and they are forgotten. And where are the gods of Rome? Doth Janus now command the temple? or do the vestal virgins now feed their perpetual fires? Are there any now that bow before these gods? No, they have lost their thrones. And where are the gods of the South Sea Islands—those bloody demons before whom wretched creatures prostrated their bodies? They have well-nigh become extinct. Ask the inhabitants of China and Polynesia where are the gods before which they bowed. Ask, and echo says ask, and ask again. They are cast down from their thrones; they are hurled from their pedestals; their chariots are broken, their sceptres are burnt in the fire, their glories are departed; God hath gotten unto himself the victory over false gods, and taught their worshippers that he is God, and that beside him there is none else. Are there gods still worshipped, or idols before which the nations bow themselves? Wait but a little while, and ye shall see them fall. Cruel Juggernaut, whose car still crushes in its motion the foolish ones who throw themselves before it, shall yet be the object of derision; and the most noted idols, such as Buddha, and Brahma, and Vishnu, shall yet stoop themselves to the earth, and men shall tread them down as mire in the streets; for God will teach all men that he is God, and that there is none else.

Mark ye, yet again, how God has taught this truth *to empires.* Empires have risen up, and have been the gods of the era; their kings and princes have taken to themselves high titles, and have been worshipped by the multitude. But ask the empires whether there is any beside God. Do you not think you hear the boasting soliloquy of Babylon—"I sit as a queen, and am no widow; I shall see no sorrow; I am god, and there is none beside me?" And think ye not now, if ye walk over ruined Babylon, that ye will meet aught save the solemn spirit of the Bible, standing like a prophet gray with age, and telling you that there is one God, and that beside him there is none else? Go ye to

Babylon, covered with its sand, the sand of its own ruins; stand ye on the mounds of Nineveh, and let the voice come up—"There is one God, and empires sink before him; there is only one Potentate, and the princes and kings of the earth, with their dynasties and thrones, are shaken by the trampling of his foot." Go, seat yourselves in the temples of Greece; mark ye there what proud words Alexander once did speak; but now, where is he, and where his empire too? Sit on the ruined arches of the bridge of Carthage, or walk ye through the desolated theatres of Rome, and ye will hear a voice in the wild wind amid those ruins—"I am God, and there is none else." "O city, thou didst call thyself eternal; I have made thee melt away like dew. Thou saidst 'I sit on seven hills, and I shall last forever;' I have made thee crumble, and thou art now a miserable and contemptible place, compared with what thou wast. Thou wast once stone, thou madest thyself; I have made thee stone again, and brought thee low." O! how has God taught monarchies and empires that have set themselves up like new kingdoms of heaven, that he is God, and that there is none else!

Again: how has he taught his great truth *to monarchs!* There are some who have been most proud that have had to learn it in a way more hard than others. Take, for instance, Nebuchadnezzar. His crown is on his head, his purple robe is over his shoulders; he walks through proud Babylon, and says, "Is not this great Babylon which I have builded?" Do you see that creature in the field there? It is a man. "A man?" say you; its hair has grown like eagles' feathers, and its nails like birds' claws; it walketh on all-fours, and eateth grass, like an ox; it is driven out from men. That is the monarch who said—"Is not this great Babylon that I have builded?" And now he is restored to Babylon's palace, that he may "bless the Most High who is able to abase those that walk in pride." Remember another monarch. Look at Herod. He sits in the midst of his people, and he speaks. Hear ye the impious shout? "It is the voice of God," they cry, "and not the voice of man." The proud monarch gives not God the glory; he affects the God, and seems to shake the spheres, imagining himself divine. There is a worm that creepeth into his body, and yet another, and another; and ere that sun has set, he is eaten up of worms. Ah! monarch! thou thoughtest of being a god, and worms have eaten thee! Thou hast thought of being more than man; and what art thou? Less than man, for worms consume thee, and thou art the prey of corruption. Thus God humbleth the proud; thus he abaseth the mighty. We might give you instances from modern history; but the death of a king is all-sufficient to teach this one lesson, if men would but learn it. When kings die, and in funeral pomp are carried to the grave, we are taught the lesson—"I am God, and beside me there is none else." When we hear of revolutions, and the shaking of empires—when we see old dynasties tremble, and gray-haired monarchs driven from their thrones, then it is that Jehovah seems to put his foot upon land and sea, and with his hand uplifted cries—"Hear! ye inhabitants of the earth! Ye are but as grasshoppers; 'I am God, and beside me there is none else.'"

Again: our God has had much to do to teach this lesson *to the wise men of this world;* for as rank, pomp, and power, have set themselves up in the place of God, so has wisdom; and one of the greatest enemies of Deity has always been the wisdom of man. The wisdom of man will not see God. Professing themselves to be wise, wise men have become fools. But have ye not noticed, in reading history, how God has abased the pride of wisdom? In ages long gone by, he sent mighty minds into the world, who devised systems of philosophy. "These systems," they said, "will last forever." Their pupils thought them infallible, and therefore wrote their sayings on enduring parchment, saying, "This book will last forever; succeeding generations of men will read it, and to the last man that book shall be handed down, as the epitome of wisdom." "Ah! but," said God, "that book of yours shall be seen to be folly, ere another hundred years have rolled away." And so the mighty thoughts of Socrates, and the wisdom of Solon, are utterly forgotten now; and could we hear them speak, the veriest child in our schools would laugh to think that he understandeth more of philosophy than they. But when man has found the vanity of one system, his eyes have sparkled at another; if Aristotle will not suffice, here is Bacon; now I shall know everything; and he sets to work, and says that this new philosophy is to last forever. He lays his stones with fair colors, and he thinks that every truth he piles up is a precious imperishable truth. But, alas! another century comes, and it is found to be "wood, hay, and stubble." A new sect of philosophers rises up, who refute their predecessors. So too, we have wise men in this day—wise secularists, and so on, who fancy they have obtained the truth; but within another fifty years—and mark that word—this hair shall not be silvered over with gray, until the last of that race shall have perished, and that man shall be thought a fool that was ever connected with such a race. Systems of infidelity pass away like a dew-drop before the sun, for God says, "I am God, and beside me there is none else." This Bible is the stone that shall break in powder philosophy; this is the mighty battering-ram that shall dash all systems of philosophy in pieces; this is the stone that a woman may yet hurl upon the head of every Abimelech, and he shall utterly be destroyed. O Church of God! fear not; thou shalt do wonders; wise men shall be confounded, and thou shalt know, and they too, that he is God, and that beside him there is none else.

"Surely," says one, "*the Church of God* does not need to be taught this." Yes, we answer, she does; for of all beings, those whom God has made the objects of his grace are perhaps the most apt to forget this cardinal truth, that he is God, and that beside him there is none else. How did the church in Canaan forget it, when they bowed before other gods, and therefore he brought against them mighty kings and princes, and afflicted them sore. How did Israel forget it; and he carried them away captive into Babylon. And what Israel did, in Canaan and in Babylon, that we do now. We too, too often, forget that he is God, and beside him there is none else. Doth not the Christian know what I mean, when I tell him this great fact? For hath he not done it himself? In certain times prosperity has come upon him; soft gales have blown his bark along, just where his wild will wished to steer; and he has said within himself: "Now I have peace, now I have happiness, now the object I wished for is within my grasp, now I will say, 'Sit down, my soul, and take thy rest; eat, drink, and be merry; these things will well content me; make thou these thy god, be thou blessed and happy.'" But have we not seen our God dash the goblet to the earth, spill the sweet wine, and instead thereof fill it with gall? and as he has given it to us, he has said—"Drink it, drink it: you have thought to find a god on earth, but drain the cup and know its bitterness." When we have drunk it, nauseous the draught was, and we have cried, "Ah! God, I will drink no more from these things; thou art God, and beside thee there is none else." And ah! how often, too, have we devised schemes for the future, without asking God's permission! Men have said, like those foolish ones whom James mentioned, "We will do such-and-such things on the morrow; we will buy and sell and get gain," whereas they knew not what was to be on the morrow, for long ere the morrow came they were unable to buy and sell; death had claimed them, and a small span of earth held all their frame. God teaches his people every day, by sickness, by affliction, by depression of spirits, by the forsakings of God, by the loss of the Spirit for a season, by the lackings of the joys of his countenance, that he is God, and that beside him there is none else. And we must not forget that there are some special servants of God raised up to do great works, who in a peculiar manner have to learn this lesson. Let a man, for instance, be called to the great work of preaching the gospel. He is successful; God helped him; thousands wait at his feet, and multitudes hang upon his lips; as truly as that man is a man, he will have a tendency to be exalted above measure, and too much will he begin to look to himself, and too little to his God. Let men speak who know, and what they know let them speak; and they will say, "It is true, it is most true." If God gives us a special mission, we generally begin to take some honor and glory to ourselves. But in the review of the eminent saints of God, have you never observed how God has made them feel that he was God, and beside him there was none else? Poor Paul might have thought himself a god, and been puffed up above measure, by reason of the greatness of his revelation, had there not been a thorn in the flesh. But Paul could feel that he was not a god, for he had a thorn in the flesh, and gods *could not* have thorns in the flesh. Sometimes God teaches the minister, by denying him help on special occasions. We come up into our pulpits, and say "Oh! I wish I could have a good day today!" We begin to labor; we have been just as earnest in prayer, and just as indefatigable; but it is like a blind horse turning round a mill, or like Samson with Delilah: we shake our vain limbs with vast surprise, "make feeble fight," and win no victories. We are made to see that the Lord is God, and that beside him there is none else. Very frequently God teaches this to the minister, by leading him to see his own sinful nature. He will have such an insight into his own wicked and abominable heart, that he will feel as he comes up the pulpit stairs that he does not deserve so much as to sit in his pew, much less to preach to his fellows. Although we feel always joy in the declaration of God's Word, yet we have known what it is to totter on the pulpit steps, under a sense that the chief of sinners should scarcely be allowed to preach to others. Ah! beloved, I do not think *he* will be very successful as a minister who is not taken into the depths and blackness of his own soul, and made to exclaim, "Unto me, who am *less than the least of all saints*, is this grace given, that I should preach among the Gentiles the unsearchable riches of Christ." There is another antidote which God applies in the case of ministers. If he does not deal with them personally, he raises up a host of enemies, that it may be seen that he is God, and God alone. An esteemed friend sent me, yesterday, a valuable old Ms. of one of George Whitefield's hymns which was sung on Kennington Common. It is a splendid hymn, thoroughly Whitefieldian all through. It showed that his reliance was wholly on the Lord, and that God was within him. What! will a man subject himself to the calumnies of the multitude, will he toil and work day after day unnecessarily, will he stand up Sabbath after Sabbath and preach the gospel and have his name maligned and slandered, if he has not the grace of God in him? For myself, I can say, that were it not that the love of Christ constrained me, this hour might be the last that I should preach, so far as the ease of the thing is concerned. "Necessity is laid upon us; yea, woe is unto us if we preach not the gospel." But that opposition through which God carried his servants, leads them to see at once that he is God, and that there is none else. If every one applauded, if all were gratified, we should think ourselves God; but, when they hiss and hoot, we turn to our God, and cry,

> *"If on my face, for thy dear name,*
> *Shame and reproach should be,*
> *I'll hail reproach and welcome shame,*
> *If thou'lt remember me."*

II. This brings us to the second portion of our discourse. Salvation is God's greatest work; and, therefore, in his greatest work, he specially teaches us this lesson, That he is God, and that beside him there is none else. Our text tells us *how he teaches it.* He says, "Look unto me, and be ye saved, all the ends of the earth." He shows us that he is God, and that beside him there is none else, in three ways. First, by the person to whom he directs us: "Look unto *me*, and be ye saved." Secondly, by the means he tells us to use to obtain mercy: "Look," simply, "Look." And thirdly, by the persons whom he calls to "look:" "Look unto me, and be ye saved, *all the ends of the earth.*"

1. First, *to whom does God tell us to look for salvation?* O, does it not lower the pride of man, when we hear the Lord say, "Look unto *me*, and be ye saved, all the ends of the earth?" It is not, "Look to your priest, and be ye saved;" if you did, there would be another god, and beside him there would be some one else. It is not "Look to yourself;" if so, then there would be a being who might arrogate some of the praise of salvation. But it is "Look unto me." How frequently you who are coming to Christ look to yourselves. "O!" you say, "I do not repent enough." That is looking to yourself. "I do not believe enough." That is looking to yourself. "I am too unworthy." That is looking to yourself. "I cannot discover," says another, "that I have any righteousness." It is quite right to say that you have not any righteousness; but it is quite wrong to look for any. It is, "Look unto *me*." God will have you turn your eye off yourself and look unto him. The hardest thing in the world is to turn a man's eye off himself; as long as he lives, he always has a predilection to turn his eyes inside, and look at himself; whereas God says, "Look unto *me*." From the cross of Calvary, where the bleeding hands of Jesus drop mercy; from the garden of Gethsemane, where the bleeding pores of the Saviour sweat pardons, the cry comes, "look unto me, and be ye saved, all the ends of the earth." From Calvary's summit, where Jesus cries, "It is finished," I hear a shout, "Look, and be saved." But there comes a vile cry from our soul, "Nay, look to yourself! look

to yourself!" Ah, my hearer, look to yourself, and you will be damned. That certainly will come of it. As long as you look to yourself there is no hope for you. It is not a consideration of what you are, but a consideration of what God is, and what Christ is, that can save you. It is looking from yourself to Jesus. O! there be men that quite misunderstand the gospel; they think that righteousness qualifies them to come to Christ; whereas sin is the only qualification for a man to come to Jesus. Good old Crisp says, "Righteousness keeps me from Christ: the whole have no need of a physician, but they that are sick. Sin makes me come to Jesus, when sin is felt; and, in coming to Christ, the more sin I have the more cause I have to hope for mercy." David said, and it was a strange thing, too, "Have mercy upon me, for mine iniquity is great." But, David, why did not you say that it was little? Because, David knew that the bigger his sins were, the better reason for asking mercy. The more vile a man is, the more eagerly I invite him to believe in Jesus. A sense of sin is all we have to look for as ministers. We preach to sinners; and let us know that a man will take the title of sinner to himself, and we then say to him, "Look unto Christ, and ye shall be saved." "Look," this is all he demands of thee, and even this he gives thee. If thou lookest to thyself thou art damned; thou art a vile miscreant, filled with loathsomeness, corrupt and corrupting others. But look thou here— seest thou that man hanging on the cross? Dost thou behold his agonized head dropping meekly down upon his breast? Dost thou see that thorny crown, causing drops of blood to trickle down his cheeks? Dost thou see his hands pierced and rent, and his blest feet, supporting the weight of his own frame, rent well-nigh in twain with the cruel nails? Sinner! dost thou hear him shriek, "Eloi, Eloi, lama sabbacthani?" Dost thou hear him cry, "It is finished?" Dost thou mark his head hang down in death? Seest thou that side pierced with the spear, and the body taken from the cross? O, come thou hither! Those hands were nailed for thee; those feet gushed gore for thee; that side was opened wide for thee; and if thou wantest to know how thou canst find mercy, there it is. "Look!" "Look unto *me!*" Look no longer to Moses. Look no longer to Sinai. Come thou here and look to Calvary, to Calvary's victim, and to Joseph's grave. And look thou yonder, to the man who near the throne sits with his Father, crowned with light and immortality. "Look, sinner," he says, this morning, to you, "Look unto me, and be ye saved." It is in this way God teaches that there is none beside him; because he makes us look entirely to him, and utterly away from ourselves.

2. But the second thought is, *the means of salvation.* It is, "*Look unto me, and be ye saved.*" You have often observed, I am sure, that

many people are fond of an intricate worship, an involved religion, one they can hardly understand. They cannot endure worship so simple as ours. Then they must have a man dressed in white, and a man dressed in black; then they must have what they call an altar and a chancel. After a little while that will not suffice, and they must have flower-pots and candles. The clergyman then becomes a priest, and he must have a variegated dress, with a cross on it. So it goes on; what is simply a plate becomes a paten, and what was once a cup becomes a chalice; and the more complicated the ceremonies are, the better they like them. They like their minister to stand like a superior being. The world likes a religion they cannot comprehend. But have you never noticed how gloriously simple the Bible is? It will not have any of your nonsense; it speaks plain, and nothing but plain things. *"Look!"* There is not an unconverted man who likes this, "Look unto Christ, and be ye saved." No, he comes to Christ like Naaman to Elijah; and, when it is said, "Go, wash in Jordan," he replies, "I verily thought he would come and put his hand on the place, and call on the name of his God. But the idea of telling me to wash in Jordan, what a ridiculous thing! Anybody could do that!" If the prophet had bidden him to do some great thing, would he not have done it? Ah! certainly he would. And if, this morning, I could preach that any one who walked from here to Bath without his shoes and stockings, or did some impossible thing, should be saved, you would start off tomorrow morning before breakfast. If it would take me seven years to describe the way of salvation, I am sure you would all long to hear it. If only one learned doctor could tell the way to heaven, how would he be run after! And if it were in hard words, with a few scraps of Latin and Greek, it would be all the better. But it is a simple gospel that we have to preach. It is only "Look!" "Ah!" you say, "Is that the gospel? I shall not pay any attention to that." But why has God ordered you to do such a simple thing? Just to take down your pride, and to show you that he is God, and that beside him there is none else. O, mark how simple the way of salvation is. It is, "Look! look! look!" Four letters, and two of them alike! "Look unto me, and be ye saved, all the ends of the earth." Some divines want a week to tell what you are to do to be saved; but God the Holy Ghost only wants four letters to do it. "Look unto me, and be ye saved, all the ends of the earth." How simple is that way of salvation! and O, how instantaneous! It takes us some time to move our hand, but a look does not require a moment. So a sinner believes in a moment; and the moment that sinner believes and trusts in his crucified God for pardon, at once he receives salvation in full through his blood. There may be one that came in here this morning unjustified in his conscience, that will go out justified rather than others. There may be some here, filthy sinners one moment, pardoned the next. It is done in an instant. "Look! look! look!" And how universal is it! Because, wherever I am, however far off, it just says, "Look!" It does not say I am to see; it only says, "Look!" If we look on a thing in the dark, we cannot see it; but we have done what we were told. So, if a sinner only looks to Jesus he will save him; for Jesus in the dark is as good as Jesus in the light; and Jesus, when you cannot see him, is as good as Jesus when you can. It is only, "Look!" "Ah!" says one, "I have been trying to see Jesus this year, but I have not seen him." It does not say, see him, but "Look unto him." And it says that they who looked were lightened. If there is an obstacle before you, and you only look in the right direction, it is sufficient. "Look unto me." It is not seeing Christ so much as looking after him. The will after Christ, the wish after Christ, the desire after Christ, the trusting in Christ, the hanging on Christ, that is what is wanted. "Look! look! look!" Ah! if the man bitten by the serpent had turned his sightless eyeballs towards the brazen serpent, though he had not seen it, he would still have had his life restored. It is looking, not seeing, that saves the sinner.

We say again, how this *humbles* a man! There is a gentleman who says, "Well, if it had been a thousand pounds that would have saved me, I would have thought nothing of it." But your gold and silver is cankered; it is good for nothing. "Then, am I to be saved just the same as my servant Betty?" Yes, just the same; there is no other way of salvation for you. That is to show man that Jehovah is God, and that beside him there is none else. The wise man says, "If it had been to work the most wonderful problem, or to solve the greatest mystery, I would have done it. May I not have some mysterious gospel? May I not believe in some mysterious religion?" No; it is "Look!" "What! am I to be saved just like the Ragged School boy, who can't read his letters?" Yes, you must, or you will not be saved at all. Another says, "I have been very moral and upright; I have observed all the laws of the land; and, if there is anything else to do, I will do it. I will eat only fish on Fridays, and keep all the fasts of the church, if that will save me." No, sir, that will not save you; your good works are good for nothing. "What! must I be saved in the same way as a harlot or a drunkard?" Yes, sir; there is only one way of salvation for all. "He hath concluded all in unbelief, that he might have mercy upon all." He hath passed a sentence of condemnation on all, that the free grace of God might come upon many to salvation. "Look! look! look!" This is the simple method of salvation. "Look unto me, and be ye saved, all the ends of the earth."

But, lastly, mark how God has cut down the pride of man, and has exalted himself *by the persons whom he has called to look.* "Look unto me, and be ye saved, all the ends of the earth." When the Jew heard Isaiah say that, "Ah!" he exclaimed, "you ought to have said, 'Look unto me, O Jerusalem, and be saved.' That would have been right. But those Gentile dogs, are they to look and be saved?" "Yes," says God; "I will show you Jews, that, though I have given you many privileges, I will exalt others above you; I can do as I will with my own."

Now, who are the ends of the earth? Why, there are poor heathen nations now that are very few degrees removed from brutes, uncivilized and untaught; but if I might go and tread the desert, and find the Bushman in his kraal, or go to the South Seas and find a cannibal, I would say to the cannibal or the Bushman, "Look unto Jesus, and be ye saved, all the ends of the earth." They are some of "the ends of the earth," and the gospel is sent as much to them as to the polite Grecians, the refined Romans, or the educated Britons. But I think "the ends of the earth" imply those who have gone the farthest away from Christ. I say, drunkard, that means you. You have been staggering back, till you have got right to the ends of the earth; you have almost had *delirium tremens;* you cannot be much worse. There is not a man breathing worse than you. *Is there?* Ah! but God, in order to humble your pride, says to you, "Look unto me, and be ye saved." There is another who has lived a life of infamy and sin, until she has ruined herself, and even Satan seems to sweep her out at the back door; but God says, "Look unto me, and be ye saved, all the ends of the earth." Methinks I see one trembling here, and saying, "Ah, I have not been one of these, sir, but I have been something worse; for I have attended the house of God, and I have stifled convictions, and put off all thoughts of Jesus, and now I think he will never have mercy on me." You are one of them. "Ends of the earth!" So long as I find any who feel like that, I can tell them that they are "the ends of the earth." "But," says another, "I am so peculiar; if I did not feel as I do, it would be all very well; but I feel that my case is a peculiar one." That is all right; they are a peculiar people. You will do. But another one says, "There is nobody in the world like me; I do not think you will find a being under the sun that has had so many calls, and put them all away, and so many sins on his head. Besides, I have guilt that I should not like to confess to any living creature." One of "the ends of the earth" again; therefore, all I have to do is to cry out, in the Master's name, "Look unto me, and be ye saved, all the ends of the earth: for I am God, and there is none else." But thou sayest, sin will not let thee look. I tell thee, sin will be removed the moment thou dost look. *"But I dare not; he will condemn me; I fear to look."* He will condemn thee more if thou dost not look. Fear, then, and look; but do not let thy fearing keep thee from looking. *"But he will cast me out."* Try him. *"But I cannot see him."* I tell you, it is not seeing, but looking. *"But my eyes are so fixed on the earth, so earthly, so worldly."* Ah! but, poor soul, he giveth power to look and live. He saith, "Look unto me, and be ye saved, all the ends of the earth."

Take this, dear friends, for a new year's text, both ye who love the Lord, and ye who are only looking for the first time. Christian! in all thy troubles through this year, look unto God and be saved. In all thy trials and afflictions, look unto Christ, and find deliverance. In all thine agony, poor soul, in all thy repentance for thy guilt, look unto Christ, and find pardon. This year remember to put thine eyes heavenward, and thine heart heavenward, too. Remember, this day, that thou bind round thyself a golden chain, and put one link of it in the staple in heaven. Look unto Christ; fear not. There is no stumbling when a man walks with his eyes up to Jesus. He that looked at the stars fell into the ditch; but he that looks at Christ walks safely. Keep your eyes up all the year long. "Look unto *him*, and be ye saved;" and remember that *"he* is God, and beside him there is none else." And thou, poor trembler, what sayest thou? Wilt thou begin the year by looking unto him? You know how sinful you are this morning; you know how filthy you are; and yet it is possible that, before you open your pew door, and get into the aisle, you will be as justified as the apostles before the throne of God. It is possible that, ere your foot treads the threshold of your door, you will have lost the burden that has been on your back, and you will go on your way, singing, "I am forgiven, I am forgiven; I am a miracle of grace; this day is my spiritual birthday." O, that it might be such to many of you, that at last I might say, "Here am I, and the children thou hast given me." Hear this, convinced sinner! "This poor man cried, and the Lord delivered him out of his distresses." O, taste and see that the Lord is good! Now believe on him; now cast thy guilty soul upon his righteousness; now plunge thy black soul into the bath of his blood; now put thy naked soul at the door of the wardrobe of his righteousness; now seat thy famished soul at the feast of plenty. Now "Look!" How simple does it seem! And yet it is the hardest thing in the world to bring men to. They never will do it, till constraining grace makes them. Yet there it is, "Look!" Go thou away with that thought. "Look unto me, and be ye saved, all the ends of the earth: for I am God, and there is none else."

II

The Narrowness of the Gospel
By D. Martyn Lloyd-Jones

From *Evangelistic Sermons* (Edinburgh:
The Banner of Truth Trust, 1983)

David Martyn Lloyd-Jones (1899-1981) was born in Cardiff in Wales and raised in Cardiganshire. After his father's financial adversity, he moved with his parents to London, where the family had fellowship in the Calvinistic Methodist (otherwise known as the Welsh Presbyterian) Church. Iain Murray's two peerless volumes, *The First Forty Years* and *The Fight of Faith* (published by Banner of Truth Trust in 1982 and 1990 respectively) trace Lloyd-Jones's study and practice of medicine as Lord Horder's clinical assistant. In his twenties but not yet converted, Lloyd-Jones was moved by the preaching of Dr. John Hutton at Westminster Chapel, of whom Murray says: "He believed in rebirth and regeneration" (*The First Forty Years*, p. 61). After Lloyd-Jones's conversion, he felt the call to the ministry and, with his wife, began serving the Bethlehem Forward Movement Church in Aberavon, Port Talbot in Wales, in February 1927. Here came the touch of the Spirit in an area where 90 percent were unchurched. In 1931, 135 people came into the membership, of whom 128 were "from the world" (*ibid.*, p. 212). In 1938 he went to London as an associate of G. Campbell Morgan at Westminster Chapel, from which pulpit he addressed the whole world in an increasingly influential ministry through his printed sermons and lectures. This majestic message was preached in Aberavon in the early days.

THE NARROWNESS OF THE GOSPEL

Enter ye in at the strait gate: for wide is the gate, and broad is the way, that leadeth to destruction, and many there be which go in thereat: because strait is the gate, and narrow is the way, which leadeth unto life, and few there be that find it.

Matthew 7:13, 14

There is no charge which is quite so commonly and frequently brought against the Christian way of life as the charge of narrowness. It is a charge also that is constantly brought against the individual Christian believer by that type of man, who, in his desire to show his own breadth of mind describes himself as a man of the world. He is so broad that nothing but world dimensions can give you a true impression of the width and largeness of his views! He is a man of the world in contrast to this narrow and confined man who calls himself a Christian! I fear at times also it is true to say that there is no charge concerning which the average Christian believer is quite so frightened as this charge of narrowness. To some Christians at the present time, it is more or less immaterial what men may say about them as long as they do not describe them as narrow. Of course, there is a sense in which that is a very good and healthy reaction. God forbid that we should ever really become narrow in the sense that the Pharisees were narrow, or that Judaism was narrow. God forbid that we should ever really reduce this glorious gospel of liberty to a mere number of prohibitions and restraints. But that is not our danger at all. Our danger is that in our fear of being thought narrow, we should so swing over to the opposite extreme as eventually to become quite nondescript.

I sometimes feel that a simple, well-known story in Aesop's Fables has a good deal to say to many modern Christians. I am referring to the well-known story of the frog and the ox. One day, it says, a little frog in a field suddenly lifted up his head and observed an ox standing near by. He looked at the ox, and began to admire him, and wished that he was as broad and as big as the ox. 'I am so small and insignificant,' he said. 'How marvellous it must be to have the breadth and width of that ox.' And the story goes on that the frog began to imitate the ox, and he began to expand, and to grow larger and larger, and broader and broader, and eventually he reached a point at which he just exploded and ceased to be. Now that, unless I am mistaken, is the precise thing which has happened to the so-called faith of many a Christian during the last fifty years. In his desire to become broad and wide, the little Christian faith that man ever had has long since exploded and ceased to be. What the exact explanation of the phenomenon is I am not quite

sure, but I think we must recognize that there has been a tendency, particularly during this century, for the church to pay great respect and
regard to the man of scientific knowledge. He has become the last
authority on all these questions. The church has gone to very great
lengths in order to please him; she has been prepared not to stress certain doctrines in her creed and to delete certain portions of the Bible and
she has in so doing wandered very far from the example set for her by
her Lord and Master. I never find Jesus Christ changing His gospel in
order to make it suit the people. Rather I find Him changing the people
in order to make them fit into His gospel. We can be perfectly certain
that there will be no true revival in this country, in spite of what may be
happening round about us, until we return to the royal pattern.

My commission is this:

> *Ye servants of God, your Master proclaim,*
> *And publish abroad His wonderful Name.*

Whether men like it, or dislike it, our business is to preach the truth
which was once and for all committed unto the saints. There is a very
real danger that we should develop a kind of inferiority complex in the
fear of being thought narrow, and ultimately make shipwreck of our
faith. But all this is merely an aside.

For my text is not a negative text, but a very positive text. It tells us
that we must not only not be afraid of being called narrow, but it actually goes on to say that if we really want to be Christians worthy of the
Name, we must go out of our way to become narrow: we must enter in
at the strait gate and walk on the narrow way! Now this, surely, is rather
a startling and amazing thing. Is it not wonderful that when our Lord
came to choose the designation to express His way of life, He should
have selected the very word by which we are most frightened—that the
very word of which we tend to be afraid is the very word in which He
exults, the very word which He puts upon His flag? I would say also,
for the purpose of encouraging and stimulating any frightened Christian
who happens to be here, the next time one of these so-called men of the
world tells you that you are narrow, instead of trying to run away, just
stand your ground, look him straight in the face, and say, 'Of course I
am narrow: and it would be a very much better thing for you, and for
your wife and children, if you also became narrow, and ceased to boast
of a largeness and a breadth which are in reality nothing but a cloak for
laxity and looseness.' He would not worry you quite so frequently in the
future!

But why does our Lord speak about entering in at the strait gate, and walking on the narrow way? Christ never said anything accidentally. He had all the letters of the alphabet at His command, yet He deliberately chose these words to describe His way of life. He spoke thus because there must be certain respects in which the gospel of Christ is really narrow. I want to try to consider with you some of the respects in which this is so.

The first respect in which we observe its narrowness is this, that the gospel confines itself to one particular subject. The gospel of Christ narrows itself down to one question—the soul of man and its relationship to God. In the Bible there is a good deal of history—history of men and nations—and geography, and some people find in it geology and biology. All sorts of subjects are dealt with in this Book, and yet it is not an encyclopedia. It is not a Book which gives us a little knowledge about many things. It is a Book which gives us much knowledge about one thing. It is the textbook of life, the handbook of the soul. It is a manual dealing with one subject, the reconciliation of man with God. If ever there was a specialist's textbook in this world it is this Book. This is true also of the Master of the Book. If ever there was a specialist on the face of the earth it was our Lord Jesus Christ. There is a sense in which He preached only one sermon, and the theme of this sermon was this—the soul of man and its relationship to the Eternal Father. All the knowledge and information He possessed, He used in order to illustrate this important and vital subject. Let me give you some instances.

One day our Lord was in the country, with His disciples standing round about Him. And He observes a farmer sowing seed into the ground. Very clearly our Lord was not only interested in agriculture, but He knew a good deal about it. But the sight of that farmer does not prompt our Lord to deliver an address on agriculture: but as He watches that farmer He sees an illustration for His sermon. 'You see that man,' says our Lord. 'He is sowing seed into the ground. There are different types of ground into which it is sown: and the ground will be judged by its response to the seed that the farmer is sowing into it. I am like that farmer: I am sowing the seed of the Word of God which leads to eternal life. Ultimately men will be judged by their reaction to that seed sown in their lives.'

On another occasion when in the country our Lord beholds the various fruit-trees in an orchard. It is quite clear that our Lord knew a good deal about horticulture, but that does not lead Him to deliver an address on that subject. 'Look at those trees,' says our Lord. 'They may bear either good or bad fruit. Ultimately they will be judged by the kind of fruit that they bear.' And turning to His disciples, He says, 'You are exactly like those trees. By your lives and by your works you will bear either good or bad fruit. So take heed.' On another occasion our Lord was in the country and He observed the lilies of the field and the birds of the air. 'If God is so concerned about the lilies of the field that He clothes them, and about the birds of the air, that He feeds them, how much more is He concerned about you,' Christ says. So I could go on taking you through our Lord's discourses, and you will find how He is constantly making use of things around Him to illustrate His one great theme—the soul of man and its relationship to God.

We hear a good deal nowadays about the simple gospel. The secret of the simplicity of the gospel is this. Jesus of Nazareth, being the Son of God, and living in perfect correspondence and communion with His Father, had all knowledge. He knew what was important, and what was unimportant: and He ignored the unimportant, and gave Himself solely and entirely to the important things of life. He disregarded the irrelevant, and gave Himself utterly and only to the relevant, and to that which ultimately matters. The secret of the simplicity of the gospel lies in the fact that He brushed aside everything but the one supreme question of the soul's need. That is, clearly, an utter contradiction of all our modern ideas and conceptions. We, today, tend to judge the greatness of a man, not by his simplicity, but by his complexity. Yet here was the very Son of God, and even little children got something from Him: ordinary fisherfolk followed Him—'the common people heard Him gladly.' Why? Because He always talked about something which they understood. You, my friend, may be very well versed in many of the arts and sciences. You may be an expert on politics: you may be an authority on quite a number of subjects. But I would like to put a very simple question to you—do you know how to live? 'What shall it profit a man if he gain the whole world,' of knowledge, as well as wealth, 'and lose his own soul?' 'Enter ye at the strait gate.' Come back to the beginning. The important and vital question is that of the soul.

But the narrowness of the gospel does not end at that point: it is merely a beginning. We discover that the gospel even narrows that. The ancient Greek pagan philosophers were very interested in the soul as a concept, as a thought, and they talked and argued much concerning the soul. But our Lord was not interested in the soul as the Greek philosophers were. It was the individual soul in which our Lord was interested. Someone says, 'I do not like such a gospel—it is so personal.' It is profoundly true that the gospel is personal, and on that account it annoys certain people. We find a perfect illustration of the personal nature of the gospel in the fourth chapter of the Gospel according to St. John in the story of our Lord's meeting with the woman of Samaria at the well. Our Lord that afternoon was very tired, too tired to accompany His disciples into the city to buy food, and He rested by the side of the well. A woman came to draw water: and immediately they had a religious discussion. Did that well really belong to the Jews or to the Samaritans, and where exactly should worship take place? This woman seems to have been very astute: she was certainly an expert in the art of repartee. They were engaged in this religious discussion, when suddenly our Lord actually becomes personal! He turns to the woman, and says, 'Go, fetch thy husband,' revealing, thereby, that He knew all about the kind of life she was living. It was as if He said, 'My dear woman, you have really no right, being what you are, to talk about worship and about God. You cannot even manage your own life, you have no right to express an opinion on these great eternal themes. Start with yourself first. "Go, fetch thy husband." When you put your own life in order then you will be entitled to speak.'

Yes, the gospel is a personal thing. We cannot be saved in families: we cannot be saved as a congregation. We cannot be saved collectively because we are all doing a certain amount of philanthropic work. We are saved one by one. It is question of you and God. Have you entered in at the strait gate? Are you prepared to meet God face to face? Are you ready for the Judgment? Do you know in whom you have believed? Is all well with your soul? Have you a personal conviction of sin, and a personal knowledge of God?

But the narrowness of the gospel does not end even there. It tends to become still narrower by insisting upon having a say in our conduct and behaviour. It is not content merely with bringing the soul into a personal contact with God. But it insists upon dictating to us the kind of life we have to live. Someone says, 'That is precisely why I have long since finished with organized religion, and turned my back upon it. It is too narrow. I maintain that I am entitled to live my own life in my own way. I will not be fettered.' Yes, the gospel is very narrow, and it is narrow with respect to this question of conduct and ethics in two main respects: we can call them, if you like, negative and positive. The negative injunctions of the gospel with regard to conduct are perfectly familiar to us all: 'Thou *shalt not* kill.' 'Thou shalt not steal.' 'Thou shalt not commit adultery.' 'Thou shalt not take the Name of the Lord thy God in vain.' 'Avoid every appearance of evil.' If a thing is doubtful, it is wrong, and you must not do it. The gospel goes so far as to say that though a thing may be perfectly right for me, if it is a stumbling block to a weaker brother, I must not do it for his sake. Says someone, 'That is exactly why I have no use for such a gospel: it makes life a misery. You have to put on a black suit, and walk to church with your head down.' But have you realized that if every man and woman were as narrow as the gospel of Christ would have us be, there would be no more drunkenness, no need of Divorce Courts, no need for the League of Nations? Why? the world would be a paradise. It would be perfect, even as God Himself is perfect! The narrowness of the gospel—I speak with reverence—is the narrowness that is in God Himself. Oh, that we all became narrow, that we might enter in through this strait gate! 'Few there be that find it,' says our Lord. Yes! because it takes an exceptional man to say 'No' to temptation, and to restrain and control himself. It takes an exceptional man to deny himself in order to make things easier for others. On the broad way there is a great crowd! 'Many there be which go in thereat.' It does not take an exceptionally great man to sin. Any fool can sin, and every fool does sin. But that broad way leadeth to destruction. There is the narrowness of the gospel in its negative injunctions.

But I want to show you its narrowness in its positive injunctions. This, of course, is the great theme of the Sermon on the Mount. If you would really see the narrowness of the gospel you must come to the Sermon on the Mount. One of the great words of this generation is the word love. But if you really want to see the greatness of the word love you must narrow it down: you must focus it. You do not know what love really means until you love your enemies. The great task which is set before the Christian is to love ugly people until they are made beautiful. Another great word today is the word brotherhood. We believe today in doing good, and in helping others. But if you want to see how great that word really is you must narrow it down. You must bless them that curse you, and pray for them that despitefully use you. The task set before the Christian is to 'do good to them that hate you.' Another great word is the word happiness. There are those who say, 'I want to enjoy myself, and I have no use for religion. Why should I bury myself alive?' Again you have a great word, but you must narrow it down and focus it, if you would discover its real size. You know not what happiness means until you can 'rejoice in tribulation,' until you can be happy even in the midst of persecution. The task for the Christian is to be happy even when the clouds have gathered and the sun has ceased to shine, and everything has gone wrong.

There, then, we see something of the essential narrowness of the gospel. It is, in other words, this narrowness of the expert, or, if you like, the narrowness of the highest circle of achievement. You are all familiar with the saying that there is always plenty of room for a good man at the top. The higher the circle of achievement, the smaller will be the number found in it. For instance, there are many who can sing remarkably well, but very few Carusos; there are many who can play the violin amazingly well, but very few Kreislers: there are many who paint extraordinarily well, but comparatively few Royal Academicians. That, it seems to me, is the very point which our Lord makes in this text. 'Do not be content with living anyhow.' He says, in effect: 'Do not be content with living on the ordinary level of life. Come up to the top. Ascend the mount. Live life tremendously, live life as an expert. Live as I live, yea, come to the very summit. Be ye perfect, even as your Father which is in heaven is perfect.'

But, lastly, if you would see the narrowest and straightest point of all, you must confront the gospel at that point at which it tells you that salvation is only possible in and through one particular Person and especially in His death. There is the point at which perhaps the majority tend to object. 'I have agreed with you entirely, so far,' says someone, 'I liked your emphasis upon the soul, your emphasis upon personal decision, and your emphasis upon ethics and conduct. But when you tell me, now, that I can only be saved by believing that Christ died my death, I find it impossible to follow you. The conception is too narrow. I cannot understand it. It seems to me, to be almost immoral. I cannot accompany you any further.' What has the gospel to say to such a man? It does not argue with him. It challenges him. It turns to him and says something like this: 'If you can find God without going via Calvary, do so. If you can find liberation from your besetting sin without the power of the cross of Christ, carry on. If you can find peace and rest to your troubled conscience without believing in the death of the Son of God for you and for your sins, go ahead. If you can lie on your deathbed and think of facing a holy God without fear and without alarm, I really have nothing to say to you. But, if ever you should feel lost and miserable and wretched; if ever you should feel that all your righteousness is but as filthy rags; if ever you are filled with terror and alarm as you think of God, and His holy Law; if ever you feel utterly helpless and hopeless, then turn back to Him, the Christ of the cross, with His arms outstretched, who still says: "Look unto me and be saved, all ye ends of the earth."' It is there that the whole of humanity is focused. He is the representative of the whole of mankind. He died for all. But still more wonderful, according to Paul it is also true to say that, 'in Him dwelleth all the fulness of the Godhead bodily.' Complete man and complete God and all in one Person! God-Man! In Him, God and man are indissolubly linked, and through Him and in Him the way is opened from hell to heaven, from darkness to light, from despair to hope.

Let me show you, as I close, how perfectly this text, and all I have tried to say with respect to it, can be illustrated from the story of our Lord's earthly life and pilgrimage. Consider His birth and the self-emptying that it involved. Try to think of the narrowness and straitness of Bethlehem, when the Word was made flesh and eternity came into time—'Strait is the gate.' Then think of Him in the wilderness at the commencement of His earthly ministry, tempted forty days and forty nights. Then watch the Scribes and Pharisees and Sadducees and Herodians, as they spread their net round about Him, and gradually draw it in—'Strait is the gate and narrow is the way.' Then look at Him in the Garden of Gethsemane—the very Son of God, by whom and through whom all things were created, confined to a garden surrounded by soldiers. And then in a few hours, in the police court, with a soldier standing one each side. In the Garden, He could at least walk backwards and forwards along the path; now He is not allowed to move—'Strait is the gate, narrow is the way.' But still it is not finished—see Him on the cross nailed to the tree—the Son of God, the Creator of the world— fixed there, unable to move hand or foot. He dies. They take down the body and place it in a grave. Peer into that grave—can you see any light there? Do not the very sides seem to fall in and to collapse?—'Strait is the gate, narrow is the way.' It leads to death, the grave, darkness, utter desolation.

And there we should have to end if we but believed what so frequently passes as gospel at the present time. But—blessed be the Name of God—the gospel goes on. It does mean Bethlehem, it does mean the wilderness and temptation, it does mean enemies and persecution, it does mean Gethsemane, trial, cross, death, yea and the grave. BUT—on the morning of the third day, behold, the resurrection! He bursts asunder the bands of death and rises triumphant o'er the grave! The darkness leads to dawn and to the light of endless day! 'Strait is the gate, narrow is the way—BUT—it leadeth unto life.'

If you accept the gospel and yield yourself to it, it will mean another birth for you; it will mean trial and temptation, it will mean persecution, it will mean the crucifixion and death of an 'old man' that is in you. BUT, it will lead to life which is life indeed, life more abundant, yea, the very life of God Himself.

'Enter ye in at the strait gate.' Come on to the narrow way!

III

The Cross as Power and Wisdom
By James S. Stewart

From *River of Life* (Nashville:
Abingdon Press, 1972)

James Stuart Stewart (1896-1990) was known as "Stewart of Morningside" in his native Scotland. In a most thoughtful personal reminiscence, Dr. Richard Longenecker speaks of Stewart's ability to bring together "a rigorous scholarship, a reverential reading of Scripture, and an effective communication of the gospel" ("Missing One of Scotland's Best," *Christianity Today*, July 22, 1991). Stewart served local congregations for twenty-two years, including the famous North Morningside Church of Scotland parish in Edinburgh. His Warrack Lectures on Preaching (*Heralds of God*) are classics, and his books of sermons (such as *The Gates of New Life*, *The Strong Name*, and *River of Life*) have been read around the world. In 1946 he was appointed Professor of New Testament Language, Literature and Theology at New College, Edinburgh. His scholarly monograph entitled *A Man in Christ: Vital Elements in St. Paul's Religion* is an extraordinary rich treasury of truth. He was, as Longenecker reminds us, Chaplain to the Queen and Moderator of the Church of Scotland. He traveled and preached on several continents, was chaplain to a local professional soccer team, and regularly preached the gospel "at a rescue mission in an Edinburgh slum." His lectures on evangelism under the title *Thine Is the Kingdom* are powerful and stirring, as is this unusual sermon.

THE CROSS AS POWER AND WISDOM

'The Jews require a sign, and the Greeks seek after wisdom: but we preach Christ crucified, unto the Jews a stumbling-block, and unto the Greeks foolishness; but unto them which are called, both Jews and Greeks, Christ the power of God, and the wisdom of God'—I Corinthians 1:22-24.

There are two demands we often make on God, in face of the tragic element of life and all the mystery of the world. The one is intervention, the other interpretation.

Intervention, action—this first. 'Let God do something! If He is really a God of righteousness, let Him prove it. If He is sovereign in His universe, let Him demonstrate His sovereignty. Why should a hurricane in the Caribbean, an earthquake in Japan, a famine in India, devastate ten thousand homes, and God give no sign? Why should man's inhumanity to man and the endemic injustice of the world sabotage the dream of progress? Why should nuclear devilry threaten the extinction of the world? Let God arise, and let His enemies be scattered!' Intervention—that is the first demand.

The second is interpretation, explanation. 'If only we could make sense out of life's jumbled pattern!' Some time ago I had a letter from a young doctor in America. She was working in a children's hospital where babies are sometimes brought in suffering from a fatal disease. 'What am I to say to these parents?' she asked me. 'When they demand, "Where is the sense, the providence, the rationality of this?" what am I to answer?' We have all felt the cutting edge of that enigma. If only there were some clue to the riddle! If only providence would explain!

These are two great demands we are constantly making on God—intervention, interpretation.

Now here is an immensely significant fact: these were precisely the demands being made when the Christian faith first launched itself upon the world. 'The Jews require a sign, and the Greeks seek after wisdom.'

'The Jews require a sign'—that is, action, intervention, a visible demonstration of God's power. That is what the Jew wants, says Paul. That is characteristic of the Jewish attitude to life. 'Let God assert Himself visibly, dramatically. Let Him make bare His holy arm in the eyes of all the nations. Let Him deal with the dictators, and ruin the aggressors. Let Him in the twinkling of an eye eliminate incurable disease and heartbreak and all the sorrow and injustice of the world.' 'Awake,' cries Isaiah, 'put on strength, O arm of the Lord!' 'The Jews require a sign.'

'And the Greeks seek after wisdom'—that is, a rational interpretation and explanation of the divine purpose. That is what the Greek wants, says Paul. That is characteristic of the Greek attitude to life— always dissecting ultimate questions; always fashioning some new philosophy to rationalise the chaos and make this unintelligible life coherent; always searching for the solving word, the hidden pattern, the correct intellectual formula—and imagining sometimes it has found it in some early Greek version of logical positivism, linguistic analysis, depth psychology, or a clever blue-print of a new order. 'The Greeks seek after wisdom.'

So, you see, the situation Paul is addressing is not an old Bible story. It is our situation precisely. It is right in the centre of the contemporary map. That Jew demanding a sign, a divine intervention, is just ourselves. That Greek seeking after wisdom, interpretation, is just ourselves. We are all in this together.

Now watch what follows. Paul here asserts that God has faced exactly these two demands, and given His answer. And God's answer to both of them is the same. It is the answer of the cross. 'We preach Christ crucified.' 'There, Jew, is your "sign"—the divine dramatic deed you clamour for. And there, Greek, is your "wisdom"—the solving word for the whole baffling enigma.' All roads lead to Calvary at last.

But now the question is—what do you think of that for an answer? I have said that the Jew and the Greek are just ourselves. So we had better see what the Jew and the Greek thought of the answer.

The Jew certainly did not think much of it. Paul tells us that. 'We preach Christ crucified—unto the Jews a stumbling-block.' The word is *skandalon*, a scandal, an embarrassing, shocking offence.

Now of course Paul knew what he was talking about. For Paul was a Jew himself. He had felt just like that once upon a time when he contemplated the cross. The thing is a scandal! So Saul of Tarsus felt. For the Messiah of the Jews was to be a warrior-king. He was to ride through rivers of blood to the conquest of the world. Ride on, ride on in majesty! God save the King! O King, live for ever! But this Man upon a gallows—a scandal indeed! Did not the law of Moses say—'Cursed is everyone who hangs on a tree'? 'Take it away,' cried the Jew. 'I want a demonstration of power, and you give me this pathetic symbol of weakness and defeat, this broken, tortured, thorn-crowned victim, nailed hand and foot, helpless. Strange token of omnipotence this! God with His back to the wall! You have given me the exact opposite of my demand. I wanted power, intervention—you have given me impotence and discomfiture. A stumbling-block indeed! Take it away.'

And we are stumbled by it too—are we not?—we who clamour for our twentieth-century sign, who think that God—if there be a God—should force His will upon recalcitrant dictators and incurable disease and all the stubborn intractability of the world: 'Put on strength, O arm of the Lord!' And what we see instead is that gaunt tree on Golgotha, love crucified there, and crucified still in a thousand thousand innocent sufferers. 'Jesus,' said Pascal, 'will be in agony till the end of the world.' A stumbling-block indeed! 'Don't look at that picture, you fool,' cries one Dostoievsky character to another who is gazing at a picture of the crucifixion. 'Don't you know a man can lose his faith by looking at that picture?' 'Yes,' comes the answer, 'that is just what is happening to me.' Christ crucified—a stumbling-block, a scandal. That is the Jew.

What of the Greek? What did he think of God's answer? The Greek did not think much of it. Paul tells us that also. 'We preach Christ crucified—unto the Greeks foolishness.' The word is *moria*, sheer absurdity.

Again Paul knew what he was talking about. For Paul had in him a considerable element of the Greek, the cosmopolitan. He had felt just like that in the old days, contemplating the cross. Folly! So Saul of Tarsus had reacted. For the Saviour the Greeks looked for was to be the apotheosis of all the culture and philosophy of the world. He was to be a super-Aristotle, a demigod for wisdom, the head of a new intellectual aristocracy. But this crucified Man, this

> *Sacred Head, sore wounded,*
> *With grief and shame bowed down—*

'Take it away!' cried the Greek. 'I want a rational explanation, and in the name of all that is irrational you offer me this! It offends my aesthetic temperament. It insults my cultured intelligence. A gallows—it is so undignified. You have given me the exact opposite of my demand. I wanted interpretation, explanation—you have given me only deeper discord and anomaly, confusion worse confounded. It is sheer absurdity! Take it away.'

And we are there too, are we not, with our perpetual 'Why?' Why is life so unjust? Why is suffering so indiscriminate? Every minister in his pastoral counselling knows these questions which, however often he tries to answer them, drain the virtue out of him. Why did my beloved die? Why could I never realise my heart's desire? Why is it so difficult to believe in God? Why is the pathway to maturity so slow and painful and humbling and bewildering? Why are there so many complications along the road?

And instead of light, it looks—this cross of Calvary—like deeper darkness: instead of the dawn of the kingdom of heaven, Christ descending into hell. Is it not mad to offer this as the clue to the mystery of life and the riddle of the world? We preach Christ crucified—to the Greeks sheer folly.

But wait! This is where the sudden exciting hopefulness of the gospel appears. Those immediate, instinctive reactions of Jew and Greek to the cross were not the last word then—nor are they the last word now.

For that Jew requiring a sign, a demonstration of power, and finding only a stumbling-block, has a second look at the cross, then a third, then a fourth, perhaps a hundredth. He is going deeper. He is changing his verdict. And suddenly, 'I see it!' he cries, 'it was true after all! I wanted God to act, and—how blind I was!—this cross which I called a stumbling-block, a scandal, of all God's mighty acts this is the mightiest! Here is the victory that conquers the world. Here is the devil's strategy defeated!'

This is the great discovery. Do let us try to get it clear today. I would put it to you like this.

The really damnable thing about evil is its self-propagating power. Injury produces resentment, resentment produces retaliation, this produces further injury, that produces further pain and evil: and so the whole miserable story drags on hopelessly for ever. This is the devil's standard strategy, individually and collectively—and it is frightfully successful: it is the vicious circle that could easily have spelt the ruin of the world.

But now look! When Christ died on the cross, forgiving, He broke right into that process. He met this whole tyranny of evil, and outmanoeuvred it. For here at last was One who refused to allow injury and pain to produce resentment. Instead, He took all the pain and injury into His own body and soul. Thus in His broken body and soul He absorbed it, neutralised it, cut short its power. This is the frustration of the devil. This is the atonement of the world.

I put it to you: there is not one of us today who believes that in the presence of the cross of Christ we are in the presence of defeat. We know we are in the presence of victory. Here is the cross, history's blackest crime—and history's brightest hope. Here is the most atrocious tragedy ever enacted—and it is precisely this which has become the supreme assurance of the sovereignty of God. They gave Him a cross, and He made it a throne. They slammed every door against Him, and flung Him outside the city gates to die; and that very act has lifted up the gates of the universe to let the King come in. They thought they had hunted God to His doom, not knowing that it was God who was tracking them down. He reigns from the tree. 'We preach Christ crucified, the power of God'—the one power big enough to take a grip of the world's desperate situation, and defy the gates of hell, and give a fresh start to humanity. If only the world today would align itself with Jesus in His victory, we should see the powers of darkness discomfited again.

Do you see where this touches your life and mine? I am not suggesting, mark you, that God wants us quietly to acquiesce in evils and scourges that can and should be removed. No, surely God wants His human race to be rebels and fighters against needless suffering and incurable disease, to fight these things with all the resources of knowledge and science and dedicated life until they are swept for ever from the earth. That is different. But suppose there is some trouble in your life that cannot be removed. Suppose there is some overwhelming enigma of desolating sorrow—as with those parents in the children's hospital about whom my friend wrote to me. Suppose there is some heavy trial you are bearing now. Suppose there is the sting of sin to make you miserable and ashamed: 'O wretched man that I am! Who shall deliver me?' And suppose you were to get your life into the way of that power of the cross, that alchemy that can turn the iron of bitterness into the gold of blessing. If it is going to heal mankind at last, and bring the harvest of the divine purpose out of the wreck and ruin of the world, do you not think it could perhaps help to heal you here and now? Even with all the monotony of defeat, the accusing voices, the bungling and the disappointment, do you not think that union with this Christ could do the miracle for us now? It is worth believing. I do not know how to fathom by any theory of atonement what it was that happened at Calvary. I do not know how deep were the waters crossed, nor how dark the night the Lord passed through. I only know that through those deep waters and that dark night the Shepherd found His sheep. I only know that John Bunyan was speaking for ten thousand times ten thousand when he said that at the sight of the cross the burden fell off Christian's back and was never seen again. I only know that when they thrust Jesus outside their city gates to die they were putting the keys of the whole world into His pierced hands for ever. 'We preach Christ crucified, the power of God.'

Finally, what of the Greek? The Greek, searching after wisdom and interpretation and explanation, and finding only foolishness—he too has a second look at the cross, then a third, then a fourth, perhaps a hundredth. He is going deeper. He is going deeper into the heart of things than his own Plato and Aristotle ever went. He is seeing right across the frontier into another world. And suddenly, 'I see it!' he cries, 'it was true after all! I wanted God to explain, to interpret, and—how blind I was!—

this cross that I called rank folly and absurdity, it is the word from heaven!'

For this is the ground-plan of the universe. This is the great Architect's design for building His new creation. This is the wisdom which created man at the first, and now at the cross it is creating the new humanity.

Are there not traces of this sometimes to be found even on the human level? A servant of Christ, working in a dreadful slum, takes in to share his humble abode a man who has been in trouble with the police for a stabbing affray. Folly? By any secular standard, rank folly. But what if it is the wisdom of God by which that broken life is to be remade? There was the headmaster of a London school who, during an air attack, shepherded all the children into the safety of the shelters; and then, going back again to make doubly certain that no one had been left behind, was himself caught by a bomb and killed instantly. Was that sacrifice needless folly? Or was it perhaps the wisdom of God by which honour comes into its heritage?

These are only dim analogies, distant and remote. Here stands the cross of Jesus. Here is the sign that gives the lie to the plausible wisdom of material security. We are being told today that scientific humanism holds the key to security. We are being told that words like faith and providence are now unintelligent sentimentalities which we must leave out of the reckoning. We are even told that as long as we can build bigger and better ballistic missiles than other nations nothing else matters: this is our best security. What a hope! Men today are beginning to see through that decrepit philosophy. For in fact it is the bankrupt logic of fatalism and despair: 'mind at the end of its tether', to use H. G. Wells' phrase. Here stands the cross of Jesus—this essential insecurity, this foolishness of faith, this hope strained to the breaking-point, this love despised and rejected. This is the wisdom of God. And it is quite certain that life will work no other way.

Let me make this quite personal. Someone may say, 'Sacrifice? I don't want sacrifice. I am sick of the sound of the word. I am bored with Christianity's reiteration about taking up a cross. It is such a dismal dirge, such an outmoded ethic. Self-realisation—that is my goal: to be the arbiter of my own destiny, going ahead and fulfilling even what Christianity would tell me was an unfulfilable desire.'

But I am only asking you to look into your heart and look up at the cross. Does not your own heart tell you that the wisdom of God is there, and that life will work no other way? Canon Streeter once put it memorably: 'The primrose path of dalliance is early overrun with briars; and if we must be pierced with thorns, it is more kingly to wear them as a crown.' More kingly, yes, and infinitely more satisfying too. For Christ will be there to help and strengthen you; and, as Principal David Cairns used to say, 'What God did with the cross of His first-born Child Jesus, He can do with all the crosses of all His other children.' He can make them shine with glory.

When you reach that point in your thinking—'Christ crucified the wisdom of God'—suddenly it flashes upon you, 'I must be in this with Jesus. I must be identified and united with Him in His sacrifice and passion—in that self-offering of which the dear Lord said, "To this end was I born, and for this cause came I into the world."' He is bearing now, this very hour, the shame and suffering of all the earth. And I know He is looking round on me and saying, 'Will you stand in and share with Me in this, or is it nothing to you?' For today Christ, the Power and the Wisdom of God, stands at the door and knocks. While the sands of time are running out, and the hurrying hours mould our destiny, He stands at the door and knocks. It is so urgent that we should make our dedication real.

> *Passionately fierce the voice of God is pleading,*
> *Pleading with men to arm them for the fight;*
> *See how those hands, majestically bleeding,*
> *Call us to rout the armies of the night.*

> *Bread of Thy Body give me for my fighting,*
> *Give me to drink Thy Sacred Blood for wine,*
> *While there are wrongs that need me for the righting,*
> *While there is warfare splendid and divine.*

This is your calling. This is your vocation. To this end were you born, and for this cause you came into the world.

IV

Peace Be Unto You
By George W. Truett

From *Who Is Jesus?* (Grand Rapids,
MI: Baker, 1973)

George Washington Truett (1867-1944) was born in Clay County in
North Carolina where his parents had a small farm. His mother
was a warm Christian woman who prayed for twenty-six years for the
conversion of her husband. In his superb biography of Truett, Dr.
Powhatan W. James relates how the young George Truett at age nineteen attended evangelistic services in his home church and heard a sermon on "The just shall live by faith; and if any man draw back, my soul
shall have no pleasure in him" (see *George W. Truett*, Nashville:
Broadman, 1939). Sensing the call to preach, he attended Baylor
University where he came under the strong influence of Dr. B. H.
Carroll. He preached for several years at the East Waco Baptist Church
and at age thirty entered the pastorate of the First Baptist Church of
Dallas, Texas, where he proclaimed Christ faithfully for forty-seven
years. Truett served as president of the Southern Baptist Convention and
the Baptist World Alliance. He was blessed with an unusually effective
speaking voice. Like Spurgeon, his heart was broken by a great personal
tragedy when he accidentally shot one of his best friends in a hunting
accident, the Chief of Police of Dallas and a member of First Baptist
Church. When he died, Truett felt he could never preach again, but the
Lord gave him special grace and strength in that trial. Used globally as
well as nationally and locally, Truett was a giant of the faith.

PEACE BE UNTO YOU

> And as they thus spake, Jesus himself stood in the midst of them,
> and saith unto them, Peace be unto you.
>
> Luke 24:36

This is one of the most notable appearances of our Lord, after His
resurrection. He made eleven distinct and different appearances during
the forty days of His sojourn on the earth after He was risen from the
dead. This is one of the most suggestive and instructive of all His appearances.

He appeared, you remember, first of all to Mary; then He appeared
to other women; He made an appearance to Simon Peter. Later He
appeared to the two disciples on the way to Emmaus, and they hurried
back to the followers of Jesus who were in an upper room conversing
and reasoning about all these matters. While they talked Jesus stood in
their midst and confirmed the several reports which had reached them
touching the fact that He had verily risen from the dead. But still all of
them did not believe it. Some of them did, for unto some of them He
had appeared and already they were convinced. But others of them were
terrified and affrighted and imagined that a ghost had made its appearance among them. They were still terrified as He began to speak to them.

Several vital truths emerge from this incident. First, is the certainty
of the resurrection of Jesus Christ from the grave. Of all the facts of history, I hazard nothing in saying that there is no more thoroughly authenticated fact in all history than the resurrection of Jesus Christ from the
grave. My conviction is that He verily came out of the grave, put death
beneath His feet, and after forty days ascended to Heaven where He ever
lives to make intercession for us.

A man has to discredit all testimony and has to discard all the laws
of evidence if he repudiates or calls in question the great teaching of the
resurrection of Jesus from the grave. There is one question at which
unbelief stumbles and staggers; that question is: What became of the
body of Jesus? Where is the body of Jesus? I repeat, a fact as thoroughly
authenticated as any fact in all history is the fact that Jesus of Nazareth,
crucified under Pontius Pilate, and buried in Joseph's new tomb, on the
third day came out of the grave, a triumphant man, a triumphant God,
over the power of death. And every one who has set out with honest
mind and heart to find out the truth of that matter has been convinced
beyond the shadow of a doubt of the truth of that claim.

Gilbert West, that noted skeptic, said, "I will overthrow the whole
scheme of the Christian religion by overthrowing the teaching that Jesus

of Nazareth came out of the grave, raised from the dead." He began this project with the result that, after faithful investigation, he bowed before Jesus Christ and sought forgiveness of his sins. Then the noted unbeliever became one of the most triumphant soldiers and witnesses for Jesus Christ in all the earth.

So must we always accept the proposition that if Christ be not risen from the dead, Christianity is a farce and a delusion from first to last. Paul was right when he said, "If He be not risen, our preaching is vain; we are yet in our sins, and we are of all men most miserable." The more you look into this proposition and ponder its testimony, the more your mind and your heart will be overwhelmed with the conviction and the consciousness that our Lord is not in the grave. He has put the grave beneath His feet, and is ascended on high, and now reigns and lives and intercedes for all whom the Father hath given Him.

But there are some lessons in this simple narrative of this fifth appearance of Jesus after His resurrection. He came to this company of dismayed disciples, and gave them several evidences of His resurrection. He gave them the evidence of hearing. He gave them the evidence of seeing. He gave them the evidence of touching. He gave them the evidence of common sense. And all these evidences stand out in this portion of scripture.

Jesus appeared to these disciples, stood in their midst unannounced and at the very first sight of Him, they heard him say, "Peace be unto you." He gave them, first of all, the evidence of hearing. There must have been something about the voice of Jesus that never echoed in any other voice. There must have been something about His speech that no man could imitate. Thus when he stood in their midst and said, "Peace be unto you," they were terrified; they were affrighted; they thought a ghost had made its appearance.

Then he continued, in effect: "Why are ye troubled, and why do ye have reasonings in your heart? I am but carrying out what Moses and the prophets foretold—all this is but the unfolding, the revealing, the opening of the things that were foretold should thus come to pass." And still they wondered, and still they were amazed, and still they were filled with fear. O, how slow to believe were even the apostles! Slow to believe! No wonder He cried out, "O, foolish men, and slow of heart to believe!"

And then He gave them the evidence of sight. "Why are ye terrified? I am not a ghost. I am not an apparition. I am not a mere spirit. Look on me; behold that it is I, myself." And He showed them the nail-prints in His hands and feet and the rent in His side.

One week later Jesus appeared again in their meeting and said to

Thomas, who was not in the first meeting, "Thomas, thou doubting, distrusting, unbelieving one, come hither and put your fingers in the nail prints in my hands and feet, and thrust your hand into the great rent in my side from which issued blood and water as I died on the tree. Come, handle me. Not only hear me, and not only look upon me, but come and touch me." A spirit does not have bones and flesh. A spirit does not have corporal existence. "Come and touch me, and see for yourself that I am Jesus risen from the dead."

Then, as if to give them the crowning proof of the certainty of the resurrection, Jesus appealed to their common sense. "Have ye anything here to eat?" He asked. "Bring it to me." And they brought Him a piece of fish and an honeycomb, and there before them, the Master did eat. And yet they were terrified and affrighted through it all, until, at the last, they were overwhelmed and convinced that He was verily risen from the grave.

The one great fact in which we rejoice is the fact of the resurrection of Jesus Christ from the grave. That is the great key-stone in the arch, for the redemption of a ruined world. We rejoice in it. Without cavil or fear, without distrust, we build our hope upon this fact that Christ who was in the grave, has been raised from the dead and has become the first fruits of them that slept.

When once this great fact of the resurrection of Jesus Christ is conceded, Christianity is accepted and all other facts of any moment in the Christian religion are adjusted. Why need men have doubts about miracles, if Christ came out of the grave? Why need men wonder about supernaturalism, if this one great fact be granted? But if this fact be denied, if this fact be repudiated, the whole great superstructure of the Christian religion shall totter and fall into ashes and death; for, if Jesus be in the grave, our gospel is a delusion, and we are of all men most miserable.

Let us look at Jesus' character after His resurrection. These verses here indicate the character of Jesus after He had been dead, and after He had come out of the grave, and had put death beneath His feet. What will He think of us now? How will He act now? What relation will He bear to us now? We see that after His resurrection, just as He was before His death, Jesus was still desirous that His followers might have peace. The very first word He spoke when He stood in that upper room where the apostles and friends were gathered was "Peace be unto you." And time and time again, when He met the apostles after His resurrection, His greeting always was, "Peace be unto you." And so in this incident, as we see Him appearing to this company of apostles, His usual salutation falls upon their ears and upon ours, "Peace be unto you." Our Lord Jesus, after His resurrection, was concerned, just as He was before, that we might have peace.

Jesus does not want us to be filled with foreboding and depression and despondency and distrust and gloom. His words were and are, "Rejoice. Be of good cheer. Be not cast down. Be not consumed with anxious care. Put distrust and doubt and unbelief far away." That was the mind and heart of our Lord, after He rose from the grave, just as it was before and just as it is even now.

We see also in this manifestation that He sought to drive away all doubt and distrust. "Why are ye troubled?" He tenderly inquired. "Why are ye cast down?" And in that tender, searching inquiry, our Master sought to drive away all unbelief and all distrust. "O, ye of little faith! Why do you doubt?" Doubt consumes; doubt depresses; doubt enslaves; doubt harms; doubt hurts. Put your doubt and your distrust and your unbelief far away. There is no occasion for it.

Thus we see in these scriptures that Jesus had the same loving fellowship with men after the resurrection that He had before His death. Think what fellowship our Lord had with men! He mingled with all classes of people. Here He dined; there He comforted; here He healed; there He warned; here He preached, and there He taught. These things He did among all kinds of people—high and low, rich and poor, young and old, good and bad. Children loved Him because they instinctively knew that He loved them.

So after He was risen from the dead He mingled with men just as before. "Have ye anything to eat?" He asked. And our Lord sat down with that company of devoted friends and ate as He did before His death. O, the fellowship of Jesus! O, brethren, born for adversity, He has a heart of sympathy for you. He had commiseration and companionship and fellowship for them after death, as well as before!

Notice here the patience of our Master with His people. How slow they were to believe! How slow they were to accept Him! How hesitant they were to acknowledge Him as Lord and Master. But He was patient with them. He revealed little by little, until men more and more came to an understanding of who He was.

See again, friends, how our Lord after His resurrection was concerned about scripture. He sat down there on this occasion and told them, "Did I not tell you before my death that all these things must be fulfilled, which were spoken by Moses and by the prophets and in the Psalms? And now I point you back to the great living word of God! That was what I told you then, and after my resurrection, I tell it to you again." Oh, the tender regard our Lord had for the divine Word; and in that there ought to be a lesson for us.

Why should we accept, unreservedly, many of the great facts of the Old Testament which unfriendly critics of the Bible so ardently dispute? Why do we accept, unreservedly, the great fact of man's fall? Because Jesus Christ magnified that awful fact in His teachings, while among men. Why do we accept the fact of the great flood that covered the earth in Noah's time? Because our Lord accepted it and drew some of His greatest lessons from it. Why do we accept the fact of the great disasters that came to Sodom and Gomorrah in the days of Lot? Because our Lord accepted it, and based some pointed lessons on it. Why do we accept the teaching that the great fish swallowed Jonah, where Jonah abode for three days? Why do we accept it? We accept it, unreservedly, because Christ accepted it, and drew some of the most pungent lessons of His public ministry from it.

And whatever our Lord hath endorsed, unreservedly we endorse. He endorsed the great facts of scriptural history. We follow Christ Jesus in His acceptance of all these great facts, and do not follow the so-called critics; for our Lord knew the sure and infallible oracles of God. Having risen from the dead, Jesus had the same tender regard for scripture that He had before. He quoted and explained both the Law and the Prophets after His resurrection just as He had done before His crucifixion.

Risen from the dead, He was concerned, just as He was before, for the salvation of men. O, friends, our Lord, when He died on the cross, ah, surely, He was concerned for the lifting up of a ruined, doomed, lost race! And He is just as much concerned now. Risen from the dead, He stands with His company of disciples, and teaches them the great plan of salvation just as He taught before. This was the divine commission that He, on this occasion, gave these disciples: "As my Father hath sent me, even so send I you." Find out why Jesus came, and you find out for what you came to the Kingdom. The redeemed of the Lord are one in their mission with Jesus of Nazareth. The only reason we need not die for a lost world, as our Lord did, is that in Him was full atonement made for a ruined race; and by living, by working, and by doing, we can do more than by dying. Otherwise, we ought to die for the redemption of men—for a ruined world. Our Lord was and is the same, great missionary Leader, the same great worldwide gospel propagandist after His resurrection, that He was before.

And now, a final word: What do these scriptures teach of our own resurrection? It remained for Christianity to give us the great truth that our bodies should be raised from the grave. Before Jesus came there were glimmerings of light, that the spirit should live forever. But it remained for Christianity to give us that great hope, that marvelous, unapproachable truth that these bodies should be raised from the grave. Christianity means to redeem the entire man. Christ came to seek and to save the lost. Our bodies are lost as well as our spirits. Christianity came to redeem these bodies. After a while they shall be fully regenerated as are our spirits, and shall come back together, forever to be with the Lord.

Our future nature, after death, is to be one filled with peace. We shall have fellowship with each other and recognition beyond the grave. Often the question is asked, "Will God's children know each other in heaven?" It would be difficult to ask a more foolish and unreasonable question. We shall certainly not know less in heaven than we know here on earth. To be sure, we will know each other, and social life shall be extended and rejoiced in in heaven infinitely beyond its highest conception on earth. Yes, just as Jesus came and knew and as these men in the flesh knew the resurrected Lord, so shall all redeemed by His blood know, and greet and rejoice with each other on the golden shore. The child shall climb up in your arms, and you will call it your child again. And the loved one, separated from you, shall sit down by you, and you will talk over the glad days again.

The resurrection of Jesus carries with it the great doctrine of our resurrection, and of our recognition and our fellowship on the other shore. That is one of the sweetest truths in our Christian religion. "We shall know, even as we are known," and we shall do just like our Lord did. We shall talk of the past, for we shall remember. He remembered the past and dwelt upon it. So shall it be in our Father's house on high.

And there is this other word: We shall be busy in our resurrection life. I do not know where we shall go. I do not know on what missions He will send us. You and I may be preachers to some far-off planet after we go to be with God. But we shall be busy. Heaven is a place of unwearied activity. Our Lord will be there, and we shall work with Him and for Him forever.

Is the resurrection and the life your portion? It is, if you are Christ's. Are you Christ's? This is the all-important matter. Are you Christ's? Do you belong to Him? Have you accepted Him as your personal Saviour? Come now and hear Him say, "Peace be unto you."

V

Heaven and Hell
By Billy Graham

From *The Challenge: Sermons from Madison Square Garden* (New York: Doubleday, 1969)

Of Billy Graham (1918–) it has been said that he has preached to more people than anyone else in the history of the Christian church. Born in North Carolina and trained in Florida and at Wheaton College, Wheaton, Illinois, his conversion through the ministry of Mordecai Ham is well-known. After serving in an independent church in Western Springs, Illinois, Graham was associated with Youth for Christ in its early post-war surge. Called to succeed Dr. W. B. Riley as president of Northwestern Schools in Minneapolis, he was quickly caught up in the greater plans the Lord had for him. The 1949 Crusade in Los Angeles (with converts such as Hamblen, Vaus, and Zamperini) catapulted the Graham Team into an international ministry which has reached into sixty-five countries. The fidelity of Billy Graham to the Scriptures and the gospel, his own consistent personal and financial integrity, and his deep humility and spiritual earnestness have been mightily blessed of God. This sermon is one actually preached in the New York City Crusade of 1969 (on June 17). Billy Graham has never wavered in proclaiming that there is not only a Heaven to be gained, but a Hell to be spurned. How many thousands around the world will gather around the "throne of God and of the Lamb" to whom they were introduced by the Lord's steadfast servant, Billy Graham.

HEAVEN AND HELL

I am going to ask that we bow our heads in prayer. Every head bowed and every eye closed. People are here from various parts of the United States and, for that matter, the world. We represent various nationalities; many of us speak with accents because we have come from abroad to be here in New York City, to live here, to work here. Or perhaps you are a tourist visiting here. Whoever you are, there is one thing we all have in common: Our hearts are the same. Whatever the color of the skin, or whatever the accent we speak with, our hearts are the same—the same fears, the same longings, the same sins—troubles, problems, difficulties. Well, I tell you tonight Christ can help you. He can take the guilt away, and He can give you a joy, a peace and a new dimension of living, if you let Him. And I am going to ask you to listen very quietly and very prayerfully tonight. My message will be brief.

"Our Father and our God we pray that Thy Holy Spirit will speak to us and draw us to the Savior. For we ask it in His Name, Amen."

Now tonight I want you to turn with me to two passages of Scripture, [first] the last part of the 23rd Psalm that was read a few moments ago—the words of David as a Shepherd: ". . . and I will dwell in the house of the Lord for ever."

Now most of the creeds of the church teach life after death.

I want to talk tonight about the future life and the choice we must make now. Now this is an election day in New York City, and you do a strange thing here that I have not seen before. The election polls did not open until 3:00 and they closed at 10:00. I think I've got that right if I read the paper correctly. And usually it is sunrise to sunset down where I live, and we thought that tonight most of our people would be away voting. Apparently, the vote must have been light because I think most of you came here [instead]. The Garden is not only packed, but people are in the overflow auditorium in the beautiful Forum watching by closed-circuit television. Lee Fisher, one of my associates, told me a little story today about Al Smith when he was Governor of New York. He went to speak at Sing Sing. He had never spoken to inmates in a prison before, and he didn't know how to start. He was a little bit embarrassed and he started out by saying, "My fellow citizens," and then he thought to himself, "Well, they've lost their citizenship." So, he cleared his throat and started over and said, "My fellow convicts." And that didn't sound exactly right, so he backed up and started over again. He said, "Well, anyway, I'm glad to see so many of you here." Politics haven't changed very much.

But the second passage of Scripture has something to do about choice. It's from the Sermon on the Mount, and it's the word of our Lord in the 7th chapter, in which He says,

> "Enter ye in at the strait gate: for wide is the gate, and broad is the way, that leadeth to destruction, and many there be which go in thereat: Because strait is the gate, and narrow is the way, which leadeth unto life, and few . . ."

Notice our Lord said, "few there be that find it."

Jesus Christ taught that there are two roads of life. He taught there are two masters. You are either mastered by self or you are mastered by God, and He said you cannot serve both at the same time.

And He said that there are two destinies, heaven and hell.

Now Christ doesn't divide men between black and white, rich or poor, or educated and uneducated. He divides us into two classes—those who are on the broad road that leads to destruction and those on the narrow road that leads to eternal life. Which road are you on?

You know, we don't hear much preaching on the subject of the afterlife any more. How long has it been since you heard a sermon on hell or heaven?

You know, Winston Churchill said a few years ago, "The moral landslide in Great Britain can be traced to the fact that heaven and hell are no longer proclaimed throughout the land."

In an article some time ago, in an editorial, a major news magazine pleaded for more hell preaching.

You know somehow we have planned everything as though this life is the sum total of our existence. The Bible teaches that this life is only a preparation for eternity. Our lives will go on for millions and millions of years. And the choice we make now decides the type of life we are going to live in the future. Now we may not like that. I know that kind of talk today is not popular.

But Jesus said, "A man's life consisteth not in the abundance of the things he possesses." Jesus taught that "man shall not live by bread alone." But we are trying to prove that if we have a high standard of living and can somehow make it to a good retirement, we are all right. But the Bible teaches that we are a mind; we need education. We are a body; we need medicine, we need food, we need drink. But we are also a spirit, and the spirit of man is going to live forever. The "real you" that lives inside your body is destined for eternity. God has put eternity in our hearts, said King Solomon many centuries ago.

Now Jesus said, "There is a broad road of life, and it is the road that leads to destruction." Many of you are on that road tonight. The extremes of humanity are there—the sex glutton, the dope pusher, the murderer, the rapist, the mugger—but a lot of church people, too. Over on the next page in the same chapter in the Sermon on the Mount, there were people who thought they were going to get to heaven, and when they got there Jesus said, "I don't even know you."

"But, Lord, I cast out demons in Your name. Lord, I was an evangelist. Lord, I was this; I was that."

Jesus is going to say, "I didn't even know you."

This broad road that leads to destruction is a *deceptive road.* "There is a way that seemeth right unto a man, but the end thereof is a way of death."

You see, it seems right to live for self. It seems right to live a selfish life and get what you can get out of life, for your own pleasures, your own appetite. But the end is death, says the Bible. We need to spend some more time thinking about the future and what the future holds.

And then Jesus said, "Not only is it a deceptive road, but *it leads to hell."*

Now I know you don't hear much preaching about it, but everybody else is using the word "hell." We use it on television now; we use it in the movies. Many of our major motion pictures use the word "hell." There is a film showing right now called *Hell's Cat.* And the film industry has been using it for years. Remember *Hell's Angels, To Hell and Back, The City of Hell, Hell's Return, Hell Bent for Glory, Hell and High Water, The Wicked Go to Hell*—every kind of motion picture using the word "hell." And I hear the word "hell" used all the time—in elevators, in airplanes, and wherever I am traveling—in hotels. I never hear the word "heaven." Why doesn't a fellow say, "To heaven with you"? You never hear that!

You know, I asked a psychiatrist friend of mine about this some time ago, and you know, he had an interesting answer. He said, "Something deep inside of our subconscious makes us afraid that we may go to hell, and so we use the word 'hell' all the time."

Now the Bible has a lot to say about it. Jesus had a lot to say about it. He talked about it a number of times. In fact He talked about it more than anybody else. And He said that hell was not prepared for man. God never meant that man would ever go to hell. Hell was prepared for the devil and his angels, but man rebelled against God and followed the devil. And the existence of hell indicates that man has freedom of choice. You have a choice—the broad road, or the narrow road, and at the end of the broad road is a place or a condition that Jesus described as hell, and every one of us is on one road or the other, leading to those two destinies.

Now the Bible teaches there is a judgment. "God will bring every deed into judgment with every secret thing whether good or evil."

The Psalmist said, "God will judge the world with righteousness and the peoples by his truth."

And the Apostle Paul wrote to the Thessalonians and said, "When the Lord Jesus shall be revealed from heaven with his mighty angels in flaming fire taking vengeance on them that know not God, and that obey not the Gospel of our Lord Jesus Christ, who shall be punished with everlasting destruction from the presence of the Lord and from the glory of his power."

Now what does that mean? What do all of those passages mean? Whatever hell may be, and there are many mysteries, and I don't intend to solve them all—whatever hell may mean, it is separation from God.

Now there are *three words* that Jesus used constantly to describe it. One is called *"fire."* Now we know that God has a fire that burns and doesn't consume, like the burning bush that Moses experienced. We know that James said, "The tongue is set on fire of hell." We know that that wasn't combustion—that actual literal fire isn't down in your throat and in your tongue. It is symbolic language. And theologians through the centuries have argued and debated over what fire means.

The Bible said, "For our God is a consuming fire."

Jesus told the story about the rich man who went to hell and he asked that Lazarus may dip the tip of his finger in water and cool his tongue.

Could it be that the fire Jesus talked about is an eternal search for God that is never quenched? Is that what it means? That, indeed, would be hell. To be away from God forever, separated from His Presence.

Jesus said, "I am the water of life," and never to know the water of life would be hell.

And then He used another word. He used the word *"darkness."* Now the Bible says, "God is light." And Jesus said, "The children of the Kingdom shall be cast into outer darkness."

He said in Matthew 22, "Bind him hand and foot and take him away and cast him into outer darkness."

The Apostle Peter said, "God spared not the angels that sin but cast them into hell and delivered them into chains of darkness."

What does that mean? There again, the darkness is separation from God. God is light. Separation from light is darkness.

And then the *third word* that Jesus used is *death—the second death* in the Bible. God is life. Hell is death to the spirit, death to the soul, separation from God. "Death and hell were cast into the lake of fire." This is the second death, says the Scripture.

Now the Bible teaches that God does not take any delight in this. God loves you. He sent His Son to keep you from being lost. He sent the Holy Spirit to prompt you and convince you so that you would not be lost. And if you are lost, and if you go to hell, it will be by your own deliberate choice, because God never meant that you go there. It is your own decision. Now that is a terrifying thought, and it should disturb all of us.

You say, "Well, Billy, I'm not sure I can accept that." I know that according to the latest national poll, sixty-five percent of Americans believe there is a hell. Thirty-five percent say there is none. Well, let's just suppose there is a ten percent chance that Jesus was right. Just a ten percent chance. Let's say there is a ten percent chance that there is an afterlife and that there is a life of destruction and separation from God. I want to ask you, "Is it worth taking that chance?" If I went out to Kennedy Airport and they told me, "There is a ten percent chance this plane you are going to get on is not going to make it. We found out there is something wrong with the motor; but we are going anyway," I tell you, I'm going to wait for a later plane!

And yet how many of us take a chance on our lives, our eternal souls. You have a choice.

Yes, there is a broad road. Jesus said many are on that road. The majority of humanity is on that road. "Many there are which go in thereat."

But now let's come to the *narrow road*. Only a few are on that road. Jesus said, "Few there be that go in thereat." Jesus said, "The entrance to that road is a narrow gate." Notice, "a narrow gate." Now we don't like that word "narrow." We are living in an age of tolerance. We are living in an age when "every man is for himself. You can believe anything you want to believe."

You know, it's not true in most realms of life.

Suppose those astronauts who are going to go to the moon in July get on the wrong path and in the wrong orbit, and the people in Houston say, "Oh, that's all right. There are a number of roads leading up there. Keep going." They would keep going; never be back. No, they go by precise laws. All of nature is run by precise laws. We know at what temperature water boils. We know at what temperature water freezes. We know all of these scientific laws work in perfect precision. We are discovering the laws of nature.

Why would God be haphazard about spiritual and moral laws? They are just as precise, if not more so. Jesus said, "The road is narrow;

the gate is narrow." And He said, "If you're going to go on the narrow road that leads to eternal life, you'll have to go through the narrow gate." Now, what is that gate? Jesus said, "I am the way. I am the door. By me if any man enter in he shall be saved." Jesus said, "Don't try to come some other way. That's like a robber." He said, "There is only one door. There is only one gate. I am the way. I am the truth. I am the light. I am the way to heaven. You have to come by me."

Now you say, "Billy, I can't accept that. I want to go to heaven. I've got a feeling there is an after-life, and I've got a feeling that maybe there is a heaven, but I just don't want to come by the way of Jesus."

Well, I am sorry, but I cannot compromise at that point. I have to go by the rule book. I cannot bargain. I have no authority from the Bible to bargain with your soul. I have no authority to lower the standards. Jesus said, "I am the door. By me if any man enter in he shall be saved."

Jesus said, "Except your righteousness exceed the righteousness of the Scribes and Pharisees, ye shall in no wise enter into heaven."

The righteousness He requires is beyond works. You cannot work your way to heaven and you cannot buy your way to heaven. It is a gift of God because of what Christ did on the Cross.

"So by grace are ye saved, through faith, and that not of yourself. It is a gift of God, not of works lest any man should boast."

You say, "Well, Billy, what do you think heaven is going to be like?"

Well, there are some things we know. But there are mysteries known only to God. There is a mystery to hell; there is a mystery to heaven. I personally believe that the Bible teaches that heaven is a literal place. You say, "Do you think it is one of the stars or do you think it is one of the planets, or where do you think it is?"

I don't know. The Bible doesn't tell us. I can't even speculate. I do know that the scientists tell us there are a hundred billion stars in our galaxy. Now we don't measure distance in miles. We measure it in light years. With light traveling at the rate of 186,000 miles a second, eleven million miles to the minute, the sun is only eight light minutes from us. One light year is six trillion miles. Our galaxy, just our galaxy, is one hundred thousand light years in diameter. There are one thousand million galaxies, and in each galaxy it is estimated there are one hundred thousand million stars and planets. I believe that out there somewhere God can find someplace to put us in Heaven. I'm not worried where it is going to be. I know it is going to be where Jesus is.

Jesus said, "I go to prepare a place for you." And I read in the Bible that Abraham looked for a city whose builder and maker was God, and I know that the Scripture says that "Here we have no continuing city."

There is nothing permanent in this life. There is only one permanent thing in life, and that is impermanence. Nothing lasts. Every day you read the obituary column in *The New York Times* or one of the other newspapers. They died and left it all. One fellow left in his will—he was a Texas millionaire—that he wanted to be buried in a gold Cadillac. And as he was going down in the grave in his gold Cadillac, one of the grave diggers said, "Boy, that's really living."

Not only is heaven a place, but the Bible teaches that heaven is going to be Home. The Bible says that those of us who know Christ—the moment you accept Christ, you become a citizen of heaven. Now we are citizens of two worlds. I am a citizen of this earth, but I'm a citizen of another world. I am a citizen of heaven because of what Christ did on the Cross. And in this world with its secularism and its materialism and all of its hostile forces I'm living for God, I'm a stranger and a pilgrim. The Bible refers to that in several places. We are strangers and we are pilgrims. "They were strangers and pilgrims on the earth," says Hebrews 11. 1 Peter 2 says, "I beseech you as strangers and pilgrims." Our citizenship is in heaven. Now as good citizens of this earth we ought to vote. As good citizens we ought to be interested in our community. As good citizens we ought to help every good project in our community. As good citizens we ought to be interested in all the social problems that we face. As good citizens we ought to do what we can to make this a better place in which to live. But we are citizens of two worlds . . . this world and the future world. We are citizens of heaven. My citizenship is there. Now I've already lived most of my life here. I am fifty years old. I'm not likely to live to be a hundred. In fact, I will be very happy if I make it to sixty or sixty-five. I'll be happy if I just make it through this service.

We never know. Most of my life, though, by the law of averages, is gone. I'm on the sunset side now. I'm already a grandfather and very proud of it. And I'm glad that I'm a citizen of the future world. Now you think of all the emphasis we put on retirement centers and senior citizens, and all the benefits of retirement. You'd have an idea, wouldn't you, by reading the ads and hearing all the propaganda that the moment you retire you are in heaven. Well, I go to a lot of these places and I know a lot of older people, and the first year they are retired, they are full of energy. But then after a while they begin to settle down and they begin to realize that the next step is the casket. And the aches and the pains and the problems of old age—it is not quite what the ad said it would be unless Christ is in your heart. Because you see, you experience heaven the moment you receive Christ. Heaven comes to live in your heart, because Christ is heaven. He said, "The kingdom of heaven is within you."

And you know, in the future life those of us who know Christ are going to be like Jesus. How would you like to live in a whole world where everybody was like Jesus? Well, that's what it says . . .

"Beloved, now are we the sons of God, and it doth not yet appear what we shall be: but we know that, when he shall appear, we shall be like him; for we shall see him as he is" (1 John 3:2).

Now in heaven there is not going to be any racial discrimination. There is not going to be any poverty. There is not going to be any war. The policemen won't have anything to do. Oh, what a glorious world it is going to be—heaven! Everything that that word means, everything that you ever dreamed of—the Utopia that we dreamed of and thought that maybe we could build on this earth, and have failed, is going to be in heaven.

And then heaven is going to be a place of service. Now you're not just going to go there and sit under a palm tree and have a pretty girl waving a palm branch over you. Lots of people have the idea that that is what heaven is like. One of the great religions of the world teaches that. It says, "You're going to have a thousand girls to wait on you." No, that's not what the Bible says. It says we are going to work. I imagine that is going to be hard on some. But we are going to work, because it says in Revelation 22:3, "His servants shall serve him."

You know, I've got the feeling that we are going to be able to travel from planet to planet, and the thing that science is now beginning to catch a glimpse of we are going to see completely and fully. And all of these scientific things are going to be an actuality in heaven. And do you know how fast I think we are going to travel? This is my own private speculation. This is not in the Bible. Don't go out of here and quote it. You know the fastest way to travel somewhere? Thought. Think it. All right, I think I am on Mars. I am there. What is that program on television where the witch twitches her nose, and instantly she is in another place? She thinks it. Well, this is a little glimpse of what it may be like. We can think our way through the universe, serving God as ambassadors to other planets, because we are going to be the Sons of God. We are going to be something that people on other planets probably never dreamed they would be. We are going to be the actual Sons of the living God who runs this whole universe. Now that's incredible. It's almost impossible to believe, but this is what the Bible teaches. We are the Sons of God.

And heaven is going to be a place where all mysteries are going to be cleared up. Why did we have a certain amount of suffering down here? Why were loved ones taken at a particular moment when they were? We are going to understand something of the enormity of sin. We are going to understand the problem of evil. We are going to understand what the devil was all about, and why God allowed him to exist as long as he did. We'll know something of the price that Christ paid on the Cross that we cannot know now. When He said, "My God, My God, why hast thou forsaken me?"—none of us can understand what went on at that moment, but on that day, we will understand.

We will know why there is a hell. We will understand why God moves in a mysterious way His wonders to perform. You know there are ten thousand questions I want to ask the Lord as soon as I get there. I want to ask Him some of these questions that these college kids have asked me that I couldn't answer, because they are just mysteries in the Bible that we don't know all the answers to. We must take them by faith.

Now I have staked personally, and many of you have, my eternal future on the fact that this Bible is true and Jesus knew what He was talking about. I can't make you do it. I ask you to do it—that's a commitment that you as an individual have a right to reject. You can reject it. You don't have to believe it. That's your privilege; that's your freedom of choice. I myself also have the same freedom, and I accepted it, and it answers many questions in my life and gives me a peace, a security, and a serenity.

You say, "Billy, you're dreaming."

Someone wrote a hymn. I think it was Gypsy Smith. He said, "If I am dreaming, let me dream on, my sins are gone." It is a wonderful dream.

And you know heaven is going to be the place of the final coronation of the King of Kings. What a day that is going to be! The Bible says, "There will be written on Him, King of Kings, and Lord of Lords." You and I are going to be present at the coronation of Jesus Christ when He is crowned King of the Universe. I am looking forward to that day. My seat is reserved. It was bought not with my silver and gold. It was bought with the blood of Christ on the Cross. What a time that is going to be!

You know when Handel—George Frederick Handel—wrote *The Messiah* he was in poor health and poor financial condition. His right arm and his right side were almost useless by paralysis, and all of a sudden the "Hallelujah Chorus" came to him. When it was first sung in 1743, I believe it was at Covent Garden in London. When they came to that chorus—"The Lord Omnipotent reigneth, King of Kings and Lord of Lords," the King of Great Britain, the most powerful country in the world at that time, rose to his feet and so did that vast audience—to acknowledge the "King of Kings and Lord of Lords."

Listen, we Christians don't have to go around with our shoulders bent and discouraged and despondent. We are on our way to heaven. This is not our home, and this is not our world. We are going to help all we can, but we are on our way to a better world.

And you know, when you get that perspective, you can be a better servant of the Lord right here. And you know, the Bible, by warnings and threats and invitations and commands, urges people to make that decision. Make that decision now and receive Christ as your Lord and your Savior.

You know *The Times* told this morning about Neil Armstrong who is scheduled to plant his foot on the moon at 2:17 A.M., Eastern Daylight Time, on July 21. And in yesterday's paper we saw pictures of Neil Armstrong practicing the landing of his craft so that he would be ready.

Now, if you intend to set your feet in heaven, you are going to have to do a little practicing down here. You've got to rehearse by planting your feet on the Rock of Ages, Jesus Christ.

Do you know Him as your Savior? Is your sin forgiven?

We had an election here as we have already heard, and I remember a story that when Mayor La Guardia was mayor of this city or when he was a judge, I guess, a man was brought before him during the depression. He had stolen a loaf of bread to feed his family. And the mayor had to fine him $50. Then the mayor looked at the audience in the courtroom and said, "This court is not only one of justice, it is one of mercy." And then he fined everyone in the courtroom $1 for allowing conditions to exist where a man had to steal to provide for his family. And he gave the money to the man and said, "Pay your fine and go your way and sin no more," and that is exactly what Jesus did. He paid the fine for us. He took the hell and the judgment and the destruction and the end of that broad road for us. Now God says, "I love you. I forgive you. Go and sin no more."

You start through that narrow gate and live on the narrow road, and you are going to be in heaven.

Which road are you on tonight? Which direction are you traveling? Are you going toward destruction or are you going toward Life? Which way? You can make the choice tonight. You can take the first step. Now it's costly. It's not easy to go through that narrow gate, and it's not easy to follow Christ. But it is a glorious and wonderful experience even here on this earth—the joy, the peace, the security, the sense of forgiveness, that He gives you—all this and heaven, too—by a choice that you make.

You say, "Well, why did God make it so simple?" He made it simple so everybody could enter—the blind man, the poor man, the deaf man—the black, the white, the yellow, the red—anybody can believe. Anybody can receive. Anybody can come by faith. He said, "Whosoever will, let him come." The offer is open to everyone here tonight. Will you come?

Notes

CHAPTER ONE: *The Priority of Evangelism*

1. For an exposition of this point, cf. Robert E. Coleman, *"Nothing to Do but Save Souls": John Wesley's Charge to His Preachers* (Grand Rapids, MI: Francis Asbury Press [Zondervan], 1990).
2. For a provocative discussion of these issues, cf. David J. Hesselgrave, "Holes in 'Holistic Mission,'" in *Trinity World Forum*, Spring 1990, pp. 1-6.
3. J. I. Packer, *Evangelism and the Sovereignty of God* (Downers Grove, IL: InterVarsity Press, 1961), pp. 37, 38.
4. *Ibid.*, p. 39.
5. John R. W. Stott, *The Lausanne Conference: An Exposition and Commentary* (Minneapolis: World Wide Publications, 1975), p. 20.
6. Richard Stoll Armstrong, *The Pastor as Evangelist* (Philadelphia: Westminster, 1984), pp. 21-26.
7. E. W. Hengstenberg, *Christology of the Old Testament* (Grand Rapids, MI: Kregel, 1872, 1956), pp. 14-29.
8. Erich Sauer, *The Dawn of World Redemption* (London: Paternoster, 1951).
9. George Smeaton, *The Doctrine of the Atonement as Taught by Christ Himself* (Grand Rapids, MI: Zondervan, 1871, 1953), pp. 190-207.
10. O. Hallesby, *Infant Baptism and Adult Conversion* (Minneapolis: Augsburg, 1924), pp. 105-108.
11. C. Jack Eichhorst, "Is 'Decision Theology' a Real Lutheran Problem?," in *Advance*, Winter 1989, p. 2.
12. R. B. Kuiper, *God-centered Evangelism* (Grand Rapids, MI: Baker, 1961).
13. B. B. Warfield, *The Plan of Salvation* (Grand Rapids, MI: Eerdmans, 1942), p. 33ff.; Lewis Sperry Chafer, *Salvation* (Findlay, OH: Dunham, 1917), p. 1ff.
14. John W. Alexander, "What Is Evangelism?," in Paul E. Little, *Guide to Evangelism* (Downers Grove, IL: InterVarsity Press, 1977), pp. 15, 16.

CHAPTER TWO: *The Theology of Conversion*

1. Michael Mott, *The Seven Mountains of Thomas Merton* (Boston: Houghton-Mifflin, 1990), p. 111.
2. Frederick Dale Bruner, *The Theology of the Holy Spirit* (Grand Rapids, MI: Eerdmans, 1970), p. 234.
3. William A. Dyrness, *How Does America Hear the Gospel?* (Grand Rapids, MI: Eerdmans, 1989), p. 5.
4. Frederick Buechner, *Wishful Thinking: A Theological ABC* (San Francisco: Harper, 1973), p. 38.
5. Newell Dwight Hillis, "'The Rediscovery of Sin,'" in Paul S. Rees, *Stir up the Gift* (Grand Rapids, MI: Zondervan, 1952), p. 65.
6. D. B. Davies, in Carl F. H. Henry, *Remaking the Modern Mind* (Grand Rapids, MI: Eerdmans, 1946), pp. 55-76.
7. C. E. M. Joad, *The Recovery of Belief* (London: Faber and Faber, 1952), p. 64ff.

8. Gustaf Wingren, *Theology in Conflict* (Philadelphia: Muhlenherg, 1958), p. 25.

9. Wick Broomall, "'Conversion,'" in *Baker's Dictionary of Theology* (Grand Rapids, MI: Baker, 1960), p. 139.

10. *Ibid.* See also J. I. Packer, *Evangelism and the Sovereignty of God* (Downers Grove, IL: InterVarsity Press, 1961), p. 13ff. for a superb handling of the evangelical concurrence on this primary concern.

11. *Vine's Expository Dictionary* (Westwood, NJ: Revell, 1940), pp. 230, 231.

12. William Barclay, *Turning to God* (Philadelphia: Westminster, 1964), p. 12.

13. *Ibid.*, p. 13.

14. A. D. Nock, *Conversion: The Old and the New in Religion from Alexander the Great to Augustine of Hippo* (New York: Oxford, 1933). Note also J. Gresham Machen, *The Origin of Paul's Religion* (Grand Rapids, MI: Eerdmans, 1925, The Sprunt Lectures), still the best written on this theme. Note also L. R. Rambo, "Conversion," in *Encyclopedia of Religion*, Vol. 4 (New York: Macmillan, 1987), pp. 73-79 and bibliography. Also, "Current Research in Religious Conversion," *Religious Studies Review*, 8:1982, pp. 148-159.

15. David F. Wells, *Turning to God: Biblical Conversion in the Modern World* (Grand Rapids, MI: Baker, 1989), p. 25.

16. *Ibid.*, p. 49ff. For a masterful analysis, cf. Timothy J. Ralston, "The Theological Significance of Paul's Conversion," in *Bibliotheca Sacra*, April-June 1990, p. 198ff. The very strong work of Seyoon Kim, *The Origin of Paul's Religion* (Grand Rapids, MI: Eerdmans, 1981) should be consulted. Reference will be made subsequently to Alan F. Segal's *Paul the Convert*.

17. Stanley Jones, *Conversion* (New York: Abingdon, 1959), p. 15.

18. *Ibid.*, p. 32.

19. Peter Toon, *Born Again: A Biblical and Theological Study* (Grand Rapids, MI: Baker, 1987).

20. Helmut Burkhardt, "The Experience of Conversion," in I. Howard Marshall, ed., *Christian Experience in Theology and Life* (Edinburgh: Rutherford House Books, 1988), p. 139ff.

21. Hugh T. Kerr and John M. Mulder, eds., *Conversions* (Grand Rapids, MI: Eerdmans, 1983). Also the older classic: Harold Begbie, *Twice-born Men: A Clinic in Regeneration* (New York: Revell, 1909).

22. John R. W. Stott, *The Cross of Christ* (Downers Grove, IL: InterVarsity Press, 1986).

23. H. D. McDonald, *The Atonement of the Death of Christ* (Grand Rapids, MI: Baker, 1985), pp. 299-302.

24. Axel Anderson, *The Christian Doctrine of the Atonement According to P. P. Waldenstrom* (Chicago: Covenant Press, 1937), pp. 90, 91.

25. Charles G. Finney, *Lectures on Systematic Theology* (Grand Rapids, MI: Eerdmans, 1878).

26. B. B. Warfield, *Biblical and Theological Studies* (Philadelphia: Presbyterian and Reformed, 1988), pp. 402, 403.

27. John D. Hannah, "The Meaning of Saving Faith: Luther's Interpretation of Romans 3:28," in *Bibliotheca Sacra*, October-December 1983, p. 322ff.

28. G. C. Berkouwer, *The Triumph of Grace in the Theology of Karl Barth* (Grand Rapids, MI: Eerdmans, 1956), pp. 262-296.

29. J. I. Packer, "'The Way of Salvation: The Problems of Universalism,'" in *Bibliotheca Sacra*, January-March 1973, p. 3ff.; also Roger Nicole, "Universalism: Will Everyone be Saved?," in *Christianity Today*, March 20, 1987, pp. 31-39.

30. Fredrick Holmgren, *The God Who Cares: A Christian Looks at Judaism* (Atlanta: John Knox, 1979), p. 130ff. (in which the author lurches toward the universalism of Hans Kung).
31. Jim Wallis, *The Call to Conversion* (San Francisco: Harper, 1981).
32. Peter Beyerhaus, *Missions: Which Way?* (Grand Rapids, MI: Zondervan, 1971), p. 101.
33. Robert Schuller, *Self Esteem: The New Reformation* (Waco, TX: Word, 1982), p. 69.
34. Michael Novak, *Will It Liberate?* (New York: Paulist Press, 1986). Cf. also J. Ronald Blue, "Major Flaws in Liberation Theology," in *Bibliotheca Sacra*, January-March 1990.
35. Edmund P. Clowney, "'Kingdom Evangelism," in Roger S. Greenway, ed., *The Pastor-Evangelist* (Phillipsburg, NJ: Presbyterian and Reformed, 1987), p. 15ff.
36. William J. Abraham, *The Logic of Evangelism* (Grand Rapids, MI: Eerdmans, 1989).
37. *Ibid.*, p. 3.
38. Arthur P. Johnston, "Trends in Theology: Evangelists Beware!," in *The Calling of an Evangelist*, Second International Conference for Itinerant Evangelists, Amsterdam (Minneapolis: World Wide Publications, 1987), pp. 193-196.

CHAPTER THREE: *The Psychology of Conversion*

1. Frederick Buechner, *The Sacred Journey* (San Francisco: Harper, 1982), p. 111.
2. Alzina Stone Dale, *T. S. Eliot* (Wheaton, IL: Harold Shaw, 1988), p. 102.
3. William James, *Varieties of Religious Experience* (New York: Modern Library, 1902), p. 186.
4. *Ibid.*, p. 224.
5. Henry Newton Malony, "Conversion: The Sociodynamics of Change," in *Theology, News and Notes*, June 1986, p. 18.
6. Svere Norborg, *Varieties of Christian Experience* (Minneapolis: Augsburg, 1937).
7. Stephen Neil, "Conversion," in *Scottish Journal of Theology*, 3 (1950), pp. 352, 353.
8. Bernard L. Ramm, *Offense to Reason: A Theology of Sin* (San Francisco: Harper, 1985), p. 37.
9. William A. Dyrness, *How Does America Hear the Gospel?* (Grand Rapids, MI: Eerdmans, 1989), p. 146.
10. *A Christian Approach to Psychological Medicine* (London: IVF, n.d.), p. 26.
11. Karl Menninger, *Whatever Became of Sin?* (New York: Hawthorn, 1973), p. 228.
12. M. Scott Peck, *People of the Lie* (New York: Simon and Schuster, 1983). See also Richard Lovelace, *Dynamics of Spiritual Life* (Downers Grove, IL: InterVarsity Press, 1979), p. 81ff. for an excellent treatment on the need for facing sin.
13. Robert Johnston, "Acculturation or Inculturation?," in *The Covenant Quarterly*, May/August 1988, pp. 209, 210.
14. Paul Tournier, *Guilt and Grace* (New York: Harper, 1962); Lewis Joseph Sherrill, *Guilt and Redemption* (Richmond, VA: John Knox, 1945); Lewis Joseph Sherrill, *The Struggle of the Soul* (New York: Macmillan, 1963); Bruce Narramore and Bill Counts, *Guilt and Freedom* (Santa Ana, CA: Vision House, 1974).
15. J. I. Packer, *A Quest for Godliness* (Wheaton, IL: Crossway, 1990), p. 164.
16. J. I. Packer, *Evangelism and the Sovereignty of God* (Downers Grove, IL: InterVarsity Press, 1961), p. 111.

17. Martyn Lloyd-Jones, *Conversions: Psychological and Spiritual* (London: IVF, 1959); reprinted Martyn Lloyd-Jones, *Knowing the Times* (Edinburgh: Banner of Truth, 1989), pp. 61-89.
18. *Ibid.*, p. 39.
19. R. T. Kendall, *Stand Up and Be Counted* (Grand Rapids, MI: Zondervan, 1985), pp. 87, 88.
20. Gordon Allport, *The Individual and His Religion* (New York: Macmillan, 1950), p. 34.
21. E. D. Starbuck, *The Psychology of Religion* (New York: Scribner's, 1899).
22. George Albert Coe, *The Religion of a Mature Mind* (New York: Fleming H. Revell, 1902).
23. Dale, *T. S. Eliot*, pp. 89, 90.
24. Gordon H. Clark, *Today's Evangelism: Counterfeit or Genuine* (Jefferson, MD: Trinity Foundation, 1990).
25. Carl G. Jung, *Psychology and Religion* (New Haven, CT: Yale, 1938), p. 113.
26. *A Christian Approach to Psychological Medicine*, pp. 35, 36.
27. Andrew Murray, *The Children for Christ* (New York: Fleming H. Revell, n.d.).
28. Samuel Southard, "The Evangelism of Children," in *Evangelism and Pastoral Psychology* (Great Neck, NY: Pastoral Psychology Press, 1956).
29. James Y. Fowler, *Stages of Faith* (San Francisco: Harper, 1981).
30. Robert Coles, *The Spiritual Life of Children* (Boston: Houghton-Mifflin, 1990).
31. David Martin, *Tongues of Fire: The Explosion of Protestantism in Latin America* (London: Basil Blackwell, 1990).
32. C. Eric Lincoln and Lawrence H. Mamiya, *The Black Church in the African American Experience* (Durham, SC: Duke University Press, 1990). Cf. David J. Hesselgrave, *Cross-cultural Communication* (Grand Rapids, MI: Zondervan, 1991 [second edition]).
33. Charles Hodge, quoted in David Wells, "The Shaping of the 19th-Century Debate Over the Atonement," *Bibliotheca Sacra*, July-September 1987, p. 249.

CHAPTER FOUR: *The Ancestry of Evangelistic Preaching*

1. William J. Abraham, *The Logic of Evangelism* (Grand Rapids, MI: Eerdmans, 1989), p. 44.
2. Vernon L. Stanfield, *Effective Evangelistic Preaching* (Grand Rapids, MI: Baker, 1965).
3. Ben Campbell Johnson, *Rethinking Evangelism: A Theological Approach* (Philadelphia:Westminster, 1988).
4. David L. Larsen, *The Anatomy of Preaching* (Grand Rapids: Baker, 1989), pp. 12-15.
5. Henry Alford, *The New Testament* (Chicago: Moody Press, n.d.), p. 404.
6. R. K. Harrison, "The Gospel in Old Testament Preaching," in *Bibliotheca Sacra*, October-December 1989, pp. 363-372. This is the basis for the superb work by Faris D. Whitesell, *Evangelistic Preaching and the Old Testament* (Chicago: Moody Press, 1947).
7. H. H. Rowley, *The Biblical Doctrine of Election* (London: Lutterworth, 1950).
8. Scot McKnight, *A Light Among the Gentiles* (Philadelphia: Fortress, 1991).
9. Ozora S. Davis, *Evangelistic Preaching* (New York: Fleming H. Revell, 1921).
10. J. Arthur Baird, *Audience Criticism and the Historical Jesus* (Philadelphia: Westminster, 1969).
11. Raymond Bailey, *Jesus the Preacher* (Nashville: Broadman, 1990).

12. W. B. Riley, *Seven New Testament Converts* (Grand Rapids, MI: Eerdmans, 1940); G. H. Gerberding, *New Testament Conversions* (Philadelphia: Lutheran Publication Society, 1889).

13. David Bahr, *Evangelism in America* (New York: Paulist Press, 1977), p. 171.

14. John Wimber, *Power Evangelism* (San Francisco: Harper and Row, 1986).

15. William L. Banks, *In Search of the Great Commission* (Chicago: Moody Press, 1991). Cf. also the older but very solid David H. Adeney, *The Unchanging Commission* (Chicago: Moody Press, 1955).

16. Michael Green, *Evangelism in the Early Church* (Grand Rapids, MI: Eerdmans, 1970), pp. 29-47. Cf. also John R. W. Stott, *The Spirit, the Church and the World* (Downers Grove, IL: InterVarsity Press, 1990).

17. Wayne A. Meeks, *The First Urban Christians: The Social World of the Apostle Paul* (New Haven, CT: Yale University Press, 1983); E. M. Blaiklock, *The Christian in Pagan Society* (Cambridge, England: Tyndale, 1951).

18. Stanley C. Brown, *Evangelism in the Early Church* (Grand Rapids: Eerdmans, 1963); C. E. Autrey, *Evangelism in the Acts* (Grand Rapids, MI: Zondervan, 1964).

19. Robert C. Worley, *Preaching and Teaching in the Earliest Church* (San Francisco: Harper and Row, 1936); Robert Mounce, *The Essential Nature of New Testament Preaching* (Grand Rapids, MI: Eerdmans, 1960); Jesse B. Weatherspoon, *Sent Forth to Preach: Studies in Apostolic Preaching* (New York: Harper and Row, 1954).

20. Green, *Evangelism in the Early Church*, p. 194. For a most helpful treatment of conversion preaching in Acts, cf. William Barclay, *Turning to God* (Philadelphia: Westminster, 1964), pp. 31-81.

21. N. B. Stonehouse, *The Areopagus Address* (Cambridge, England: Tyndale, 1949).

22. Rudolf Stier, *The Words of the Apostles* (Edinburgh: T. & T. Clark, 1899); Roland Allen, *Missionary Methods: St. Paul's or Ours?* (Chicago: Moody Press, 1959), pp. 82-101.

23. Green, *Evangelism in the Early Church*, p. 117.

24. Alan F. Segal, *Paul the Convert* (New Haven, CT: Yale University Press, 1990).

25. *Ibid.*, p. 14.

26. *Ibid.*, p. 73.

27. *Ibid.*, p. 113. Cf. also John Eadie, *Paul the Preacher* (London: Richard Griffin, 1859); O. Moe, *The Apostle Paul* (Grand Rapids, MI: Baker, 1950); C. H. Dodd, *The Meaning of Paul for Today* (London: Fontana Books, 1920).

28. As argued by Thomas D. Bernard, *The Progress of Doctrine in the New Testament* (Grand Rapids, MI: Eerdmans, 1949), p. 151ff.

29. Meeks, *The First Urban Christians*, pp. 74-110.

30. F. F. Bruce, *The Spreading Flame* (Grand Rapids, MI: Eerdmans, 1958); also, *The Defense of the Gospel in the New Testament* (Grand Rapids, MI: Eerdmans, 1959).

31. F. F. Bruce, *Paul and His Converts* (Downers Grove, IL: InterVarsity Press, 1985); Abraham Malherbe, *Paul and the Thessalonians* (Philadelphia: Fortress, 1987).

CHAPTER FIVE: *The Continuity of Evangelistic Preaching*

1. Adolph Saphir, *Epistle to the Hebrews* (Grand Rapids, MI: Kregel, 1983), p. 41.

2. D. Martyn Lloyd-Jones, *Knowing the Times* (Edinburgh: Banner of Truth, 1989), p. 5.

3. For a classic treatment, see A. Schlatter, *The Church in the New Testament Period* (London: SPCK, 1955).

4. Robert D. Sider, *The Gospel and Its Proclamations* (Wilmington, DE: Michael Glazier, n.d.), p. 14.

5. Edward Gibbon, *The Decline and Fall of the Roman Empire* (Chicago: Great Books of the Western World, 1952), pp. 179-185.

6. John Broadus, *History of Preaching* (New York: Sheldon Co., 1876), p. 47.

7. Michael Green, *Evangelism in the Early Church* (Grand Rapids, MI: Eerdmans, 1970), p. 203.

8. M. A. Smith, *From Christ to Constantine* (London: IV Press, 1971), pp. 39, 40.

9. Green, *Evangelism in the Early Church*, p. 155.

10. *Ibid.*, p. 160.

11. Ramsay MacMullen, *Christianizing the Roman Empire* (New Haven, CT: Yale University Press, 1984), pp. 59-57.

12. Adolf Harnack, *The Mission and Expansion of Christianity* (New York: Harper, 1961), p. 94.

13. Eusebius, *Ecclesiastical History*, 5.10.2; 3.37.2. Also of great interest is his two-volume work, *Preparation for the Gospel*.

14. Carl A. Voltz, *Pastoral Life and Practice in the Early Church* (Minneapolis: Augsburg, 1990); Thomas K. Carroll, *Preaching the Word: Message of the Fathers of the Church* (Wilmington, DE: Michael Glazier, 1984); Philip L. Culbertson and Arthur Bradford Shippee, *The Pastor: Readings from the Patristic Period* (Minneapolis: Fortress, 1990).

15. T. F. Torrance, *The Doctrine of Grace in the Apostolic Fathers* (Grand Rapids, MI: Eerdmans, 1948), p. 138.

16. Kenneth Scott Latourette, *A History of the Expansion of Christianity: The First Five Centuries* (Grand Rapids, MI: Zondervan, 1937).

17. Thomas Carlyle, "Signs of the Times," in *Critical and Miscellaneous Essays*, in V. Raymond Edman, *The Light in Dark Ages* (Wheaton, IL: Van Kampen, 1949), p. 40.

18. William R. Cannon, *History of Christianity in the Middle Ages* (New York: Abingdon, 1960).

19. G. S. M. Walker, *The Growing Storm* (Grand Rapids, MI: Eerdmans, 1961), p. 16.

20. Edman, *The Light in Dark Ages*, pp. 142-163.

21. Bernard of Clairvaux, *Sermons on Conversion* (Kalamazoo, MI: Cistercian Publications, 1981).

22. Jean Lecercq, Introduction, *Sancti Bernardi Opera, IV* (Rome: n.p., 1966), p. 61.

23. Lloyd Perry and John Strubhar, *Evangelistic Preaching* (Chicago: Moody Press, 1979), p. 44.

24. Walker, *The Growing Storm*, p. 183. Cf. also Robert Payne, *Fathers of the Western Church* (New York: Viking, 1951); Duane W. H. Arnold and C. George Fry, *Francis: A Call to Conversion* (Grand Rapids, MI: Zondervan, 1988).

25. Perry and Strubhar, *Evangelistic Preaching*, pp. 25-53.

26. Lloyd-Jones, *Knowing the Times*, p. 102.

27. Philip S. Watson, *Let God Be God: An Interpretation of the Theology of Martin Luther* (Philadelphia: Fortress, 1947), p. 3.

28. *Ibid.*, p. 34.

29. Roland H. Bainton, *Here I Stand: A Life of Martin Luther* (New York: Mentor, 1950), p. 45ff.

30. Martin Luther, *A Treatise on Christian Liberty*, in *Three Treatises* (Philadelphia: Muhlenberg, 1947), p. 255.
31. Fred W. Meuser, *Luther the Preacher* (Minneapolis: Augsburg, 1983); Bainton, *Here I Stand*, p. 272ff.
32. Walter Conn, *Christian Conversion: A Developmental Interpretation of Autonomy and Surrender* (New York: Paulist Press, 1986), p. 6.
33. Lloyd-Jones, *Knowing the Times*, p. 103.
34. Perry and Strubhar, *Evangelistic Preaching*, p. 52.
35. Jerald C. Brauer, "Conversion: From Puritanism to Revivalism," in *Journal of Religion*, 1958, p. 232.
36. J. I. Packer, *A Quest for Godliness: The Puritan Vision of the Christian Life* (Wheaton, IL: Crossway Books, 1990), p. 74.
37. *Ibid.*, p. 166.
38. A. Skevington Wood, *The Inextinguishable Blaze* (Grand Rapids, MI: Eerdmans, 1960), pp. 23-36.
39. Iain H. Murray, *Jonathan Edwards* (Edinburgh: Banner of Truth, 1987); John H. Gerstner, *Steps to Salvation: The Evangelistic Message of Jonathan Edwards* (Philadelphia: Westminster, 1960); Harold Simonson, *Jonathan Edwards: Theologian of the Heart* (Grand Rapids, MI: Eerdmans, 1974).
40. Peter Y. DeJong, *The Covenant Idea in New England Theology* (Grand Rapids, MI: Eerdmans, 1945).
41. Timothy L. Smith, *Whitefield and Wesley on the New Birth* (Grand Rapids, MI: Zondervan, 1986).
42. Milton J. Coalter, Jr., *Gilbert Tennent: Son of Thunder* (New York: Greenwood, 1986).
43. Christmas Evans, *Sermons and Memoirs of Christmas Evans* (Grand Rapids, MI: Kregel, 1986).
44. Lewis A. Drummond, *The Life and Ministry of Charles G. Finney* (Minneapolis: Bethany Press, 1983); Keith J. Hardman, *Charles Grandison Finney* (Syracuse, NY: Syracuse University Press, 1987).
45. William G. McLoughlin, *Modern Revivalism* (New York: Ronald Press, 1959).
46. J. Edwin Orr, *The Second Evangelical Awakening* (London: Marshall, Morgan and Scott, 1949).
47. Arnold Dallimore, *Spurgeon* (Chicago: Moody, 1984).
48. Stuart Henry, *Unvanquished Puritan: A Portrait of Lyman Beecher* (Grand Rapids, MI: Eerdmans, 1973); Charles Cunningham, *Timothy Dwight: 1752-1817* (New York: Macmillan, 1942).
49. Lyle Dorsett, *Billy Sunday and the Redemption of Urban America* (Grand Rapids, MI: Eerdmans, 1991); Roger Martin, *R. A. Torrey: Apostle of Certainty* (Murfreesboro, TN: Sword of the Lord, 1976); Ford C. Ottman, *J. Wilbur Chapman* (New York: Doubleday, 1920); Ray E. Garrett, *William E. Biederwolf* (Grand Rapids, MI: Zondervan, 1948).

CHAPTER SIX: *The Sociology of Evangelistic Preaching*

1. Charles Jardine, *The Classic Guide to Fly-fishing for Trout* (New York: Random House, 1991), reviewed in *National Review*, June 10, 1991.
2. For discussion of this issue, cf. David L. Larsen, *The Anatomy of Preaching* (Grand Rapids, MI: Baker, 1989), p. 35ff.
3. Frank Feather, *G Forces: The 35 Global Forces Restructuring Our Future* (New York: William Morrow, 1989).

4. *The Covenant Companion,* June 1991, p. 41.
5. *Time* magazine, April 8, 1991.
6. Woody West, "Ground Shifts Under the West," in *Insight,* November 26, 1990, p. 64.
7. Stanley J. Samartha, "A Revised Christology for a Religiously Plural World," in *Christian Ministry,* May-June 1991, p. 15ff. Also cf. John Macquarrie, *Jesus Christ in Modern Thought* (London: Trinity Press, 1990). The latter is a pathetic effort to do Christology from below.
8. Leslie Bennetts, "Marianne's Faithful," in *Vanity Fair,* June 1991, p. 131ff.
9. *Ibid.,* p. 134.
10. *National and International Religion Report,* May 20, 1991.
11. Garry Wills, *Under God: Religion and American Politics* (New York: Simon and Schuster, 1990). Here is a thoughtful treatment of secularization in America which sees evangelical Protestantism as America's chief cultural foundation.
12. Typical of these is Leith Anderson, *Dying for Change* (Minneapolis: Bethany, 1990).
13. Robert W. Glasgow, *In the Twilight of Authority: The Obsessive Concern with Self* (an interview with Robert Nisbet), in *Psychology Today,* December 1973.
14. James Davison Hunter, *American Evangelicalism: Conservative Religion and the Quandary of Modernity* (New Brunswick, NJ: Rutgers, 1983).
15. David Riesman, in *Man and Mind: A Christian Theory of Personality* (Hillsdale, MI: Hillsdale College Press, 1987).
16. James Patterson and Peter Kim, *The Day America Told the Truth* (New York: Prentice Hall, 1991).
17. Samuel R. Schutz, "Ministry Groups: A Means for Personalizing Evangelistic Witness," in *Covenant Quarterly,* May 1989, p. 42ff.
18. J. A. Davidson, *The Prairie Overcomer,* November 1977, p. 628.
19. H. Richard Niebuhr, *Christ and Culture* (New York: Harper, 1951).
20 Kenneth A. Myers, *All God's Children and Blue Suede Shoes: Christians and Popular Culture* (Wheaton, IL: Crossway, 1990).
21. Nathan O. Hatch, *The Democratization of American Christianity* (New Haven, CT: Yale University Press, 1989).
22. J. Gresham Machen, *Christianity and Liberalism* (New York: Macmillan, 1923).
23. Altina L. Waller, *Reverend Beecher and Mrs. Tilton* (Amherst, MA: University of Massachusetts Press, 1982, p. 27.
24. *Ibid.,* p. 70.
25. Henry Alford, *The New Testament* (Chicago: Moody Press, n.d.), p. 932.
26. Maurice D. Irwin, *Alliance Witness,* June 5, 1991, p. 31.
27. Bruce Buursma, *Chicago Tribune,* May 3, 1986, Section I, p. 6.
28. "USA Weekend," *Chicago Tribune,* December 19-21, 1986, p. 4ff.
29. Udo Middelmann, *Pro-Existence* (Downers Grove, IL: InterVarsity Press, 1974), p. 81.
30. Isaiah Berlin, *The Crooked Timber of Humanity: Chapters in the History of Ideas* (New York: Knopf, 1990).

CHAPTER SEVEN: *The Technology of the Evangelistic Sermon*

1. Quoted in *A Passion for Preaching: Essays in Honor of Stephen F. Olford* (Nashville: Thomas Nelson, 1989), p. 33.
2. *Ibid.,* p. 34.

3. Earl V. Comfort, "Is the Pulpit a Factor in Church Growth?," in *Bibliotheca Sacra*, January-March 1983, p. 66.
4. *Ibid.*, p. 66ff.
5. David L. Larsen, *The Anatomy of Preaching* (Grand Rapids: Baker, 1989), pp. 157-169.
6. Martin P. Marty, *Context*, June 15, 1991, p. 4.
7. *Ibid.*, July 1, 1990, p. 4.
8. Richard Koenig, "A Lutheran Debate on Theological Integrity," in *The Christian Century*, June 27-July 4, 1990, p. 623.
9. Larsen, *The Anatomy of Preaching*, "When Does Persuasion Become Manipulation?," pp. 131-143.
10. James D. Berkley, ed., *Preaching to Convince* (Waco, TX: Word, 1986).
11. Jack Kuhatschck, *Taking the Guesswork out of Applying the Bible* (Downers Grove, IL: InterVarsity Press, 1990). Cf. also Elliott E. Johnson, *Expository Hermeneutics* (Grand Rapids, MI: Zondervan, 1990), pp. 215-306.
12. *Evangelistic Preaching: A Self-study Course* (book and cassettes) (Minneapolis: Grason, 1990).
13. James M. Wall, *The Christian Century*, May 1, 1991, p. 475.
14. "The Storytelling Renaissance," *Utne Reader*, March/April 1991, p. 46ff.
15. Robert Coles, *The Call of Stories* (Boston: Houghton-Mifflin, 1989).
16. S. Hauerwas and L. G. Jones, *Why Narrative? Readings in Narrative Theology* (Grand Rapids, MI: Eerdmans, 1989), p. 295.
17. Gabriel Fackre, *The Christian Story* (Grand Rapids, MI: Eerdmans, 1978, 1984). Volumes I and II are published as of this date.
18. Robert Alter, *The Art of Biblical Narrative* (New York: Basic Books, 1981).
19. Frank Kermode, *The Genesis of Secrecy: On the Interpretation of Narrative* (Cambridge, MA: Harvard University Press, 1979).
20. Eugene L. Lowry, *The Homiletic Plot* (Richmond, VA: John Knox, 1980).
21. William Barclay, *Fishers of Men* (Philadelphia: Westminster, 1966), p. 41.
22. Calvin Miller, "Zeal vs Art: The Preacher's Dilemma," *Leadership*, Spring 1984, p. 36ff.
23. *Ibid.*, p. 43.
24. Thomas H. Troeger, *Imagining a Sermon* (Nashville: Abingdon, 1990).
25. Denise Shekerjian, *Uncommon Genius: How Great Ideas Are Born* (New York: Viking, 1990).

CHAPTER EIGHT: *The Controversy over the Evangelistic Appeal*

1. Bishop John Shelby Spong, "Evangelism When Certainty Is an Illusion," *Christian Century*, January 6-13, 1982, pp. 11-16.
2. John F. MacArthur, Jr., *The Gospel According to Jesus* (Grand Rapids, MI: Zondervan, 1988).
3. Gary R. Collins, *Beyond Easy Believism* (Waco, TX: Word, 1982).
4. The North American church is obviously suffering from a vicious pendulum swing from legalism to a therapeutic fixation on "feeling good" rather than "finding God." Cf. "The Curse of Self-esteem: What's Wrong with the Feel-good Movement," *Newseek*, February 17, 1992, p. 46ff.
5. MacArthur, *The Gospel According to Jesus*, p. 15.
6. *Ibid.*, p. 56.
7. *Ibid.*, p. 79.
8. *Ibid.*, p. 196.

9. Quoted in Thomas G. Lewellen, "Has Lordship Salvation Been Taught Throughout Church History?," in *Bibliotheca Sacra*, January-March, 1990, p. 66.

10. Everett F. Harrison, "Must Christ Be Lord to Be Savior?," in *Eternity*, September 1959, p. 16.

11. Charles C. Ryrie, *So Great Salvation* (Wheaton, IL: Victor Books, 1989).

12. Henry Alford, *The New Testament* (Chicago: Moody Press, n.d.), p. 938 on Romans 11:6.

13. Rich Wager, "Lordship Salvation: Another Gospel?," in *Signal*, November-December 1986, pp. 12, 13.

14. Dave Breese, "The Gospel of Grace: Are You Clear About It?" in *Signal*, March-April, May-June, July-August 1986.

15. Ryrie, *So Great Salvation*, p. 40.

16. *Ibid.*, p. 84.

17. J. I. Packer in Foreword, MacArthur, *The Gospel According to Jesus*, p. ix.

18. Darrell Bock, "A Review of *The Gospel According to Jesus*," *Bibliotheca Sacra*, January-March 1989, p. 27.

19. Ryrie, *So Great Salvation*, p. 98.

20. Carl G. Kromminga, "Repentance," in *Baker's Dictionary of Theology* (Grand Rapids, MI: Baker, 1960), p. 444.

21. Joseph A. Fitzmyer, *Luke the Theologian* (New York: Paulist Press, 1989), pp. 117-145.

22. Zane C. Hodges, *Absolutely Free!* (Grand Rapids, MI: Zondervan, 1989).

23. *Ibid.*, p. 18.

24. John R. W. Stott, in Harrison, "Must Christ Be Lord to Be Savior?," p. 17.

25. Hodges, *Absolutely Free!*, pp. 208, 209.

26. *Ibid.*, p. 84.

CHAPTER NINE: The Methodology of the Evangelistic Invitation

1. Iain Murray, *D. Martyn Lloyd-Jones: The Fight of Faith* (Edinburgh: Banner of Truth Trust, 1990), p. 777.

2. J. I. Packer, *A Quest for Godliness: The Puritan Vision of the Christian Life* (Wheaton, IL: Crossway Books, 1990), pp. 283, 284.

3. J. I. Packer, *Evangelism and the Sovereignty of God* (Downers Grove, IL: InterVarsity Press, 1961), p. 92.

4. *Ibid.*, p. 104. Indeed, Packer states: "Evangelizing includes the endeavor to elicit a response to the truth taught. It is communication with a view to conversion. . . . It is an attempt to gain, or win, or catch, our fellow-men for Christ" (p. 50). I could not agree more.

5. John R. W. Stott, *The Preacher's Portrait* (Grand Rapids, MI: Eerdmans, 1961), pp. 44-59.

6. G. Campbell Morgan, *Evangelism* (Westwood, NJ: Revell, n.d.), p. 67.

7. Derke P. Bergsma, "Preaching for Modern Times," in *Practical Theology and the Ministry of the Church 1952-1984: Essays in Honor of Edmund P. Clowney*, ed. Harvie M. Conn (Phillipsburg, NJ: Presbyterian and Reformed, 1990), p. 183.

8. Packer, *A Quest for Godliness*, p. 164.

9. Alan Walker, *Evangelistic Preaching* (Grand Rapids, MI: Zondervan, 1983), p. 71.

10. R. Alan Streett, *The Effective Invitation* (Old Tappan, NJ: Revell, n.d.), p. 55ff.

11. *Ibid.*, p. 61.

12. David L. Larsen, *The Anatomy of Preaching: Identifying the Issues in Preaching Today* (Grand Rapids, MI: Baker, 1989), pp. 131-143.
13. Streett, *The Effective Invitation*, p. 69.
14. R. T. Kendall, *Stand Up and Be Counted: Calling for Public Profession of Faith* (Grand Rapids, MI: Zondervan, 1984).
15. Lloyd M. Perry and John R. Strubhar, *Evangelistic Preaching* (Chicago: Moody Press, 1979), p. 106.
16. Roy L. Laurin, *Help Yourself to Life* (Chicago: Moody Press, 1973), p. 11.
17. Harry S. Stout, *The Divine Dramatist: George Whitefield and the Rise of Modern Evangelicalism* (Grand Rapids, MI: Eerdmans, 1991).
18. Arnold A. Dallimore, *George Whitefield*, Vol. II (Edinburgh: Banner of Truth Trust, 1973), p. 482.
19. Murray, *D. Martyn Lloyd-Jones: The Fight of Faith*, p. 339.
20. John Piper, *The Supremacy of God in Preaching* (Grand Rapids, MI: Baker, 1990), p. 93.
21. Craig Skinner, *Lamplighter and Son: The Forgotten Story of Thomas Spurgeon and His Famous Father* (Nashville: Broadman, 1984), pp. 47, 157, 167, 168, 246, 249, 255.
22. William G. McLoughlin, *Modern Revivalism* (New York: Ronald Press, 1959), p. 216.
23. R. B. Kuiper, *God-centered Evangelism* (Grand Rapids, MI: Baker, 1961), p. 163ff.
24. Iain Murray, *The Puritan Hope* (Edinburgh: Banner of Truth Trust, 1971), p. 5.
25. Peter Masters, "Is It—Christ Receiving Sinners," *Sword and Trowel*, January 1980, pp. 16-19.
26. D. Bruce Lockerbie, "Let's Rethink the Altar Call," *Eternity*, October 1962, pp. 11-13.
27. Leighton Ford, "How to Give an Honest Invitation," *Leadership*, September 1984, pp. 104-108.
28. W. A. Criswell, *Criswell's Guidebook for Pastors* (Nashville: Broadman, 1980), p. 244.
29. Vernon L. Stanfield, *Effective Evangelistic Preaching* (Grand Rapids, MI: Baker, 1965).
30. Streett, *The Effective Invitation*, p. 116. There are also choice chapters in this book on music in relation to the invitation, Billy Graham's invitation, and children and the invitation.
31. Faris D. Whitesell, *Sixty-five Ways to Give Evangelistic Invitations* (Grand Rapids, MI: Zondervan, 1945), p. 54.
32. Ralph G. Turnbull, *A Minister's Opportunities* (Grand Rapids, MI: Baker, n.d.), p. 157.

CHAPTER TEN: *The Energy for the Evangelistic Enterprise*

1. Erick Dahlhielm, *A Burning Light* (Chicago: Covenant Press, 1951), pp. 17-37.
2. Don Richardson, *Peace Child* (Ventura, CA: Regal, 1974); *Lords of the Earth* (Ventura, CA: Regal, 1977) (on why the cross was used).
3. Classic treatments on the Holy Spirit would include Abraham Kuyper, John Walvoord, Morris Inch, H. B. Swete, and A. B. Simpson's two volumes.
4. F. Dale Bruner, *A Theology of the Holy Spirit: The Pentecostal Experience and the New Testament* (Grand Rapids, MI: Eerdmans, 1970).
5. Henry Alford, *The New Testament* (Chicago: Moody Press, n.d.), p. 494.

6. George Smeaton, *The Doctrine of the Holy Spirit* (Edinburgh: Banner of Truth, 1958), p. 176ff.

7. H. C. G. Moule, *Veni Creator* (London: Hodder and Stoughton, 1890), p. 97.

8. E. F. Kevan, *The Saving Work of the Holy Spirit* (London: Pickering and Inglis, 1953), p. 7.

9. Samuel Chadwick, *The Way to Pentecost* (London: Hodder and Stoughton, 1921), p. 43.

10. Bernard L. Ramm, *Rapping About the Spirit* (Waco, TX: Word, 1974), p. 68.

11. James Montgomery Boice, *Awakening to God* (Downers Grove, IL: InterVarsity Press, 1979), p. 63.

12. John F. Walvoord, *The Holy Spirit* (Grand Rapids, MI: Zondervan, 1954), p. 158; Martyn Lloyd-Jones, *God's Ultimate Purpose* (Grand Rapids, MI: Baker, 1978), pp. 243-300. An excellent treatment on sealing is F. E. Marsh, *Emblems of the Holy Spirit* (Grand Rapids, MI: Kregel, 1957).

13. Leon Morris, *Spirit of the Living God* (Downers Grove, IL: InterVarsity Press, 1960), p. 98.

14. Roland Allen, *The Ministry of the Spirit* (Grand Rapids, MI: Eerdmans, 1960), p. 22.

15. Dean S. Gilliland, *Pauline Theology and Mission Practice* (Grand Rapids, MI: Baker, 1983).

16. Iain Murray, *D. Martyn Lloyd-Jones: The Fight of Faith* (Edinburgh: Banner of Truth, 1990), p. 28.

17. Frederick Buechner, *The Book of Bebb* (New York: Atheneum, 1979)—the probing fictionalization of an American evangelist's life and ministry.

18. Richard Baxter, *Reformed Pastor* (Portland: Multnomah, n.d.), pp. 145, 106.

19. Charles Haddon Spurgeon, *Lectures to My Students* (Grand Rapids, MI: Zondervan, n.d.), from chapter XXIII, "On Conversion as Our Aim," p. 337. A most outstanding more recent volume on the Holy Spirit in relation to preaching is Dennis Kinlaw, *Preaching in the Spirit* (Wilmore, KY: Francis Asbury Press, 1985).

CHAPTER ELEVEN: *A Survey of the Contemporary Evangelistic Scene*

1. Paul G. Hiebert, "World Trends and Their Implications for Missions," in *Trinity World Forum*, Winter 1990, p. 1.

2. *Ibid.*, p. 2.

3. *National and International Religion Report*, July 29, 1991, p. 1.

4. James Spencer, *Hard Case Witnessing* (Old Tappan, NJ: Chosen/Revell, 1990).

5. Carl F. H. Henry, "Can the Church Save our Culture?," in *Trinity's Wellspring*, Spring 1991, p. 4. Cf. also Carl F. H. Henry, "Evangelical Impact on U.S. Society," in *Los Angeles Times*, Part II, November 7, 1987, p. 6.

6. Ben J. Wattenberg, *The First Universal Nation* (New York: Free Press, 1991).

7. C. Howard Hopkins, *John R. Mott* (Grand Rapids, MI: Eerdmans, 1979).

8. E. Stanley Jones, *Motives for Evangelism* (Nashville: Tidings, 1966), p. 3.

9. J. I. Packer, *A Quest for Godliness: The Puritan Vision of the Christian Life* (Wheaton, IL: Crossway Books, 1990), p. 307.

10. D. James Kennedy, *Evangelism Explosion* (Wheaton, IL: Tyndale House, 1973).

11. George W. Peters, *Saturation Evangelism* (Grand Rapids, MI: Zondervan, n.d.), pp. 51-85.

12. *Evangelism in Depth* (Chicago: Moody Press, 1961), p. 25.

13. Peters, *Saturation Evangelism*, pp. 87-142.

14. Ramon Carmona, "The Gospel Can Impact an Entire Nation," in *Latin American Evangelist*, July-September 1991, p. 3.

15. Tom Allan, *The Face of My Parish* (London: SCM Press, 1954).

16. David L. Larsen, *Caring for the Flock: Pastoral Ministry in the Local Congregation* (Wheaton, IL: Crossway Books, 1991), pp. 23-30, "The Mission of the Church."

17. Jerry White, *The Church and the Parachurch* (Portland: Multnomah, 1983).

18. Paul S. Rees, in *Cooperating in World Evangelization: A Handbook on Parachurch Relationships* (Wheaton, IL: Lausanne Committee, 1983), p. 91.

19. White, *The Church and the Parachurch*, p. 84.

20. Frank R. Tillapaugh, *The Church Unleashed* (Ventura, CA: Regal, 1982), pp. 10-25.

21. Thom S. Rainer, ed., *Evangelism in the Twenty-first Century: Essays in Honor of Lewis A. Drummond* (Wheaton, IL: Shaw, 1989), p. 189.

22. The most helpful volume is John Pollock, *To All the Nations: The Billy Graham Story* (San Francisco: Harper, 1985). Pollock's 1979 title *Billy Graham: Evangelist to the World* is also well done, as are titles by Stanley High, Sherwood Wirt, George Burnham, and Helen Kooiman. Studies of the results of Graham crusades are found in Curtis Mitchell, *Those Who Came Forward* (Philadelphia: Chilton Books, 1966). Other important studies are Marshall Frady, *Parable of American Righteousness* (Boston: Little Brown, 1979) and Marion Bell, *Crusade in the City* (Philadelphia: Bucknell University Press, 1977). A very solid study on the basis of cooperative crusades is Robert O. Ferm, *Cooperative Evangelism* (Grand Rapids, MI: Zondervan, 1958). Attention must be directed to the newly released and very comprehensive work: William Martin, *A Prophet with Honor* (New York: William Morrow, 1991). This is the monumental and massive study of Billy Graham for which we have been waiting.

23. John H. Gerstner, *Wrongly Dividing the Word of Truth* (Brentwood, TN: Wolgemuth and Hyatt, 1991), see particularly pp. 103, 138ff.

24. Bill Hybels and Oswald C. J. Hoffmann, "Turn the Gospel Loose," in *Leadership*, 6, Fall 1985, pp. 12-23; "Preaching for Total Commitment," *Leadership*, Summer 1989, pp. 35-40; "Speaking to the Secular Mind," *Leadership*, Summer 1988, pp. 28-34; "Well-Focused Preaching," *Leadership*, 10, Winter 1989, pp. 88-94. Cf. also Leslie R. Keylock, "Pastor to the Unchurched," *Moody Monthly*, October 1988, pp. 100-103.

25. John MacArthur, Jr., *Our Sufficiency in Christ* (Waco, TX: Word, 1991), pp. 146-151.

CHAPTER TWELVE: *Our Ecclesiology and Evangelism*

1. Thomas Carlyle, *Reminiscences of My English Journey in 1949* (New York: Harper, 1882), p. 41, quoted in William Abraham, *The Logic of Evangelism* (Grand Rapids, MI: Eerdmans, 1989), p. 117.

2. Cf. David L. Larsen, *Caring for the Flock: Pastoral Ministry in the Local Congregation* (Wheaton, IL: Crossway Books, 1991), where I have attempted to argue, in Chapters 1 and 2, for a theological priority with respect to the church.

3. Jurgen Moltmann, *The Church in the Power of the Spirit* (San Francisco: Harper, 1977), p. 19.

4. Howard A. Snyder, "The Church as God's Agent in Evangelism," in *Let the Earth Hear His Voice* (Lausanne Congress) (Minneapolis: World Wide, 1975), p. 327ff.

5. Kenneth Hamilton, *Earthly Good: The Churches and the Betterment of Human Existence* (Grand Rapids, MI: Eerdmans, 1990).

6. Francis A. Schaeffer, *The Church at the End of the Twentieth Century* (Downers Grove, IL: InterVarsity Press, 1970). There is in that book a splendid discussion of form and freedom in the church, pp. 59-67.

7. Joseph Aldrich, *Life-style Evangelism* (Portland: Multnomah Press, 1988), pp. 102, 103.

8. Martin P. Marty, "In the Belly of Illness," *The Christian Century*, May 15-22, 1991, p. 561.

9. Joe Ford and Robert M. Saul, in "Prayer and Evangelism," quoted by Edward C. Lyrene, Jr., *Evangelism in the Twenty-first Century* (Wheaton, IL: Shaw, 1989), p. 90.

10. Lewis Sperry Chafer, *True Evangelism: Winning Souls Through Prayer* (Findlay, OH: Dunham, 1919), p. 83.

11. Curtis Mitchell, "Evangelistic Praying," *Grace Theological Journal*, 5:1, 1984, pp. 127-133. Mitchell has done an excellent study of "The Holy Spirit's Intercessory Ministry," *Bibliotheca Sacra*, July-September 1982, pp. 230-242.

12. Bethan Lloyd-Jones, *Memories of Sandfields* (Edinburgh: Banner of Truth, 1983), p. 85.

13. Gene A. Getz, *Sharpening the Focus of the Church* (Chicago: Moody, 1974), p. 47.

14. Robert E. Coleman, *The Master Plan of Evangelism* (Westwood, NJ: Revell, 1963); Bill Hull, *The Disciple Making Pastor* (Old Tappan, NJ: Revell, 1988). With all of the strengths of the latter, I am uneasy about the emergence of a kind of elitism which does not insist the pastor be the pastor to the whole flock. Sharing of burdens cannot mean the abrogation of responsibility.

15. William R. Bright, ed., *Ten Basic Steps Toward Christian Maturity* (Arrowhead Springs, CA: Campus Crusade, 1965).

16. J. I. Packer, *A Quest for Godliness: The Puritan Vision of the Christian Life* (Wheaton, IL: Crossway Books, 1990), p. 181.

17. L. Berkhof, *Systematic Theology* (Grand Rapids, MI: Eerdmans, 1953), p. 508.

18. Robert E. Webber, *Celebrating Our Faith: Evangelism Through Worship* (San Francisco: Harper, 1986); Patrick R. Keifert, *Welcoming the Stranger: A Public Theology of Worship and Evangelism* (Minneapolis: Fortress, 1991).

19. Dr. Nathan Hatch, in Christian Thought Lectures on Francis Asbury at Trinity Evangelical Divinity School, May 31, 1988.

20. John Pollock, *To All the Nations: The Billy Graham Story* (San Francisco: Harper, 1985), p. 41.

CHAPTER THIRTEEN: *A Strategy for All-out Evangelization*

1. A case is made for a plan and a case study is shared in David L. Larsen, *Caring for the Flock: Pastoral Ministry in the Local Congregation* (Wheaton, IL: Crossway Books, 1991), pp. 29, 30, 231, 232.

2. B. H. Lidell Hart, *Strategy: The Classic Book on Military Strategy* (second revised edition) (New York: Meridian, 1991).

3. I am indebted to my former Th.M. student and teaching fellow Todd Olson for this perspective.

4. Edward R. Dayton and David A. Fraser, *Planning Strategy for World Evangelism* (Grand Rapids, MI: Eerdmans, 1990).

5. Jim Peterson, *Evangelism for Our Generation* (Colorado Springs: NavPress, 1985); Donald C. Posterski, *Reinventing Evangelism* (Downers Grove, IL: InterVarsity Press, 1989).

6. I am grateful to my brother, Dr. Paul Larsen, who introduced me to David W. Bebbington, *Evangelicalism in Modern Britain: A History from the 1730's to the 1980's* (London: Unwin Hyman, 1989).

7. George G. Hunter, *The Contagious Congregation* (Nashville: Abingdon, 1979).

8. Kenneth L. Callahan, *Effective Church Leadership* (San Francisco: Harper & Row, 1990), p. 26.

9. Roger S. Greenway, ed., *The Pastor-evangelist: Preacher, Model, and Mobilizer for Church Growth* (Philippsburg, NJ: Presbyterian and Reformed, 1987), p. 182. Some thoughtful titles by Dr. Richard Stoll Armstrong include *The Pastor as Evangelist* (Philadelphia: Westminster, 1984) and *The Pastor-evangelist in the Parish* (Louisville: Westminster/John Knox, 1990).

10. D. M. Lloyd-Jones, *Knowing the Times* (Edinburgh: Banner of Truth, n.d.), p. 181.

11. Luis and Pat Palau, *How to Lead Your Child to Christ* (Portland: Multnomah, 1991).

12. Gerald Renner, "Phone Home," *Works*, August 1991, p. 7ff.

13. Kenneth Vetters, "Evangelism in a Small Town," and Marshall Shelley, "Home Visitation: How Well Does It Work?," *Leadership*, Spring 1984, pp. 74-83.

14. Bob and Betty Jacks, *Your Home a Lighthouse: Hosting an Evangelistic Bible Study* (Colorado Springs: NavPress, 1990). Of interest is Gabriel Fackre's· "engagement evangelism" and relevant titles such as Wesley W. Nelson, *The Art of Bridge Building for the Common Man* (Chicago: Covenant Press, 1989) and Rebecca Pippert, *Pizza Parlor Evangelism* (Downers Grove, IL: InterVarsity Press, 1976).

15. One of the choicest publishers of excellent tracts (such as *You Can Be Born Again*) is Good News Publishers, 1300 Crescent Street, Wheaton, IL 60187.

16. Bebbington, *Evangelicalism in Modern Britain: A History from the 1730's to the 1980's.*

17. Tom Phillips, "Evangelismo," *Works*, August 1991, p. 321.

18. Lyle E. Schaller, *Looking in the Mirror: Self-appraisal in the Local Church* (Nashville: Abingdon, 1984), p. 190ff.

19. John Stackhouse, "Church Growth Fine Tunes Its Formulas," *Christianity Today*, June 24, 1991, p. 45.

20. C. Peter Wagner, *Church Planting for a Greater Harvest* (Ventura, CA: Regal, 1990).

21. Luis Palau, "Evangelism Is Social Action," in *World Vision*, April-May 1990, pp. 4-8.

CHAPTER FOURTEEN: *The Intelligibility of the Christian Truth-claim*

1. James F. Engle and Wilbert Norton, *What's Gone Wrong with the Harvest?* (Grand Rapids, MI: Zondervan, 1975).

2. "Letters," *Time* magazine, August 19, 1991, p. 8.

3. Christopher Lasch, *The True and Only Heaven* (New York: Norton, 1991).

4. David McKenna, *Megatruth* (San Bernardino, CA: Here's Life, 1986), p. 63. Note also Herbert Schlossberg and Marvin Olasky, *Turning Point: A Christian Worldview Declaration* (Wheaton, IL: Crossway Books, 1987).

5. Richard Brookhiser, "Of Church Pews and Bedrooms," *Time* magazine, August 26, 1991, p. 70.

6. Francis A. Schaeffer, *The God Who Is There* (Downers Grove, IL: InterVarsity Press, 1968), p. 141. *The Complete Works of Francis A. Schaeffer* are published by Crossway Books (Wheaton, IL).

7. Donald G. Bloesch, *The Future of Evangelical Christianity* (New York: Doubleday, 1983).

8. Will Durant, *The Story of Philosophy* (New York: Time Reading Program, 1962), pp. 257-267.

9. Carl F. H. Henry, *God, Revelation and Authority*, six volumes (Waco, TX: Word, 1976). This is a massive, magnificent exploration of all relevant areas of Biblical doctrine and is highly recommended. See also Edward John Carnell, *An Introduction to Christian Apologetics* (Grand Rapids, MI: Eerdmans, 1948); Gordon H. Clark, *A Christian View of Men and Things* (Grand Rapids, MI: Eerdmans, 1952); Elton Trueblood, *A Place to Stand* (New York: Harper and Row, 1969). A superb new statement is George Carey (Archbishop of Canterbury), *Why I Believe in a Personal God: The Credibility of Faith in a Doubting Culture* (Wheaton, IL: Shaw, 1989).

10. F. F. Bruce, *Are the New Testament Documents Reliable?* (Downers Grove, IL: InterVarsity Press, 1943). Newer studies include Paul Barnett's *Is the New Testament History?* (Sydney: Hodder and Stoughton, 1986) and *Behind the Scenes of the New Testament* (Downers Grove, IL: InterVarsity Press, 1990).

11. Clark H. Pinnock, *Set Forth Your Case* (Nutley, NJ: Craig Press, 1968), p. 40ff.

12. Josh McDowell, *Evidence That Demands a Verdict* (San Bernardino, CA: Campus Crusade, 1972).

13. C. S. Lewis, *Mere Christianity* (London: Fontana, 1952).

14. Wilbur M. Smith, *Therefore Stand* (Boston: W. A. Wilde, 1945) and *The Supernaturalness of Christ: Can We Still Believe in It?* (Boston: W. A. Wilde, 1940).

15. J. V. Langmead Casserly, *Apologetics and Evangelism* (London: Mowbrays, 1962), pp. 182, 183.

16. "Who Was Jesus?," *Time* magazine, August 15, 1988, pp. 34-42.

17. "Fast Track," *Chicago Tribune Magazine*, August 11, 1991, p. 12.

18. Lawrence Shames, *The Hunger for More: Searching for Values in an Age of Greed* (New York: Times Books, 1989).

19. Gordon H. Clark, "Special Divine Revelation as Rational," in *Revelation and the Bible*, ed. Carl F. H. Henry (Grand Rapids, MI: Baker, 1958), p. 41.

20. Schaeffer, *The God Who Is There*, p. 152.

21. Father Walbert Buhlmann, "The New Missionary," *Time* magazine, December 27, 1982, p. 52.

22. Mike Bryan, *Chapter and Verse: A Skeptic Revisits Christianity* (New York: Random House, 1991).

23. Thomas C. Reeves, *A Question of Character* (New York: Free Press, 1991).

24. Emile Cailliet, *Journey into Light* (Grand Rapids, MI: Zondervan, 1968), p. 15ff.

25. Ray Monk, *Wittgenstein: The Duty of Genius* (New York: Free Press, 1990). Wittgenstein had this to say of Origen's view that all would be saved: "It would make nonsense of everything else, if what we do now is to make no difference in the end, then all the seriousness of life is done away with," p. 540.

CHAPTER FIFTEEN: *The Corollary of Revival—Evangelism*

1. For a helpful discussion on the definition of revival, see John Gerstner, "The Great Awakening," *Baker's Dictionary of Practical Theology* (Grand Rapids, MI: Baker, 1967), pp. 150-156.
2. George Mallone, *Furnace of Renewal: A Vision for the Church* (Downers Grove, IL: InterVarsity Press, 1982).
3. Stephen F. Olford, *Heart-cry for Revival* (Westwood, NJ: Fleming H. Revell, 1962), p. 75.
4. Charles G. Finney, *Revivals of Religion* (Chicago: Moody, 1962, from a condensation published in 1868), p. 14ff.
5. Robert E. Coleman, *The Spark That Ignites: God's Promise to Revive the Church Through You* (Minneapolis: World-wide, 1989), p. 20.
6. Arthur Fawcett, *The Cambuslang Revival: The Scottish Evangelical Revival of the Eighteenth Century* (Edinburgh: Banner of Truth, 1971), pp. 114, 166ff.
7. A. Skevington Wood, *The Inextinguishable Blaze: Spiritual Renewal and Advance in the Eighteenth Century* (Grand Rapids, MI: Eerdmans, 1960), p. 93.
8. Wilbur M. Smith, *The Glorious Revival Under King Hezekiah* (Grand Rapids, MI: Zondervan, 1937), pp. 6, 7.
9. C. E. Autrey, *Revivals of the Old Testament* (Grand Rapids, MI: Zondervan, 1960); Walter C. Kaiser, Jr., *Quest for Renewal: Personal Revival in the Old Testament* (Chicago: Moody, 1986).
10. Brian H. Edwards, *Revival! A People Saturated with God* (Durham: Evangelical Press, 1990), p. 208.
11. Don Wooding and Ray Barnett, *Ugandan Holocaust* (Grand Rapids, MI: Zondervan, 1980).
12. Donald W. B. Robinson, *Josiah's Reform and the Book of the Law* (London: Tyndale, 1951), p. 26ff.
13. H. C. Fish, *Handbook of Revivals* (Harrisonburg, VA: Gano Books, 1874 [1988]).
14. Edwards, *Revival! A People Saturated with God*, pp. 100, 106.
15. James D. Smart, *The Strange Silence of the Bible in the Church* (Philadelphia: Westminster, 1970), p. 15.
16. Charles Cunningham, *Timothy Dwight* (New York: Macmillan, 1942), pp. 110, 333ff.
17. Timothy Smith, *Revivalism and Social Reform* (New York: Abingdon, 1957).
18. James Burns, *Revivals: Their Laws and Leaders* (Grand Rapids, MI: Baker, 1960).
19. Martyn Lloyd-Jones, *The Puritans: Their Origins and Successors* (Edinburgh: Banner of Truth, 1987), p. 289.
20. Earle E. Cairns, *An Endless Line of Splendor* (Wheaton, IL: Tyndale, 1986); J. Edwin Orr, *The Second Evangelical Awakening* (London: Marshall, Morgan and Scott, 1949).
21. Jonathan Edwards, *The Narrative*, ed. James A. Stewart (Grand Rapids, MI: Kregel, 1957), p. 25.
22. Iain H. Murray, *Jonathan Edwards* (Edinburgh: Banner of Truth, 1987).
23. Eric W. Hayden, *Spurgeon on Revival* (Grand Rapids, MI: Zondervan, 1962).
24. John D. Hannah, "The Layman's Prayer Revival of 1858," *Bibliotheca Sacra*, January-March 1977, pp. 59-73.
25. Eifion Evans, *Revival Comes to Wales* (Cardiff: Evangelical Press of Wales, 1979), pp. 97, 99; also George T. B. Davis, *When the Fire Fell* (Philadelphia: Million Testaments Campaigns, 1945), pp. 63-96.

26. George W. Peters, *Indonesia Revival* (Grand Rapids, MI: Zondervan, 1973).
27. Robert E. Coleman, *One Divine Moment* (Westwood, NJ: Revell, 1970).
28. Finney, *Revivals of Religion*, p. 211. Cf. also Finney's *Principles of Revival* (from Finney's *First Messages on Revival*), ed. Louis Gifford Parkhurst, Jr. (Minneapolis: Bethany, 1987).
29. Leonard Ravenhill, *Why Revival Tarries* (Minneapolis: Bethany, 1959).
30. Martyn Lloyd-Jones, *Revival* (Wheaton, IL: Crossway Books, 1987).
31. *Ibid.*, p. 7.
32. James A. Stewart, *Let Go and Let God! Meditations on Revival* (Philadelphia: Continental Press, n.d.), p. 67ff.
33. Iain H. Murray, *D. Martyn Lloyd-Jones: The Fight of Faith (1939-1981)* (Edinburgh: Banner of Truth, 1990), p. 384.
34. Olford, *Heart-cry for Revival*, p. 79ff.

Scripture Index

General Index